"It is very likely that Vin Scully's voice reached the ears of more sports fans than any in the history of our country. Anyone who loved listening to him, which means pretty much everyone, will enjoy this look at the man behind those memories, and the extraordinary life he led."

—**Mike Greenberg**, ESPN host

"Vin Scully loved to tell stories yet shied away from being one, so it's only fitting that Tom Hoffarth has expertly crafted a narrative weaving stories told by those who knew and revered the man behind the mic. If you've ever loved Scully's voice, now you'll value his heart even more."

—**Andrea Kremer**, Emmy and Peabody Award–winning TV sports journalist and Pro Football Hall of Fame honoree

"For Vin-o-philes like me, this book is like a free buffet to a starving man. Wonderful, fun, new stories about the best announcer who ever lived."

—**Rick Reilly**, National Sportswriters and Sportscasters Hall of Fame inductee

"It's impossible for any one person to do Vin Scully justice on the page—I know because I've tried. But this collection of essays, by colleagues, friends, and folks like me who just felt like they were listening to a friend, does him more than justice. We were lucky to listen to Vinny for all those years. And now we're lucky Tom Hoffarth has put together this book."

—**Eric Nusbaum**, author of *Stealing Home: Los Angeles, the Dodgers, and the Lives Caught in Between*

"When Vin Scully passed in 2022, his memorial service was private. Now, thanks to Tom Hoffarth, we have the public eulogy he deserves. They don't make them like Vin Scully anymore, and Hoffarth's celebration of life shows us exactly what made him the GOAT."

—**Brad Balukjian**, author of *The Wax Pack*, an NPR Best Book of 2020

"Tom Hoffarth has edited the definitive book on Vin Scully—the most iconic voice in sports broadcasting history. His collection of glowing tributes from some of the giants in the baseball and entertainment worlds give fitting praise to the soundtrack of summer of nearly seven decades."

—**Erik Sherman**, author of *Daybreak at Chavez Ravine: Fernandomania and the Remaking of the Los Angeles Dodgers*

"As baseball fans living in an era where an obsession with numbers frequently takes the humanity out of the way the game is broadcast, we hunger for story more than ever. In response Tom Hoffarth has given us just what we need: a highly entertaining and insightful collection of stories from an impressive roster of admirers about the best storyteller America's Pastime has ever known, Vin Scully. Pull up a chair and enjoy!"

—**Andrew Maraniss**, *New York Times* best-selling author of *Singled Out: The True Story of Glenn Burke*

"Tom Hoffarth puts his considerable standing among the LA sports media to full use, soliciting vibrant essays from the crème de la SoCal crème about the greatest broadcaster of all time. Bravo on both effort and result. This book is aces."

—**Jason Turbow**, best-selling author of *Dynastic, Bombastic, Fantastic: Reggie, Catfish and Charlie Finley's Swingin' A's*

"I loved hearing Vin Scully's stories about the Dodgers-Giants rivalry and how he grew up a Giants fan, emulated Mel Ott, and considered Willie Mays the best player he ever saw. Now Tom Hoffarth has compiled a million more Scully stories, and the world is grateful. It's a must-read collection of everything that was right about the greatest sports broadcaster ever."

—**John Shea**, coauthor (with Willie Mays) of the *New York Times* bestseller *24: Life Stories and Lessons from the Say Hey Kid*

PERFECT ELOQUENCE

PERFECT ELOQUENCE

An Appreciation of

VIN SCULLY

Edited by
TOM HOFFARTH

Foreword by
RON RAPOPORT

University of Nebraska Press
Lincoln

Bob Costas's essay previously appeared as "Memories of Vin
Scully," *Peacock North Magazine* 22, no. 4 (Fall 2022): 14–15. Dale
Marini's essay was previously published as "My Meeting with
Dodger Icon Vin Scully," *LMU Magazine*, December 5, 2016. An
earlier version of Sammy Roth's essay appeared as "Vin Scully's
Last Dodgers Games: What I'll Remember about the Man behind
the Voice," *Desert Sun* (Palm Springs CA), September 28, 2016.

The University of Nebraska Press is part of a land-grant institution
with campuses and programs on the past, present, and future
homelands of the Pawnee, Ponca, Otoe-Missouria, Omaha,
Dakota, Lakota, Kaw, Cheyenne, and Arapaho Peoples, as well as
those of the relocated Ho-Chunk, Sac and Fox, and Iowa Peoples.

Library of Congress Cataloging-in-Publication Data
Names: Hoffarth, Tom, 1961– editor. |
Rapoport, Ron, author of foreword.
Title: Perfect eloquence : an appreciation of Vin Scully /
edited by Tom Hoffarth ; foreword by Ron Rapoport.
Description: Lincoln : University of Nebraska Press, [2024] |
Includes bibliographical references.
Identifiers: LCCN 2023052293
ISBN 9781496238788 (hardback : acid-free paper)
ISBN 9781496240156 (epub)
ISBN 9781496240163 (pdf)
Subjects: LCSH: Scully, Vin, 1927–2022. | Baseball announcers—
United States—Biography. | Sportswriters—United States—
Biography. | Los Angeles Dodgers (Baseball team)—History. |
National Baseball Hall of Fame and Museum. | BISAC: SPORTS &
RECREATION / Baseball / Essays & Writings |
SPORTS & RECREATION / Baseball / General
Classification: LCC GV742.42.S38 P47 2024 |
DDC 796.092 [B]—dc23/eng/20231213
LC record available at https://lccn.loc.gov/2023052293

Designed and set in Garamond Premier Pro by L. Welch.

To Vin and his family.
To my parents and family and
our shared appreciation of Vin.

Peace, love, and mercy.

Vin met my mom, Terry Hoffarth, at the Dodger Stadium press box on her birthday in 2011. She looked him in the eye and told him how much he meant in her life. He had this sheepish reaction. Vin always asked how my mom was doing after every conversation we had. He called her on her eightieth birthday to welcome her to the club. Courtesy of Rhonda Hoffarth.

Contents

Illustrations

Foreword

Ron Rapoport

The first time I asked Vin Scully if I could work with him on a book was way back in the 1960s. He said no.

I can't swear that I asked him at least once every decade afterward, but I'll bet I came pretty close. He always said no.

Other people had asked him, he said once when I pressed him—no surprise there—but he just didn't want to. The only reason he ever gave was that Walter O'Malley never wrote a book and if it was good enough for Walter O'Malley it was good enough for him.

I tried to reason with him. It didn't have to be an autobiography, I told him—no barefoot boy in Brooklyn, no sad memories he'd just as soon forget—but a memoir, one that I sometimes found myself composing in my mind.

Vin would tell stories about Walt Alston and Don Zimmer. He would talk about Jackie Robinson and Pee Wee Reese, about Willie Mays and Hank Aaron, about Bob Gibson and Sandy Koufax, about Tom Lasorda and Leo Durocher, about Bobby Thomson and Ralph Branca—and on and on. Sure, he'd told a lot of these stories over the air, but that was just the point. They were in the air now, gone with the wind and not preserved in print. Nor were they preserved in what would have been an audio book for the ages. It hurt just to think about it.

In June 2022 the Dodgers retired Gil Hodges's number, and a reporter called Vin and got some wonderful stories from him about the great Dodgers' first baseman, which I had never heard before. *Lord*, I thought all over again, *what an irreplaceable resource this man is*. Two months later, Vin died, and I went into mourning, for him and for the book that got away, that never truly ended—until now.

Perhaps it took someone who has spent much of his career writing about sports broadcasting, someone like Tom Hoffarth, to realize something that had been right before our eyes all along: Vin was as interesting as many of the people he talked about, and remembrances of him from the people who knew him best would go a long way toward filling the void.

Tom has scoured his alarmingly large contacts list to bring this book to life. He has reached out to Vin's fellow broadcasters and friends; to the writers who knew him; to the players, umpires, and baseball executives he talked about in his broadcasts; to historians, celebrities, and fans—and, perhaps most touchingly, to some of the families of the players he talked about.

And just look at some of the stories Tom has collected:

- Ray Charles telling Bob Costas the one person he wanted to meet in all this world was Vin.
- Gil Hodges Jr. telling how his mother, sedated after just giving birth, woke up in her hospital room to Vin's voice telling the Dodgers' audience—and her—that the baby was a girl.
- Bryan Cranston telling about what sixty years of listening to Vin's broadcasts meant to him and, later, to his family.
- Kevin Fagan, the creator of the *Drabble* comic strip, saying he would turn his television set off if the broadcast wasn't in sync with what Vin was saying on the radio.
- Former Dodgers general manager Ned Colletti describing his rescue of Vin's golf clubs at an auction, which sounds straight out of a TV movie.
- Bruce Froemming, a Major League umpire for thirty-seven years, telling how Vin never—can this be true?—second-guessed an umpire during a broadcast.
- Joe Davis and Jessica Mendoza relating how they handled the painful assignment of announcing Vin's death on the air.
- Ann Meyers Drysdale describing how Vin and his wife, Sandi, all but adopted her and her children after her husband, the great Dodgers pitcher Don Drysdale, died unexpectedly at age fifty-six.

- Lisa Nehus Saxon relating the loneliness of being the only woman reporter on the Dodgers beat and how Vin would talk to her, cheer her up, and, in the ultimate gesture of friendship, ask her to sit next to him in church.

One of the things that struck me as I read the remembrances of Vin in this book is his capacity for friendship. He seemed to go out of his way to help people who crossed his path, to advise them, to mentor them, to simply be there for them—often when they needed a lift the most.

And so here we are, not with the book in which Vin talks about the people he discussed during his amazing career, but the book in which so many of those people talk about *him*.

I am glad Tom reached out to them. And glad they said yes.

Preface

An elegant *New York Times* summary of all the global luminaries who died in 2022 asked if any of them had a common thread. Queen Elizabeth and Pope Benedict XVI? Pelé and Sidney Poitier? Bill Russell and Barbara Walters?

Writer William McDonald also patched in this paragraph: "Four figures in Los Angeles Dodgers history departed within a few months: Roz Wyman, who as a member of the Los Angeles City Council was central to luring the team from Brooklyn to the West Coast in the late 1950s; Maury Wills, who stole bases with blazing regularity for the team in the '60s; Tommy Davis, a batting star who led Los Angeles to two World Series titles before injuries derailed a potential Hall of Fame career; and Vin Scully, who sat in the broadcast booth marveling at their exploits as one of the game's most venerated announcers."

Scully might have considered this an appropriate way to be sentenced into the great beyond—well punctuated, no dangling participles. His mention came after the others, no more "fuss and feathers," as he would say.

He might even be agreeable with the label *announcer*. Many use it interchangeably with *broadcaster*. By definition, an announcer is one who announces; a broadcaster presents and discusses information. Scully was far more the latter.

Going a step further, *Los Angeles Times* columnist Jim Murray once wrote about Scully, "He didn't broadcast a game. He narrated it."

At the end of the 2015 season, Scully announced (that's the proper use) the next summer would very likely be his last calling games for the Dodgers. It came as a blessing. He wasn't going to pull an Irish goodbye and just disappear on us. He gave a clear runway. We all had time to prepare countless bouquets of thank-yous.

Five more years went by. Scully showed what retirement past the age of ninety could look like: just being there for his ailing wife, Sandi, and his children, grandchildren, and great-grandkids; popping into the ballpark for ceremonial moments of playoff pomp and circumstance; accepting even more lifetime achievement awards; reciting poetry before a live audience at the Hollywood Bowl; making public appearances to boost charity fundraising.

When Scully died, obituary writers leaned most into his professional life and times. Very few knew about his very personal and often private endeavors. That was the tricky part. Scully wasn't an open book. He politely declined any attempts to cooperate, or authorize, a self-indulgent biographical project. So, writing about him became a bit of a *Citizen Kane*–type excavation project for those who had connections and resources to capture, perhaps, his true Rosebud.

McDonald's *Times* essay wrapped up with a somewhat esoteric point: There was "no particular lesson to be drawn from these clusters of contemporaneous deaths." He declared that, like any death, those in 2022 were "experienced alone and mourned individually. . . . It's for those of us who record such deaths, and read about them, to notice the remarkable parallels. And there we have to leave it, perhaps a little mystified. Death, in its inscrutability, doesn't explain itself. . . . All made a difference, but all died knowing that their work was unfinished, that as the world spun on without them, others would have to pick up their banners and carry them into the next year, and the next."

So much communal grief had already been laid heavily on the planet by the COVID-19 pandemic to that point. Yet Scully's passing of natural causes may have hit too many of us like a supernatural experience. On August 2, 2022—the deuces were wild—Southern Californians who tuned into the midweek night game between the Dodgers and Giants from San Francisco heard Dodgers broadcaster Joe Davis take a deep breath and deliver the news during the game.

When information like that brings people to their knees, there is a reason. We prayed. For decades, Scully's presence at Dodgers games had been a communal experience for baseball fans and beyond. This moment wasn't any different.

If our world was about to spin ahead, there had to be a way to pick up the banner for him and unfurl it forward—as he did with his own banner from the Dodger Stadium broadcast booth on his final home game, thanking all for their impact on his life.

Broadcasting may have been Vin Scully's universally appreciated vocation. He was considered the best of the best at it, in ways we all could validate from under the blanket as he tucked us into bed each night with his stories.

Ultimately, that is not what defined him. Vin Scully's actions spoke louder than his Hall of Fame words.

If given a chance to offer a personal eulogy, a tribute of thanks, what might anyone want to share? What about him do we carry with us today? That's the goal here.

A public celebration of his life was limited to a brief pregame ceremony before a Dodgers home game days after his passing. His funeral Mass shortly thereafter was private.

I am not seeking some sort of poetic closure. It is more about creating a platform for those, like me, who want something to preserve: character and ideas and a template for living, especially if we can figure out a way to play it forward.

In the weeks leading up to his retirement in September of 2016, one reporter asked Vin how he would want to be remembered.

"I really and truly would rather be remembered—'Oh yeah, he was a good guy.' Or, 'He was a good husband, a good father, a good grandfather.' The sportscasting? That's fine if they want to mention it. But that'll disappear slowly as—what is it, the sands of time blow over the goose?

"The biggest thing is I just want to be remembered as a good man, an honest man, and one who lived up to his own beliefs." I believe that to be the case. Many want to make more precise analogies, and that's natural.

"He ranks with Walter Cronkite among America's most-trusted media personalities, with Frank Sinatra and James Earl Jones among its most-iconic voices, and with Mark Twain, Garrison Keillor, and Ken Burns among its preeminent storytellers," *Sports Illustrated*'s Tom Verducci wrote in a 2016 profile on Scully. Five years later, under the headline "The Beautiful Life of Vin Scully," Verducci added that he was "a modern Socrates, only more revered, simultaneously a giant and our best friend."

These points are well taken. In today's Google-fied world, a few quick keystrokes can find a plethora of archived work. Take these interesting examples I happened to stumble on: a strikeout that ended Don Larsen's 1956 World Series perfect game, Orel Hershiser's last out to clinch the Dodgers' title in the 1988 World Series, and Clayton Kershaw's 2014 no-hitter. Scully was on the call for all three, spanning nearly sixty years. Yet he exclaimed the same thing after each ending strikeout: "Got him." And then the crowd took over.

But as much as Cronkite was a trusted source in his day, Scully might also be easily overlooked as time marches on. Too many other new people, places, and things somehow are referred to as "the best." We need testimonials of what we know happened in our lifetimes, as reference points for the future.

I understand the profound personal connection so many had with Scully. It feels a lot like falling in love—that is something of the moment. By nature of the broadcast medium, Vin's descriptions and stories were often things of the moment. And moments can evaporate.

As Bob Nightengale, the *USA Today* baseball writer, explained in his 2022 tribute piece, "If you knew Vin, if you ever met Vin, if you just listened to Vin, you loved Vin."

On what would have been Vin Scully's ninety-fifth birthday, I started reaching out to colleagues and sifted through storage boxes of notes and clippings, trying to connect dots and dashes. Common themes emerged. Bob Costas could explain not just how Scully found himself in another important moment but also the way he could elevate it even more. Al Michaels felt a personal connection as a native Brooklyn Dodgers fan moving to Los Angeles. Baseball Hall of Fame president Josh Rawitch and Gil Hodges Jr. could explain Scully's patriotic call to duty. Former Dodgers owner Peter O'Malley considered Scully like a brother. What other baseball owner can say that about a star employee?

1. Vin Scully Way, a street sign dedicated to Vin Scully at Dodgertown in Vero Beach, Florida, on display at Dodger Stadium, 2016. Courtesy of Tom Hoffarth.

Add to that another layer, deeper than just what you heard or saw. Vin's devotion to his faith and family, his sincerity, and his efforts to inspire dozens to attempt his career path weren't often revealed to the general public. He was never caught up in the trappings of celebrity and fame but could laugh along with it. As Steve Garvey says, Vin handled it all with grace.

In 2016 the Dodgers petitioned the City of Los Angeles to change the name of the main road coming to the stadium from Elysian Park Avenue to Vin Scully Avenue. It was a missed opportunity. Back at the team's Vero Beach, Florida, home, they once had a small road named for him called Vin Scully Way.

Vin Scully's way was to provide an example of what humility, dignity, and humanity look like, which is especially poignant these days as we search our past for principled answers amid a turbulent point in existence. When a lack of integrity, common decency, and respectful communication skills threaten to chip away at society, Vin was a reminder, a compass of the true foundation of patriotism, hard work, and family values.

In his story in *Sports Illustrated*, Verducci explained that, when Scully attended Fordham University, all freshmen took a seminar class called Eloquentia Perfecta. Translated from Latin, it means "perfect eloquence." "It emerged from the rhetorical studies of the ancient Greeks, codified in

Jesuit tradition in 1599," Verducci elaborated. "It refers to the ideal orator: a good person speaking well for the common good. It is based on humility: The speaker begins with the needs of the audience, not a personal agenda. Vin Scully was that ideal orator. A modern Socrates, only more revered. He was an amazing firsthand witness and chronicler of history. . . . And yet never did Vin place himself above the people and events he was there to chronicle."

Scully's friend Jackie Robinson once said it: "A life is not important except in the impact it has on other lives."

That impact is what I am trying to quantify. He was perfectly eloquent in many ways.

I created nine chapters—innings, as it turned out—that capture prominent themes of Vin's life, professional and personal. They often fed into each other. I start each theme with my interpretation based on my experience, then other writers follow with their perspective. This started with just a small number of contributors—journalists and broadcasters, mostly—whose creative prose could take things to new levels. It was by some divine intervention perhaps that as the project gained momentum, I landed on exactly sixty-seven essays at the deadline to submit the manuscript. That is one for each year Vin broadcast games for the Dodgers.

Here is my attempt to show Vin Scully's impact on others, based on the way he lived, which reverberates to this day.

TOM HOFFARTH

A Vin Scully Timeline

1927–2022

For the Vin Scully Marching and Chowder Society, here is a reference for key moments in his life and career:

1927 Five days after Thanksgiving, on November 29, Vincent Edward Scully is born in New York City. He grows up in the Washington Heights section of Manhattan. His father, Vincent Aloysius Scully, is a silk salesman. His red-haired mother, Bridget, stays home with him and his younger sister, Margaret Ann. His father dies of pneumonia when Vin is four. His mother remarries Allan Reeve, whom Vin considers his dad.

1936 On October 2 eight-year-old Vin walks by a laundromat window that shows the New York Giants lost, 18–4, to the New York Yankees in Game Two of the World Series. He lives near the Giants' home field, the Polo Grounds, and his favorite player is Mel Ott. His empathy takes over, and the team become his favorite.

1944–45 A year of service in the U.S. Navy bridges his high school graduation at Fordham Prep and entering Fordham University.

1947 Scully, majoring in English, lands a role as a Fordham University student broadcaster and helps establish the school's WFUV-FM radio station. He does play-by-play for university games; additionally, he plays center field on the varsity baseball team, is assistant sports editor for the *Fordham Ram* newspaper, and sings barbershop quartet.

1949 His first major play-by-play assignment out of college comes at CBS Radio Network. The legendary Red Barber sends him to the University of Maryland–Boston University college football game on a frigid November Saturday. Stationed on the press box roof at Fenway

Park, with a small light and not much microphone chord, Scully offers no grouse about the conditions despite leaving his coat and gloves at the nearby hotel. That impresses Barber enough to assign Scully to the iconic Harvard-Yale game the next weekend.

1950 Scully, at age twenty-two, joins Barber and Connie Desmond in the Brooklyn Dodgers radio and TV booth, his opening created by Ernie Harwell's departure. Scully calls just the third and seventh innings, as he works his way into the rotation. Jackie Robinson, at thirty-one, is starting his fourth season. Don Newcombe is the twenty-four-year-old pitching ace. Only sixteen teams exist, split between the National League and American League. In spring training, Scully meets eighty-seven-year-old Connie Mack, who started his baseball career as a player in 1886 and was managing his final season with the American League's Philadelphia Athletics (with a 52-102 record). The National League's Boston Braves are two seasons from moving to Milwaukee. Scully lives with his mother in their fifth-floor walkup apartment and says he was thoroughly intimidated doing his first game on April 18 at Shibe Park in Philadelphia when the Phillies hosted the Dodgers.

1953 Scully, at twenty-five, becomes the youngest ever to do a national TV broadcast of the World Series. Red Barber has a dispute with the broadcast sponsors, so Scully is picked to join Mel Allen for the Dodgers-Yankees faceoff.

1955 For the franchise's first World Series title after years of coming up short, Scully describes the final out on national TV: "Ladies and gentlemen, the Brooklyn Dodgers are champions of the world." He adds that if he had tried to say something other than that, he likely would have broken down and wept.

1956 A month shy of his twenty-ninth birthday, Scully, selected for the broadcasting crew as a representative of the Brooklyn Dodgers, calls the final half of the perfect game of New York Yankees pitcher Don Larsen in World Series Game Five, for a national audience.

1958 With some reluctance, Scully moves to the West Coast with the Dodgers. In the cavernous Los Angeles Memorial Coliseum as the team awaits Dodger Stadium to be constructed, Dodgers baseball is introduced to Southern California primarily through Scully's voice over the transistor radio.

1959 On May 7 at the Coliseum on Roy Campanella Night, with more than ninety-three thousand in attendance lighting a match in Campanella's honor, Scully illuminates, "Perhaps the most beautiful and dramatic moment in the history of sports. Let there be a prayer for every light. And wherever you are, maybe you, in silent tribute to Campanella, can also say a prayer for his well-being."

1965 On September 9, Dodger Stadium, Scully makes this call: "It is 9:46 p.m.... 2-2 to Harvey Kuenn ... one strike away.... Sandy into his windup ... here's the pitch.... Swung on and missed, a perfect game!" Scully's call of Sandy Koufax's perfect game is only heard on local LA radio. A month later, Scully describes to a national T V audience Koufax's complete-game, 2–0, Game Seven win in the World Series, as the Dodgers claim the title in Minnesota.

1974 On April 8 at Atlanta Fulton County Stadium, the Braves' Henry Aaron breaks Babe Ruth's career home run record with number 715: "What a marvelous moment for baseball. What a marvelous moment for Atlanta and the state of Georgia. What a marvelous moment for the country and the world. A Black man is getting a standing ovation in the Deep South for breaking a record of an all-time baseball idol. And it is a great moment for all of us, and particularly for Henry Aaron."

1975–82 Scully spans eight years calling CBS's NFL and golf coverage. In 1982 he calls San Francisco's NFC Championship Game win—Joe Montana's touchdown pass to Dwight Clark, known as "The Catch": "Third-and-three.... Montana looking, looking, throwing in the end zone; Clark caught it! Dwight Clark.... It's a madhouse at Candlestick." Scully explains that after the game that he was exhausted by the work. He turns down a ten-year contract extension with CBS.

1976 Scully is voted by the team's fans as the Most Memorable Personality in Los Angeles Dodgers History.

1982 After thirty-three seasons with the Dodgers, Scully receives the Ford C. Frick Award from the National Baseball Hall of Fame for lifetime achievement. Just the sixth recipient of the honor, Scully's Cooperstown bio notes his qualifications as "entertaining, precise, proficient, charming, friendly, outgoing, smooth, relaxed, warm, knowledgeable, intelligent, literate, concise, well-prepared and colorful." Yet Scully is not even halfway through his Dodgers career. He will broadcast thirty-four more seasons.

1983 Scully joins NBC's Saturday *Game of the Week* MLB broadcasts, which includes World Series and All-Star Games, most often paired with Joe Garagiola.

1986 On October 25 at Shea Stadium in New York, World Series Game Six between the New York Mets and Boston Red Sox, Scully describes the following: "Little roller up along first. Behind the bag! It gets through Buckner! Here comes Knight, and the Mets win it!"

1988 October 8 at Dodger Stadium, World Series Game One between the Los Angeles Dodgers and Oakland Athletics, brings the following exclamation: "In a year that has been so improbable, the impossible has happened."

1989 Scully shares the first inning of NBC's All-Star Game coverage in Anaheim with his friend, former president Ronald Reagan, highlighted by calling Bo Jackson's lead-off home run.

1989 Scully pulls off perhaps the most impressive single feat by a modern baseball broadcaster—calling forty-six innings in twenty-seven hours in two cities. It starts with the Dodgers-Astros game in Houston on a Friday night. A red-eye takes him to St. Louis for NBC's *Game of the Week* on Saturday afternoon, which goes ten innings. He immediately flies back to Houston, arriving as the national anthem is playing prior to the Dodgers-Astros affair on Saturday night. That game goes twenty-two innings, and Scully calls them all—including the last thirteen innings by himself, allowing partner Don Drysdale to rest an ailing voice. The Dodgers' 5–4 loss comes early Sunday morning at 2:52 a.m., lasting seven hours. Up after five hours of sleep, Scully comes back Sunday to call the Dodgers' thirteen-inning loss to the Astros.

1990 Scully returns to CBS Radio Network to cover the World Series on an annual basis, partnered with Sparky Anderson.

2005 *Voices of Summer: Ranking Baseball's 101 All-Time Best Announcers*, a book by noted baseball broadcast historian Curt Smith, creates ten categories on a scale of 1 to 10 to measure dozens of broadcasters who have spanned the game's history. He notes aspects such as voice, popularity, continuity, and knowledge. Scully is ranked number 1 on each list, creating the only perfect score of 100. "Baseball's fate has profited from an artful Dodger's character," Smith writes.

2008 Scully receives a lifetime achievement award from his alma mater, Fordham University.

2014 Scully serves as the grand marshal for the New Year's Day Rose Parade in Pasadena, California.

2016 After calling an estimated ten-thousand-plus games in his career—including twenty no-hitters and three perfect games—Scully makes good on his decision to retire after his sixty-seventh season, just short of his eighty-ninth birthday. His last Dodger Stadium game is calling a walk-off homer by Charlie Culberson, as the Dodgers clinch the NL West title. His final game comes at San Francisco's AT&T Park on October 2, as he does all nine innings simulcast on TV and radio.

2016 Scully receives the Presidential Medal of Freedom at the White House from President Barack Obama.

2017 The Dodgers Ring of Honor adds a placard for Scully among the franchise's retired jersey numbers.

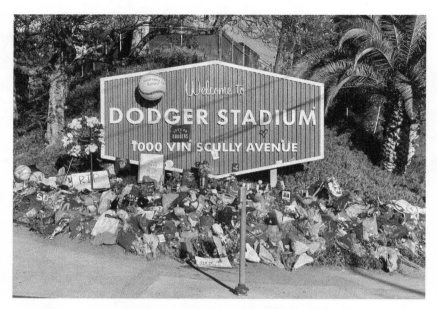

2. Fans leave flowers and memorabilia at a sign outside Dodger Stadium after Vin Scully's passing in early August 2022. Courtesy of Tom Hoffarth.

2022 Scully passes away at age ninety-four on August 2. Fans begin to leave signs and items in his memory at the Vin Scully Avenue signs around the ballpark. The Dodgers honor him before their August 5 home game. Broadcasters Joe Davis and Orel Hershiser hang a banner out of the TV broadcast booth that reads "Vin: We'll Miss You!" A video presentation with the song "Somewhere over the Rainbow" by Israel Kamakawiwo'ole is played. Dodgers manager Dave Roberts leads the crowd into reciting of Scully signature line before every game: "It's time for Dodger baseball." The Dodgers defeat the Padres, 8–1.

PERFECT ELOQUENCE

FIRST INNING

"The Shelf Where I Live"

Mastering the Craft

Days before the 1992 Major League Baseball season was about to start, the idea came to my newspaper editors: what if Vin Scully shared with readers his top-ten Dodger Stadium moments?

It made sense. Dodger Stadium was celebrating its thirtieth anniversary, after all.

You sure you don't want Vin to give his top-thirty moments? I considered asking the editors. *It would make for a longer interview.*

I showed up at about 10:00 a.m. in the Dodger Stadium press box dining room where I was told to meet him, but no one was around. The team was back at Dodgertown in Vero Beach, Florida, finishing the exhibition season. I had talked to Vin a few times on the phone before this, and a few years into writing a regular sports media column, I felt up to speed on what to expect for our first in-person chat.

In my scorebook, this would be the start to a thirty-year professional and personal relationship. The previous thirty years were growing up in Southern California, starting a family, covering the team, trying to chronicle Scully's impact. Maybe Scully helped influence my own journalism career, by virtue of his storytelling.

When Vin came into the room, introduced himself, pulled up his chair, and started the conversation, it was textbook example of how to be accommodating and make someone else comfortable.

I had a sense of what he'd pick as his most outstanding memories but wanted to hear them all over again:

- The 1962 Opening Day at Dodger Stadium: "It had tremendous meaning for me, having been with the Dodgers back in New York. This was the culmination of a dream for Walter O'Malley. It meant permanence.

1

The Coliseum was now someone else's park. This was going to be our home. The fact the Dodgers lost that game (to Cincinnati) didn't mean a thing."

- Any game when Sandy Koufax pitched: "Even on the road, when he'd walk out to warm up in the bullpen, he'd get a round of applause. That was almost like the conductor to the symphony would get when he ascended the podium."
- Kirk Gibson's 1988 World Series Game One walk-off home run: Scully explained in detail about asking NBC director Harry Coyle to come out of the commercial with a wide shot of the stadium, then pan the Dodgers' dugout without Gibson, then follow him up to the plate. "Without a doubt, the most theatrical moment," Scully said, with a tint of drama coming in his words again. "I was just trying to set the scene as a fan would if he was in the park. I wasn't carrying any special message except for the fact 'he's not in the dugout, so we're not going to see him.' Then to see him stuffing in his shirt . . . never before in my mind was the stage so dressed for the leading character." And Scully dressed it up for the occasion, of course.

Dodger Stadium five years earlier was the site of a Catholic Mass celebrated by Pope Saint John Paul II and drew the largest crowd in stadium history, more than sixty-three thousand. Scully was on the road with the Dodgers at the time and could not attend in person.

In 1966 John, Paul, George, and Ringo—the Beatles—were drowned out by screams as they played in concert on a stage near second base. That same year, Elvis Presley shot a movie, *Spinout*, around the ballpark.

Eventually, the place would be a venue for the Three Tenors—Plácido Domingo, Luciano Pavarotti, and José Carreras. There would be iconic performances by Elton John, Bruce Springsteen, the Rolling Stones, U2, Michael Jackson, among others.

But for all those who entered and left the building, Scully was and remains, even all this time after his passing, Dodger Stadium's most relevant and long-term resident, his name now on a street nearby.

And he even sang there—his recording of "Wind beneath My Wings" was his walk-off moment in September 2016.

Let's get back to 1992. Because of this in-person interview opportunity, I asked if he could expand a bit on how he approached and perfected his craft. I gulped. He obliged:

- Because he sounded so much today as he did decades ago, did he ever have a sense he was a broadcaster locked in time? He reshaped my question: "I don't know about that. I think all of us are aware of our shortcomings and our failings and our struggles. But I think what happens when I'm actually broadcasting a game for that three-hour period, I really am, I guess you could say, locked into time. I'm totally oblivious of everything else that might have happened to me that day or week or month. It's where I'm most familiar and where I'm most relaxed and, in a sense, I guess that's the shelf where I live."
- Every other MLB team employed multiple broadcasters in the booth. Scully stayed with a one-man, one-mic setup with the Dodgers, even though he showed graciousness sharing the call on a national TV game broadcast. Why? He said he believed in the end game: "The reason I think that it is valid is that when I'm doing local baseball—and I qualify that by saying local baseball—one of the jobs of the announcer is to get people to come to the ballpark, to sell the game, to sell the teams, sell the players. The best way to sell is for me to talk directly to you. Okay, so I might say, 'Oh, wow, where were you last night? Oh my gosh, was that a game. . . . Hope you'll be out tomorrow.' I'm talking directly to you, and I know somewhere I'm getting a response. The other way is to block you out and let you just listen to me having a conversation with somebody else. To me, that doesn't work. That really began with the networks. This is my own opinion and philosophy, but if I owned a team, and I wanted to sell my fans on coming to the ballpark, I would not want a lot of voices cluttering up the air. I would want one man at a one time talking to that fan. I really think that's a valid way."
- Labor negotiations made headlines off the field in '92. Scully's approach was not to talk about those kinds of things while the game was in progress. Was that fair? "I've tried very hard to stay away from salaries and arbitration and all the things that go on. Basically, I like to do the

game, and I think the fan does too. The only time I stress big money would be if the two fellows who are personally involved have overwhelmingly different salaries. Say one team brings in a pitcher making the minimum as a rookie and he's facing Darryl Strawberry with a $25 million contract. Otherwise, I don't think people care. I know I'm not that interested. I just want to concentrate on the game. It was that bit of philosophy that caused a brouhaha a few years ago prior to the strike [of 1981, when Scully was criticized for avoiding talk about the pending midseason shutdown], but it was because I just felt there was nothing we could do. We couldn't provide any news. I thought anyone who followed baseball at all had it up to here with arbitration and clauses and agents and lawyers. So, I said, 'Hey guys, let's just do the ball game.' There were those who thought I was withholding information, and in all honesty, I wasn't trying to fool anybody. I just wanted to say, 'Give 'em a game, give 'em the best we've got, and let the people who decide make the decision on what's going to happen.'"

- Even then, I had to ask, "When do you retire?" At that moment, Tommy Lasorda, not yet sixty-five, was in the news. Some wondered if it was best for him to step away after sixteen seasons as manager and forty-two years in the organization. The team eventually gave him a two-year extension. "I still get thrilled to my toes when there are great plays and dramatic moments. I think as long as it's a genuine feeling, as long as I don't have to manufacture an emotion, I think my body and my mind is telling me to keep doing it. I enjoy it immensely. It's so much part of my life. It's really been a lovely marriage. I don't want to bring it to an end."

No one did.

In 1992 the Dodgers would lose an MLB-worst ninety-nine games, finishing thirty-five games out in the NL West. Opening Day was followed about a month later by the LA riots, and the Dodgers' schedule would endure cancellations and doubleheader make-up dates. The Dodgers, and baseball, would be a tough sell and a true test of Scully's ability to offer a diversion and keep things in perspective.

At this point, I turned off my Sony microtape recorder, fumbled through a thank you, and got up to find an exit before security could usher me out.

"Want to have some breakfast?" Scully asked. "It's just us now, two guys talking." He must have seen someone else at another table—except no one else was around.

Here was my first squint into the spotlight. Scully's presence could illuminate a room, adjust the settings, and remove any perceived status barrier. Even a dimwit like me could see it happen.

I left the ballpark wondering if the interview really happened. I never thought of Scully in any sort of idolized way, but since his voice had been part of my life for so long, the first time looking him in the eye, shaking his hand, and getting a pat on the shoulder made it all finally feel real. The post-interview conversation felt as normal as anything. It was a common experience many would share with me years later.

As the years went on and I compiled an annual list of the best and worst of Los Angeles broadcasters for the Southern California News Group, the challenge was how to come up with a fresh way to keep Scully in the number one spot among play-by-play men.

Decade after decade, he was Vin-describable, in-Vin-cible. I felt Vindicated by my rankings, having the opportunity so many times to find an empty chair in the broadcast booth and watch him work before first pitch, careful not to disrupt his preparation routine, which often included greeting waves of visitors who just wanted to share a hello and a story.

I recall as he was preparing for the home opener of 2014, I slipped into the broadcast booth and snapped a few iPhone photos. That eventually led to another conversation about the somewhat lost art of the scorebook and where he might have kept all those from past years with which he documented games. He said he wasn't sure—probably in a closet somewhere. I hoped they were saved for future archeologists who might be able to translate them.

During our back-and-forth, I got a phone call—my father-in-law had been taken ill in Arizona. My wife was driving out there to be with her family. I excused myself; left the ballpark before the game started, going

3. Vin Scully works on his scorebook in the TV press box at Dodger Stadium in October 2009. Courtesy of Tom Hoffarth.

upstream against the traffic coming in; collected some things at home; and made the five-hour drive. I was there for his eventual passing by week's end.

Looking back, I recognize this as another example of the realities of life and baseball and of appreciating time—the rebirth of an Opening Day intersecting a family member's eminent departure. When I told Scully later what had happened, he was remarkably consoling and asked me for stories about my father-in-law's love of baseball, leading to stories about Ted Williams and the Boston Red Sox.

Even as a sports media writer, I can't fully explain Scully's ability to excel at his craft. It is best to let those more experienced in this area share their insights from their vantage point.

Bob Costas
Hall of Fame network broadcaster

As a Christmas present when I was fifteen, I received a box set of three books called the Fireside Books of Baseball. It was a wonderful and eclectic collection of literature, newspaper and magazine pieces, poetry, comedy, lyrics, first-person recollections of long-ago people and events, all connected to baseball.

Included was a transcript of Vin Scully's radio call of the full ninth inning of Sandy Koufax's perfect game in September of 1965. At first, the fact it was a transcript escaped me. As I read it, I honestly thought it was a very well-written piece, designed to evoke the moment-by-moment atmosphere and to build tension and excitement as Koufax approached and then achieved perfection. If that had been the case, it would have been worthy of praise.

But no. It was a word-for-word transcript of the live broadcast. In the moment, extemporaneously, Scully composed a masterpiece in the booth equal to Koufax's on the mound: a perfect game somehow elevated by a beyond-perfect description.

That ninth inning is one of the best-remembered examples of Scully's unique brilliance. It's all on display: the pleasing and distinctive voice, the command of language and phrasing, the grace notes, the eye for the telling detail, the sense of the moment, and the ability to capture and enhance it without ever resorting to shouting.

Which brings us to this: To truly appreciate Scully's mastery, it's not enough to replay standard highlights. Other great broadcasters have also risen to big moments in memorable fashion—the climactic home run, the great catch, the last out of a World Series. What set Scully apart was the framing of those moments—the buildup, the payoff, and then the postscript.

Listen to that entire Koufax ninth inning, to the entire extended at bat that culminates in Kirk Gibson's impossibly theatrical pinch-hit homer in the 1988 World Series, and then the coda: "In a year that has been so improbable, the impossible has happened!"

Or listen to the call of Henry Aaron's 715th home run, the one that took him past Babe Ruth to the top of the all-time list. The call is exciting and precise, but the aftermath is a first draft of history.

4. Sandi and Vin Scully with Bob and Jill Costas. Courtesy of Bob Costas.

Nearly thirty years ago, I interviewed Ray Charles for the NBC newsmagazine *Now* with Tom Brokaw and Katie Couric. When the cameras and microphones had been shut off, we continued to converse. At one point, Ray said, "You know who I would really like to meet? Vin Scully. Could you introduce me to him?"

Well, sure I could. But this was Ray Charles. He must have met countless interesting and accomplished people. Why Vin?

"Well, I love baseball. And you have to understand, Bob, the pictures mean nothing to me. It's all the sound. And Vin Scully's broadcasts are almost musical."

I called Vin, and we arranged to have the two of them meet and spend time together before a game at Dodger Stadium. Vin came into the booth, and as he walked toward Charles, he said, "Ray, my name is Vin Scully, and it's a pleasure to meet you." He might as well have said, "A pleasant good evening to you wherever you may be," because that's how it struck Ray. They sat down, and we had a combination baseball and music discussion. Vin had a nice experience. And Ray Charles—and I mean this sincerely—had one of the great experiences of his life.

Given his surpassing talent and approach, Vin Scully would have been unforgettably great with any team at any time. But the circumstances of his career can never be equaled. And those circumstances amplified his greatness.

The big moments Vin described so well resonated in a way comparable moments perhaps no longer do. Vin called sports other than baseball, of course. His golf and football work was—no surprise—excellent.

Still, it was baseball that called forth the full range of his abilities and sensibilities. The game's rich history, much of which he witnessed, with its gentle rhythms and leisurely pace, all played to Vin's many strengths.

In the closing seasons of his career, Vin's broadcasts were simultaneously present and nostalgic—the story of that night's game and a flashback to every game or time in your life his voice transported you to. In a world of seemingly fewer constants and enduring connections, that was deeply appealing. No matter how things around him changed, Vin was grandfathered in.

If, somehow, a twenty-two-year-old broadcaster with talent comparable to Scully's was to materialize today, that broadcaster would surely wind up in the Hall of Fame, would surely be celebrated. But the circumstances that shaped that broadcaster, as a person and a professional, and shaped how sports are presented and received, would never be close to the same.

For so many reasons, there will never be another Vin Scully. He wasn't once in a generation or once in a lifetime. He was once in forever.

David J. Halberstam
Broadcast historian

In putting together my book *Sports on New York Radio: A Play-by-Play History*, I documented Vin Scully's broadcasting birth in Brooklyn—eight seasons with the Dodgers there, then fifty-eight more in Los Angeles.

There were moments where his career could have pivoted—a job came open to call his childhood favorite New York Giants in 1950, but the team went with eventual Hall of Fame voice Ernie Harwell. That opened the door for Red Barber to hire Scully for the Dodgers, at $5,000 a year.

When the Dodgers moved west in 1958, owner Walter O'Malley had three broadcasters on his payroll but wanted to only take two with him. He resisted the way TV was prevalent in New York and was unwilling to give away what he was trying to sell in LA. Scully made the move, with Jerry Doggett. Al Helfer and Red Barber stayed.

SoCal erupted with baseball on radio. And never was there a better duo. The Dodgers world erupted, too, through radio and Vin's magical delivery, an unequaled artist, loved by all.

In 1964 the New York Yankees let go longtime voice Mel Allen and asked if Scully would like to come back to the East Coast and do games for the storied franchise. Scully considered it, then declined.

As for the essence of Scully's broadcasting career, some of the things I noted in my book still resonate today more than thirty years later.

Broadcasters became local and national voices when the World Series came around. Through 1978 the broadcast booth was graced by a member of each participating club's announce team. On either television or audio, it would be a special treat each fall, sprinkling the sports broadcasting landscape. The booth was a melting pot, and from the speakers came a multicultural sound. It was Broadway on tour.

Scully's introduction to this rotation came in 1953, again, as a business decision. Barber was the Brooklyn Dodgers' voice and had been appointed to work with Mel Allen of the New York Yankees. The talent fee was predetermined by Gillette, and it was apparently nonnegotiable. Barber was adamant and wanted more compensation. He was stunningly left off the broadcast. After the 1950 season, Branch Rickey was bought out of his team ownership share, and Walter O'Malley was in full control. Red's relationship with O'Malley and the club soured, and the Dodgers didn't intercede with Gillette on Red's behalf.

Connie Desmond, who had been with the club eleven years, was considered Brooklyn's number two man at the time. He was more than sufficiently talented to be a number one man in any Major League booth. But Connie was drinking, and the Dodgers and Gillette would take no chances with him on a national telecast.

O'Malley then nominated Scully, who had been with Brooklyn all of four years and was just twenty-five years old when the '53 Series started. Unseasoned perhaps, Vin was certainly ready and drilled. When offered the assignment, there was one piece of business remaining. He first checked with Barber. Red gave him his blessing, and as much as offered Scully his scorebook as a gesture of genuine endorsement. O'Malley approached Allen, now in his third decade of Fall Classic broadcasting, and said, "Take care of my boy Scully."

The sports world was shocked Scully was given the gig. The sports world might have been equally as shocked by Scully's performance. He handed the exalted booth with verbal aplomb and vocal grace.

Commissioner Ford Frick also had reminded all radio and television talent of a philosophy Commissioner Kenesaw Mountain Landis disseminated starting in 1935 that, among other things, interdicted play-by-play people from inserting opinions and particularly critiquing the work of the umpires. Scully thought Whitey Ford had tagged early on a fly ball and exclaimed as such immediately. Ford did not try to advance. For Scully and the outcome, it never became an issue.

For the 1955 World Series, Scully worked again with Allen on NBC, which lined up 185 stations for carriage. Scully did the last four and a half innings of the ultimate encounter, and at the moment of victory he was close to tears.

Two years later, the Dodgers announced they were headed for Los Angeles, and the golden-voiced Scully, not quite thirty at the time, was going along. Barber was adored by a generation; Scully would be for several generations.

If "radio is a blank canvas," as Scully would say, then he was Picasso. Blessed with the blarney of his Irish descent, the absolute command of the English language, and, most importantly, in-depth baseball knowledge, Scully owned October radio.

In 1992 Atlanta and Toronto faced one another, and Scully broadcast the game's first World Series from Canada. As he described it, "I come with a canvas, brushes, paints, and a palette. I paint broad strokes, and I mix the colors. I paint fine lines and the shadows and delineations. And eventually at the end of the three hours, the canvas is full, and that's the best I can do for the day." Dick Enberg lived in Los Angeles, calling Angels games and having a chance to listen and study Scully. He would describe him as someone who "has the patience to hold off using a note in the first inning when it might be better to sustain the drama of the eighth inning." So, when Joe Carter homered in the ninth of Game Six in '93, Scully, as usual, let the crowd paint the frenzied picture.

Red Barber died as the 1992 fall drama ended. After the sixth and final game on October 24, 1992, Vin proceeded to Tallahassee for the funeral of his mentor.

As network deals changed the landscape of the game's coverage again, maybe life's best lesson came again from Scully, and it had nothing to do with language or baseball. Barry Jackson of the *Miami Herald* asked him about the prospects of the 1997 World Series being his last.

"You should always look at everything you do as the last one you're ever going to do," he said. That's an unbelievable attitude for anything in life.

Andy Rosenberg

NBC Major League Baseball and golf director
and producer (1979 to 2014)

I first met Vin in January 1983, when he began his tenure at NBC as the host announcer on the network's golf coverage. Over the next seven years, we also worked many baseball games, culminating with a full season of Major League Baseball in 1989. Later on, we also worked together on some Dodgers telecasts.

As soon as Vin joined our golf coverage, it was immediately evident we had a different feel. It sounded so much better. He added a presence that hadn't been there previously. Alongside Lee Trevino in the eighteenth tower, Vin elevated our golf. Our shows were now hosted by one of the greatest announcers in sports history along with one of golf's all-time greatest players.

When Vin arrived, I was fairly young in my NBC career, and I wasn't quite sure what to expect from someone whom I'd heard for years and was already considered the best in the business. Broadcasting is full of type A, high-powered egos, some of whom can be very demanding. Vin was gracious, a gentleman, and simply a joy to work with.

Most compelling to me was Vin's wonderful use of language, without being patronizing or condescending. Unique about Vin, other than his classic introduction to the audience, was that he didn't rely on a signature catch phrase as a personal watermark on the action, all too common in sports broadcasting. Vin was a wordsmith who was very creative. An elegance and intelligence set him apart, like a good novel. If a novelist relies too much on repeated phraseology, the novel feels flat and unimaginative. If it's written with unique word combinations to describe characters and everyday situations, it's more engaging, and readers' mental pictures are fuller and more enriched. In the same way, while I provided the pictures the audience saw, Vin's descriptions added so much depth and texture. That, to me, is genius.

I recall a favorite story regarding his descriptive language. Vin and I were heading to New York on a red-eye after a ball game on the West Coast. We sat next to each other on a TWA L-1011, so that tells you how long ago it was. As the plane took off and I was ready to nod off, I peeked over, curious to see what Vin was reading, expecting it to be sports-related. Many broadcasters scour the sports sections of newspapers to find tidbits. Others watch lots of broadcasts to glean things they can add to their own shows.

But what was Vin reading? *The Poems of Dylan Thomas*. No wonder. He's reading another great wordsmith for his own joy and maybe to enhance his own verbal creativity. To me, it encapsulated his preparation. He had developed his own craft and style over a long period and wasn't searching to copy others. He simply didn't watch other broadcasters. Vin was a well-read Renaissance man who wasn't obsessed with sports to the exclusion of his other interests. Though his career took much of the time of his life, he was never one-dimensional. His career wasn't his whole life.

Working with Vin on baseball and golf, I was able to appreciate his storytelling at close range. Those two sports have a different pace than the rat-a-tat-tat, back-and-forth of sports like basketball and football. Baseball and golf are both long-form. Golf is a multiday event, and baseball has three- and four-game series. Each not only provide time to craft stories to engage viewers but also almost demand it. And frankly, keeping viewers glued to their set is the bottom line of TV.

Our research showed some viewers stay tuned primarily to see who wins. Yet there is a significant portion who watch because they like the stories about the people participating. So, to balance those desires and to try to keep people watching if there's an 11–2 baseball game or the leader of the golf tournament is ahead by ten strokes, we need to get viewers to care about the players as much as the outcome, and that's best done through storytelling. I don't think that was at all the motivation behind Vin's storytelling—to hook people to watch longer—he was just naturally inviting viewers to join in, as nonvocal participants, in his afternoon conversation—simply brilliant.

It's important to develop a trust with the audience, a trust that what you want to see and want to hear will be provided without asking for it. Vin consistently did that well, and most noticeably in the biggest moments he knew when to back off and let the moment tell everything that he could have said and more without interfering. Too many announcers want to hear their voice when the highlights of their game are shown later rather than letting the moment breathe. I'm not sure if Vin pioneered the concept, but certainly his senses were in tune with the game to consistently know when it was time to let the pictures speak for themselves.

Vin was also terrific working with the production crew to establish stories. A well-done broadcast is almost like watching a great dance duo glide across the floor. At different times, each dancer takes a turn as the leader. When skillfully done, no one at home has an idea who's leading the dance or broadcast. The reality is we took turns. To help me, in addition to the speakers for everyone in the control room to listen to, I always asked for a small speaker right in front of me, maybe four-by-six inches, that only had the broadcasters' voices, without the sound of the crowd. I could focus on what they were saying over the din of the control room. I wanted to know exactly what Vin said so I could complement his narrative with my pictures.

In that regard and unique to golf, most of the show is driven by the producer and director in the control room. The broadcasters in the eighteenth tower can only see the green right in front of them and nothing else taking place around the course. That dance is led by that decision-making, and the announcers have to seamlessly wrap the whole package together. Vin, a consummate raconteur, effortlessly did that.

Another aspect of Vin's skills that impressed me, and is easily overlooked, was how he broadcast the first three innings of local Dodgers games on TV, the middle three on radio, and then back to TV for the last three innings. There are different priorities and needs on TV versus radio. To go back and forth within a single game is very hard and almost requires a split personality. Vin bounced back and forth without a glitch.

A unique example of Vin's professionalism occurred during the 1984 World Series. Vin was in his second year at NBC, calling the series with Joe Garagiola. The final out was made, and the Detroit Tigers won. While we wrapped up our broadcast, the fans stormed the field. In the celebration, they ripped out hunks of grass and were throwing it everywhere—including up at the booth, which at Tiger Stadium in those days was one of the closest to the field of any stadium. As Vin provided his closing thoughts and read the credits, he had to dive under the console to avoid being hit with clumps of sod.

Huddled under the table, with the monitor and his notes above, he somehow finished his remarks without any attention drawn to his hidden position, and we smoothly went off the air. Easily the most bizarre way to finish a broadcast, that's grace under pressure.

Jeff Proctor

Sports TV executive

I was the executive producer at Fox Sports West when we did Dodgers games in the late '90s and early 2000s. In that role, I also got to produce about twenty events a year, and invariably I'd make sure that I did a few Dodgers games so I got to work with Vin.

Working with him was vastly different than with any other play-by-play announcer and not just because he was the best that ever did it. He was a throwback to a different era when announcers weren't intruded upon by their producers who needed them to read promos, describe replays, and send the telecast to the sideline reporter. Additionally, Vin didn't work with a partner.

In deference to his desire to speak to his audience and to not be interrupted by a producer who had an agenda that might differ from his, I very rarely talked to him in his headset during a game. He had a stage manager, Boyd Robertson, whom I'd communicate with to hand him the promos, alert him to graphics or replays, and point out things on his monitor that I felt that he needed to know. It was a completely different way of producing a game, but it was clearly the right way to do it. Vin called the game as he saw fit, and I was there to support him, not produce him.

An unwritten rule in the production truck is to not follow the announcers but lead them. In other words, the truck provides the announcer with the pictures, graphics, and replays, and the announcer reacts to them. That was not the case (nor should it have been) with Vin. When he said that the wind was gently blowing out to left-center, the director knew to follow him by getting a shot of the flags waving in the breeze. When he started a story

5. Vin Scully, *center*, enjoys a visit by a group of Little Leaguers from Manhattan Beach, California, 2009. Courtesy of Jeff Proctor.

about the third base coach, even on his radio and television simulcast, the director knew to get a shot of the third base coach.

All of us in the production truck wanted to support him and his stories, and we reacted in a way that really wasn't done with other announcers. The best at doing this was longtime director Mike Ireland, who worked with Vin for years. He suggested to me prior to my first couple of Dodgers games that it would be better to react as opposed to act, and it was great advice. There was no way that I wanted to get in Vin's way!

Clearly, in a city of great announcers, he was the very best that any of us had ever heard, much less worked with. But he was also as nice and generous a man as one could hope. We saw that as all the politicians, actors, other broadcasters, and starstruck fans were constantly making pilgrimages into the booth to say hi to Vin. I never saw him be anything but gracious, warm, and engaging with whomever he was speaking. I took my Little League All-Star team to the booth to get a picture with him, and he spoke to each member of the team and made them all feel special.

6. Vin Scully and Hannah Proctor at Vero Beach, Florida, in 2006. Courtesy of Jeff Proctor.

But my favorite Vin story is a personal one.

I took my daughter Hannah, who was eleven at the time, to spring training at Vero Beach in 2006, and we spent the day with Vin. Over lunch, he asked her if she had a boyfriend, encouraged her to have ice cream for lunch, and generally couldn't have been nicer to her. Because of my role at Fox Sports, my daughter had been to a number of sporting events in her brief life. Although she enjoyed going, she didn't have much of a grasp of how special this day was.

Fellow announcer Rick Monday and general manager Ned Colletti came over and said hi to her during the meal. It was just a fun father-daughter day for her as far as she was concerned.

Later, during the game that afternoon, the two of us sat in the small press box behind Vin and listened to him as he announced the game back to Southern California. When the game was over, we said our goodbyes and thanked him for an amazing day, and he made a point of telling Hannah how much he had enjoyed spending the day with her.

As we left, a crowd formed, about two hundred or three hundred people who hoped to get an autograph or picture with Vin as he left his perch. Hannah looked at me as we passed the line and said, "Daddy, is Mr. Scully famous?" That line has lived in our family lore ever since.

To me, Vin will always embody a guy who lived up to every bit of his reputation. He was as great a baseball broadcaster as there was, but, more importantly, he was even nicer than you might have expected.

Tom Villante
Brooklyn and Los Angeles Dodgers
broadcast director (1952 to 1959)

When I first met Vin Scully in 1952, I was with the BBDO advertising agency. The company's two biggest clients, Schaefer Beer and Lucky Strike cigarettes, were the two cosponsors of the Brooklyn Dodgers on radio and TV. So, BBDO had me as the director of the games. As it turned out, I was the only guy who worked with both Red Barber and Vinny, so that was kind of unusual.

I very seldom had to give Vin any advice on the broadcast; I only offered help on the technical side. When Vinny first came up, he had a tendency to be very nasal, but his voice mellowed as it went on.

Red was his mentor but was very tough on him. I remember the first thing he told Vinny: "When you get to the ballpark, the first people you should talk to are both trainers. Then talk to the players on the other side to see how they wanted their names pronounced. Get your notes together."

As it turned out, sometimes Vinny would use up his notes by the end of the first inning. Red said, "You gotta use it when it's relevant."

He explained to him that the crowd noise in baseball was more unique than in any other sport. If you turned on a radio and heard crowd noise, you knew when it was from a baseball game. Red explained how that crowd noise was a continuity thread. It worked forward. Don't ever talk over it. You could always tell the amateurs who would talk over the crowd noise.

So, if there is a double play, let the crowd roar, and after it died down, you could fill in the particulars: It was hit to Reese, who threw to Jackie Robinson, who whipped it to Hodges.

I think the most interesting thing Red passed on to Vinny was the value of having one person on the air. The key was to imagine just talking to one person—your mother, your brother, your best friend—instead of to thousands. Red didn't like the idea of several guys in the booth because the announcer talked to them rather than the audience. That's why I think Vin understood why he was best at working alone. He had the confidence of the audience, which also meant when he did commercials, he could talk straight to that one person.

So many commercials were on the games in those days; some were live. Vinny was good with ad-libs at the appropriate moments in the commercial. People could believe him. He had their trust. Obviously, this was back when there wasn't a ban on cigarette ads like today, or as much with alcohol. But that relates to another thing Red taught Vin: "Before a game, don't be seen having a beer in the press room. It will lead to people becoming suspicious. You don't want that."

Through the years I could see how Vinny had that extra quality of sensing and developing drama. When something was happening, he could picture it as an event that might someday be historic, so he always set the stage—perhaps the date and time, or anything needed for a historic film clip. He learned anticipation from Red. On radio, Red was the master. He had complete control. A lot of the games in Brooklyn were in the afternoon, so Red knew the broadcast would often air when people were going home from work and the car radios were very important. Red knew when people turned on that radio, they wanted to know the score, the inning, what's going on. Red insisted Vin give the score and paint a scene every three minutes and supported that with a sandglass egg timer, which he impressed on Vinny to use.

As Vinny's voice mellowed, I think he had greater confidence in himself, and that made him a master storyteller. He could interject stories and not interfere with the play-by-play.

When we first moved to LA, everyone had their radio tuned into Scully, and you hear the broadcast as if it were coming through one huge loud-speaker. Vinny would deliberately play into it. It was easy to know they were out there. As he went on, his voice was better and better, very distinctive and personal.

One of my favorite stories concerns a shortstop from Taiwan named Chin-lung Hu, who played for the Dodgers from 2007 through 2010. His last name was pronounced *who*. One time, he was at bat and drew a walk. At last, Vin reported, "All my life I've been waiting to say this: Hu's on first."

SECOND INNING

"I'm with Them"

Family and Faith

Vin Scully's family and friends gathered for a small private funeral Mass at St. Jude the Apostle Catholic Church in Westlake Village, California, on August 8, 2022, six days after his passing. Fr. Steve Davoren, the Catholic priest who presided over the services, said from where he stood at the altar he could see the faces of Dodgers history—Sandy Koufax, Kirk Gibson, Clayton Kershaw, Jaime Jarrin, Steve Garvey, Dave Roberts—making it easy to mention all of Scully's great professional moments. But during his homily, Father Davoren emphasized why he thought Scully was much more in tune with St. Augustine's acronym of FAMILY—Forget about me, I love you. "No matter how many famous people may have been there in attendance, it was still about the ordinary person that Vin was, and the extraordinary friend he was to all," Father Davoren said.

At the end of the funeral Mass and before the burial at Holy Cross Cemetery in Culver City, Scully's children took turns offering memories and sharing stories. His daughter Erin explained how she had searched her dad's office to find something that might comfort her. She came across a prayer from Catholic theologian St. John Henry Newman. In essence, it says, "God has created me to do Him some definite service. . . . Therefore, I will trust Him. . . . If I am in sorrow, my sorrow may serve Him. . . . He may make me feel desolate, make my spirits sink, hide my future from me. Still, He knows what He is about." Father Davoren added that "in the context of everything, the passage Erin picked was so beautiful because it showed how Vin was a man of deep abiding faith in our Lord Jesus and had a tremendous love of his family."

The family picked the readings—Proverbs 3:1–18; Psalm 23; 1 Thessalonians 4:13–18; and the Gospel of Matthew 5:13–16—and also wanted a version of "The Prayer" song made famous by Josh Groban. The prelude was "Go Rest High on that Mountain." A tenor sang "Danny Boy" for the procession, while "Ave Maria" was sung at the presentation of the gifts. The procession out of the church was "I Can Only Imagine." A song of farewell was also included: "May the Angels Be Your Guide." Many of the six hundred mourners in attendance talked about how they came away comforted by the moment.

If members of Scully's family were able to lean into their faith as a way to cope with his departure, they had a shining example. Vin Scully showed how he was able to do it time and time again over the course of his ninety-plus years:

- He was only four when the father he was named after died of pneumonia. He recalled his immigrant mother, Bridget, took him back to Dublin, Ireland, in time for the Thirty-First International Eucharistic Congress in June 1932. Reports were that a quarter of the entire country's population attended a Mass in Phoenix Park. "My mother, heartbroken, brought me back home and spent quite a bit of time not only in Ballyconnell but out on the farms and wherever the family was," Scully said.
- In January 1972 Scully said he heard his dog barking at 3:30 a.m. and turned in bed to check on his wife, Joan. She had died. She was thirty-five. The coroner's report was that the mother of his three children had had an accidental reaction to taking medications prescribed for a severe cold and bronchitis. The couple had been married almost sixteen years, wed in February 1958, right after the Dodgers moved to LA.
- Michael Scully, the oldest of those three children, died in 1994 at age thirty-three in a helicopter crash in the San Fernando Valley while inspecting pipelines after the Northridge earthquake.
- In January 2021 Scully's second wife, Sandi, died at seventy-six from complications brought upon by the neuromuscular disease amyotrophic lateral sclerosis (ALS, better known as Lou Gehrig's disease) after a long struggle. Scully called her "a true saint if there ever was one." She belonged to the Calvary Community Church of Conejo Valley in Westlake Village. That often meant the couple went to two church services on Sundays, a respect of their union of forty-eight years.

Scully explained his faith in a 2019 interview with *Angelus News*: "Thank God, my faith has always kept things in perspective. Completely. It has not wavered. As many who've known me know, I've had some pain in my life. Faith is the one thing that makes it work, makes me keep going. You appreciate what you've been given.

"I used my faith to keep me straight and narrow and strong, for sure. I think about that every week when I'm in line going up to the rail to receive Communion. That's a pretty important moment. It always was and always will be."

In a 1986 interview with the *Sporting News*, Scully mentioned that because he was brought up Irish Catholic, death was an ordinary subject: "From the first day I can remember, I was told about death. Death is a constant companion in our religion. You live with it easily; it is not a morbid thought. That has given me the perspective that whatever I have can disappear in 30 seconds. And being out on the road as much as I am, I realize I am killing the most precious thing that I have—time. You never know how much of it you have left."

That was evident on a Dodgers road trip on Fourth of July weekend in 1993. On the air, Scully had to inform viewers during a Saturday televised Dodgers-Expos game in Montreal that Dodgers Hall of Fame great and fellow broadcaster Don Drysdale had died in his hotel room. "Never have I been asked to make an announcement that hurts me as much as this one," Scully said at that time. "And I say it to you as best I can with a broken heart."

Sports Illustrated's Tom Verducci wrote in a 2016 cover story that the "benevolence of Vin was rooted in his faith. He emphasized that 'the most essential thing' he learned from his faith and the church was 'the importance of continual communication with God.'"

Scully grew up in New York's Catholic Youth Organization (CYO), which landed him tickets to games at the Polo Grounds to see his favorite team, the New York Giants. One time outside the park, he met Babe Ruth.

Scully said he recalled in grammar school how teachers from the good Sisters of Charity tried to correct one of God's apparent mistakes—he wrote left-handed. "A whack across the knuckles with a ruler every time I used my left hand," he told me. "Once in a while, out of frustration, they would turn the ruler so I would get hit on the edge, which would break the skin. It's prehistoric to think of this now, isn't it?

"So one night at dinner, I'm home and passing the bread, and my mother saw my beaten-up left hand. She immediately thought I did something wrong and was being punished. Well, 99 percent of the time, she'd be right. I explained how the nuns didn't want me to use my left hand.

"What made it interesting to me when I heard her tell the story years later was that we had a Jewish family doctor named Dr. Rose. He wrote this wonderful letter to the nuns saying: 'If you force this boy to write right-handed, against his natural bent, it could very well cause him to stutter.' And not only that, but he finished by writing: 'Dear sisters, why would you wish to change God's work?'

"Boom! A grand slam! From that moment on, they allowed me to be left-handed or else that would have changed my life dramatically."

If one listened close enough, Scully revealed the foundation of his faith and the respect and love he had for family in his broadcasts. When explaining years later why he verbally stamped the date and time on Sandy Koufax's 1965 perfect game amid his live call, Scully admitted it was so Koufax's family would have that reference point.

Following an infrequent mistake, Scully might exclaim the Latin phrase "mea culpa," which translates to "through my fault" and is used in a prayer of confession in the Catholic Church.

One of the most referenced of Scully's recognizable quotes focused on his appreciation of time given to all of us. The Dodgers were playing a game against the Chicago Cubs, and he told listeners about an injured player: "They say Andre Dawson is day-to-day . . . aren't we all?" When asked how that came about, Scully told me, "That was a weekday game on the radio and I'm sitting there, my chin in my hand, very low key and I was handed a note that Andre Dawson was listed as 'day-to-day' and . . . I just paused and really spoke out loud. It was such a simple thing"—a simple thing often repeated to put things into perspective.

Scully may have been present for the Miracle on Coogan's Bluff (the 1951 home run by the New York Giants' Bobby Thomson that ruined the Brooklyn Dodgers' season) and described Kirk Gibson's "impossible" 1988

World Series Game One homer. But the one home run call that he said impacted him most deeply was one he didn't even do.

In the 1963 World Series, Scully shared the national TV microphone with Mel Allen—again—for a Dodgers-Yankees battle. In Game Four, with the Dodgers ready to sweep the series, Scully did the first four and a half innings and was told that, if the Dodgers won, he was to go downstairs to conduct interviews in the locker room. But there was an ongoing problem in the booth with Allen's voice. Doctors warned him not to put too much stress on it. Scully was on standby.

In the seventh inning, Mickey Mantle hit a game-tying home run off Sandy Koufax. "Mel had a great call: 'Going, going... gone!' but he forgot all about the constraints," said Scully. "When he hit the word 'gone!' the whole voice went. It was awful.

"That really affected me emotionally.... I really could have cried for Mel at that instant. It's a national stage, I had done my part, no reason to come back, but I had to because Mel couldn't finish after that.

"That home run always has been with me because of the thought: There but for the grace of God go I. When I rank the most memorable home runs for me—Bobby Thomson, Kirk Gibson, Henry Aaron (his 715th career home run in Atlanta against the Dodgers), I think Mickey Mantle's is there in my book because of the impact it had on me spiritually. Really."

It's a reminder of one of Scully's famous fallback lines: "If you want to make God smile, tell him your plans." "Maybe as a child I heard a priest say it and it just stuck," he said. "It makes good sense. You know, we try to write our own script and it's a mistake. There's a script already written for us."

Scully admitted there was nothing scripted when first met Sandi Hunt as a secretary for the Los Angeles Rams and eventually courted her. She had two children of her own. Vin had his three. Together, they added one more. The blended family of six kids worked. The story goes that, in the 1970s when *The Brady Bunch* was one of the popular TV shows, Scully met actress Florence Henderson at Dodger Stadium during the Hollywood Stars Night festivities. She played the family's mother, Carol Brady, a widow who shepherded her three daughters into a new marriage with a man who brought his own three sons for a blended, six-child family.

"Miss Henderson, I have my own 'Brady Bunch,' and I have news for you: Our problems cannot be solved in 28 minutes," Scully told her.

In the final years of his broadcasting career, on Sunday mornings prior to an afternoon ball game at Dodger Stadium during the season, Scully could arrive early for a specially arranged Mass. It was organized by Catholic Athletes for Christ (CAC) for players and team personnel at MLB ballparks across the country. Vin and Sandi Scully joined decades-long friend and one-time Dodgers traveling secretary Billy DeLury at a makeshift chapel inside Dodger Stadium down near the locker rooms. When DeLury died at eighty-one in 2015, Scully made sure to drape DeLury's blue Dodgers jacket over an empty chair next to him.

Scully would often do the liturgical readings at those ballpark Masses. Former Dodgers outfielder Andre Ethier said that, considering all he achieved in his twelve-year career in LA, his favorite memory remains listening to Scully as a lector. "There was something probably not many got a chance to hear—Vin reading from the Bible, in his typical voice and presentation," Ethier told SportsNet LA during a Scully tribute show. "It kind of would always perk me up when you hear Vin say something out of context from what we were used to hearing."

In 2016 Scully left a lasting tribute to CAC by reading an audio narration of the Catholic Rosary prayer, which was widely acclaimed and remains requested by listeners nationally and internationally. Church was on Scully's mind as his ninetieth birthday arrived in 2017. He committed to be in Pasadena to meet Rachel Robinson and dedicate a statue outside the Rose Bowl for Jackie Robinson. Hours before, Scully said, he went to St. Jude's daily Mass to give grace for this milestone, "and I asked for a couple more going forward," he added.

Scully's faith was a large influence on others in his inner circle.

In 2022 Ed White, Scully's attorney and executor of his estate, delivered donations of $1 million to both his high school and college alma maters in New York. White, senior partner with Edward White & Company in Woodland Hills, California, also revealed Scully sponsored him during his own conversion to Catholicism.

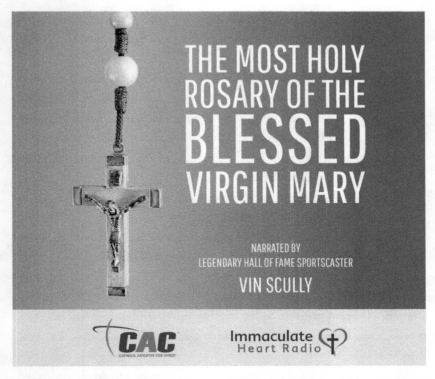

7. A compact disc of the Catholic Rosary as produced by the Catholic Athletes for Christ (CAC), voiced by Vin Scully. Courtesy of CAC.

"He loved the foundation that he received, spiritually and academically," said White. "Every time he spoke of Fordham, it was glowing."

In March 2023 Fordham arranged for a Scully memorial Mass at St. Patrick's Cathedral in New York presided by His Eminence Timothy Cardinal Dolan. At the end, the Scully family in attendance again shared the words of St. John Henry Newman, describing the prayer as "Dad's North Star—his own personal mission statement."

During the Mass, Fr. Joe Parkes, a former president of Fordham Prep, told a story he had heard about some Brooklyn Dodgers players who had been out late on a night of celebration after a playoff victory. The next morning at 6:00 a.m., reporters and photographers showed up at the team hotel to chastise all who were out cavorting. Scully filtered in among them. It was natural to suspect he was included in the revelry. Scully honestly had an alibi: he was come back from attending morning Mass at St. Patrick's Cathedral.

In June 2016, the summer leading up to his retirement, Scully was bestowed the Gabriel Award by the Catholic Academy of Communication Professionals. Unable to attend the ceremony in Saint Louis, the eighty-eight-year-old Scully created a five-minute video acceptance speech. It gave him an opportunity to recapture the time in 1956 when he was with a group that met Pope Pius XII in Rome.

The Dodgers organization made a trip to Japan for several exhibition games. On its way back to New York, Scully joined pitcher Ralph Branca and his wife, Ann, to divert through Europe for an audience with the pope. It was arranged by Ann's father, James, part owner of the Brooklyn Dodgers and a member of the Order of Malta.

Scully tried to stay calm; as he said, "My knees were trembling." He wanted to keep a promise to his mother to remember every detail. That meant describing the pope as "somewhat gaunt, with black olive eyes, wearing glasses."

After the Pope greeted the Branca couple, he turned to Scully and asked, "Are you with them?"

Scully said, "Yes."

The pope then walked over to the next guests.

"How would you like to tell that to your mother?" Scully asked.

But as he could do, Scully took that line and found its context with his Catholic roots. "As I've gotten older I realized that those couple of words 'Are you with them?' really sums up why I'm here," he said as he addressed a Catholic audience that included priests and sisters. "Oh yes. 'Are you with them' for the thousands of baseball games that I saw, the hundreds and hundreds of home runs to end exciting games, the no-hitters—I was with them. . . .

"The more I think about it now I realize not all of us can be heroes. Certainly for me, a hero goes by and I'm standing on the curb applauding as I was with them.

"I remember: To whom much is given, a great deal is required. And I pray that I will be able to fill the definition of what was required before I leave this mortal coil."

Scully then asked if he could have a picture of all the priests and sisters who were present at the banquet that night.

"I'd like to have that so when I am finally called upon on Judgment Day, I will go up and I will hold that picture and I will say, 'I'm with them.' God bless and good night."

Ann Meyers Drysdale
Naismith Memorial Basketball Hall of Fame inductee (1993)
Wife of the late Dodgers pitcher Don Drysdale

When Don passed away in July 1993, Vin spoke at his service. It was very hard on everyone. Vin and his wife Sandi helped me so much get through the funeral. Don was only fifty-six, and no one expected his death. Just a few years earlier, at our new home in Pasadena, we had a surprise party for Don on his fifty-third birthday. Vinny was there, with John Wooden and Gene Mauch. We were all so glad to be back home in LA.

Dodgers owner Peter O'Malley made the team very family orientated. When Don started doing games for the Dodgers in 1988, Vin was always very welcoming. Don was excited to be back where he pitched for so many years. We brought our two young boys, D.J. and Darren, to stop in the press box and see Vin, Ross Porter, and Jaime Jarrin.

The Dodgers had so much respect for Don that when he died, our family felt taken care of. Vin treated me like a daughter and our three children like his grandkids. He and my youngest, Drew, had a special relationship. She was only three months old when Don died.

Part of my healing process was going to the ballpark at about 1:00 p.m., and Tommy Lasorda would have our boys down at the batting cage. Up in the press box, Vin always had time for Drew. During that period, Vin and his wife, Sandi, were so generous with their time. She was always there for me, which wasn't easy.

8. Vin Scully with Ann Meyers Drysdale, 2016. Courtesy of Ann Meyers Drysdale.

When I was inducted into the Catholic Youth Organization's Hall of Fame, Vin Scully and Peter O'Malley came for me. We always had that Catholic connection. My older sister, Patty, had also taught two of Vin's daughters at Corpus Christi Catholic Church in the Pacific Palisades. On the road trips, I would go to church with Don, Vinny, and Coach Joe Amalfitano. When Vin passed away, Drew and I were at his funeral. It was very uplifting. His children were wonderful talking about their dad. We were also at Sandi's funeral when she passed away. That was so difficult for Vin and his family, especially for the limitations caused by COVID-19.

When Sandi wasn't doing very well with her health, I would love to send her cards. After she passed, I kept sending Vin cards every couple of weeks just to make him laugh.

When I think of Vin, I can't help but think of Papa—John Wooden— and how they both came from that same generation, after World War II. There was something about their character, their values, their generosity toward others. That's what was important.

Steve Garvey

Los Angeles Dodgers All-Star first baseman (1969 to 1982)
1974 National League MVP

Vin Scully was about grace.

If life is God's gift to us and what we do with it is our gift to Him, what a fabulous gift Vin gave to all of us. He was able to transcend being a voice of baseball to being a beloved figure of each person's family. That's extremely difficult to do. You do that not because of *what* you are. It's because of *who* you are—in Vin's case, a wonderful Christian gentleman.

When I do public speaking, I emphasize it's not *what* someone is— ballplayer, announcer, bus driver—but what that person believes in. What do you stand for? How are you trying to accomplish that in your life?

We all strive for that. We can realize our values in a variety of different ways and to different degrees. In his case, he was just a consistently great man. He just happened to do what he did better than anyone else.

Consistency in life is maybe the great virtue any of us could have. Life can be so challenging, but you have to handle anything that comes to you with dignity and honor and learn from it. We are not infallible. We just try not to make the same mistake twice. To be able to touch millions of lives was his gift back to God.

I was blessed to be a bat boy for five spring training seasons with the Brooklyn Dodgers. I grew up in the Tampa area of Florida, and it was the spring of 1956—the year after the Dodgers beat the Yankees in the World Series. My dad, who drove a Greyhound bus, asked me one day, "Do you want to skip school?" He drove the charter bus that would take the Dodgers from Saint Petersburg to Tampa. I brought my brand-new mitt. We see the Kay O, the Dodgers' team plane, land, and there are Robinson, Campanella, Snider, and so forth. I was probably seven, eight, nine years old then, hanging out with the Boys of Summer.

I clearly remember the first person out of uniform who really impressed me. This handsome young guy with red hair walked up; he's immaculately dressed—great loafers on and a jacket with silk pants—in the dugout, and he's carrying one of those old tape machines with a mic. And I remember thinking, *Who is this guy?* It was Vin. I watched him and listened to his voice, but that was the first day I ever saw him in person.

So now, thirteen years later, I was right out of Michigan State, drafted in the first round, in spring training with the Dodgers at Vero Beach. The third day I'm there, I walked down the path, and there was Vin Scully, twenty yards away.

"Mr. Scully, I'm Steve Garvey, and I just signed."

And Vin said, "Oh, I know, son, welcome to the organization."

I told him that he probably wouldn't remember, but I was a batboy many years ago for Brooklyn in spring training when the team was in Tampa.

Vin said, "Oh, I think I remember you. You were the pudgy kid with the flat top and butch wax?"

"Yes, sir."

"Well good luck, hope you have a long career."

"Yes, sir."

When he called a game, you never knew he was the Dodgers' announcer. He was that fair and unbiased. Having Vin call our games was special to all of us.

I remember a day in August 1971 when I was playing third base and trying to earn the position. The team was struggling. We were trying to find our way. For me, it was a rough day. I dove at a hard-hit ball, got up, threw it away. Two batters later, I bobbled a ball—back-to-back errors.

In those days of transistor radios throughout Dodger Stadium, a player could actually hear Vin's voice on the field. It gets quiet; I have my head down. I hear Vin say something like, "Well, the young man is struggling at third base, but I know he's working hard, and I think he's going to have a long career, so keep trying, kid."

Mr. Scully has saved me. That was like absolution right there. If Vin's on a player's side, that goes a long way with the fans.

Vin was like family. He fit some category for everybody. For me he was a father figure, maybe a grandfather figure. Now, to the Dodgers' credit, you can hear his voice to welcome guests to Dodger Stadium and hear that classic "It's time for Dodgers baseball." His voice is still in the air, a comforting feeling for everyone. He is there in spirit.

I've said that if the players were the authors of the game, Vin was the poet. He became special to millions of people because of how he affected them. We're in the memory business. Vin brought all our individual memories collectively to all the fans and the listeners. To be able to do that is truly special.

Kevin O'Malley
Catholic Athletes for Christ MLB ministry coordinator

Vin Scully was passionate about his Catholic faith, and it was omnipresent in every aspect of his life. He often spoke with great thanksgiving for his Catholic upbringing and education, and he confidently and comfortably allowed himself to be led by God's grace. The life lessons learned from his parents and the nuns and priests who taught him at Incarnation Grammar School, Fordham Preparatory School, and Fordham University influenced him greatly throughout his life.

Vin was a pillar at Catholic Mass on Sunday mornings at Dodger Stadium and always read the first reading—there is nothing quite like Vin Scully reading from the Old Testament of the Bible.

Shortly after I met Vin for the first time in 2014 at Dodger Stadium in my role as the MLB ministry coordinator for Catholic Athletes for Christ, he and I quickly became friends. As someone who grew up in the 1970s and 1980s with dreams of becoming a baseball broadcaster and one day meeting or working with Vin, I could never have guessed our friendship some forty years later would be based on our Catholic faith and not on baseball.

I asked Vin at the end of the 2015 baseball season if he would be willing to help CAC with an audio recording of the Rosary of the Blessed Virgin Mary as a fundraiser for the nonprofit organization. My thought was to have the greatest stories ever told from the Bible narrated by the greatest storyteller of all time. His immediate response, as was his reply for most charitable organization requests that came his way, was, "Whatever you need."

In March 2016 we met at a local home studio in Southern California to record the project. Vin said to me, as we walked together to the studio,

"Kevin, this is the most humbling thing I have ever been asked to do." He felt so unworthy to be the voice of the Rosary recording, and I assured him that this project would have far-reaching impacts greater than any of us could imagine.

Released in September 2016, CAC's Rosary of the Blessed Virgin Mary led by Vin Scully was one of the best-selling faith-based audio recordings for two straight years. Orders came pouring in month after month from all fifty states and several countries around the globe. It remains popular even today and is featured on several streaming sites.

I listened to countless stories from people who were so thankful for the opportunity to pray the Rosary led by Vin. Many told me how they were now praying the Rosary daily for the first time in decades while sitting in traffic and often would stay in the car to finish the prayers before walking into the office. The impact of Vin lending his voice to that prayer recording was seismic. Vin was amazed and humbled by the immeasurable personal and spiritual impacts felt worldwide from his voice leading Mother Mary's prayer.

The success of the Rosary CD brought with it significant media coverage, and one article mentioned Vin's home parish by name—St. Jude the Apostle Catholic Church in Westlake Village, California. As one would imagine, the following Sunday when Vin drove to Mass at St. Jude, several fans and autograph seekers waited in the church parking lot. As he relayed the story to me, he respectfully wished them a happy Sunday morning and said he was there to attend Mass—but if anyone wanted to join him inside, he would gladly sign an autograph or take a picture afterward. Over the next few Sundays Vin was able to recruit several new attendees to the Mass. True evangelization in action!

Vin lived his life the right way and always kept his vision on the ultimate prize—eternity in Heaven. His solid Catholic roots helped him through many difficult moments, and he practiced his Catholic faith by words, deeds, and actions rather than preaching from the Bible. I have learned so many lessons from Vin that I hope and pray will lead me to love my wife and children more and always make them my priority and to treat my

9. Kevin O'Malley with Vin Scully, 2015. Courtesy of Kevin O'Malley.

neighbors, coworkers, and strangers with greater love, care, and concern. Knowing him made my life better than it was.

Prior to the start of his sixty-seventh and final season of broadcasting Dodgers baseball in 2016, I had the rare opportunity to do something every resident in Southern California and baseball fan in America wishes they could have done—thank Vin and express to him what he meant to the collective audience.

In a March 2016 email to Vin, I wrote the following:

Vin, I know you are not one who is comfortable with the praise and adulation you often receive but the many acknowledgments coming your way in 2016 are as much for us to say "thank you" and "goodbye" as they are to honor you. The perfection with which you have called God's greatest game is only a small part of what has made you so special to so many of us. It is your joyfulness, kindness, humility, and welcoming spirit, both in and out of the booth, that has set you apart and had the greatest impact on those watching and listening. No matter how bad a day we may have had or if we are stuck in rush-hour traffic, your broadcasts always immediately take us to a place of comfort, peace, and simplicity. You inspire us to be better people by your examples of kindness and happiness and you have taught us that even during life's most difficult moments and tragedies, you can pick yourself back up and press forward. You have always remained true to who you are.

In speaking about how we should treat others, Saint Mother Teresa of Calcutta once said: Let there be kindness in your face, in your eyes, in your smile, in the warmth of your greeting. Always have a cheerful smile. For me, and millions of others across the country, this is what has set you apart from the rest. As you have said many times, there will be someone to come after you to call balls and strikes and the games will continue and, to that point, you are correct. However, the positive and lasting impact you have left on people and their lives can never be duplicated. For that, we are all humbly grateful.

As I have often said to people who knew of my connection with Vin, however much you think Vin Scully was a nice and kind gentleman based on how he carried himself on the air, multiply it by ten, and you'll be getting only a bit closer. Greatness is defined as the impact an individual makes on others' lives for generation after generation. Vin lived a full life centered on charity, humility, faith, hope, and love, and those qualities and virtues are why millions of people loved and adored him and why his memory and legacy will live on for generations to come (in addition to him being the greatest sports broadcaster ever).

After spending time with him and seeing firsthand how he treated everyone, regardless of name or status, I quickly learned that I would much rather be Vin Scully the fine gentleman, husband, and father, than Vin Scully the Hall of Fame broadcaster I dreamed of becoming earlier in my life.

August 2, 2022, was the day I received the phone call I knew would come one day but had hoped would not come so soon. Vin's daughter Catherine relayed the news of her dad's peaceful passing earlier in the day. After a few moments of reflection, I was not filled with the grief and sadness I expected. Instead, my soul felt a tremendous sense of peace and joy knowing that Vin crossed the finish line in first place by twenty lengths and was soon to be crowned with the gold medal of eternal rest.

Brian Golden
Journalist

My first time in the Dodger Stadium press box in 1982 was a revelation. Not only was it the best seat in the house and free, but the press box also had a press dining room that was free too. The greatest revelation, though, was the man who sat down with me and fellow broadcasting Hall of Famer Marty Brennaman of the Cincinnati Reds—or, I should say, asked to sit down.

"May I join you?" the familiar voice asked, immediately freezing me with amazement. It was Vincent Edward Scully. And immediately, I began learning that Vin Scully was a nicer man than he was a broadcaster. And he was a greater Catholic than anything else.

I was blessed to help found the Catholic Athletes for Christ Dodger Stadium Mass Ministry in 2008. We bounced around some dark, dank corners of the dugout club behind home plate during that first year, which Vin affectionately dubbed as the Catacombs Mass.

Vin and Dodgers traveling secretary Billy DeLury, both hired by the Brooklyn Dodgers in 1950, were in the front row for every Mass, and Vin was the reader for the first reading each week. On the last weekend of the 2008 regular season, Vin approached me in the press box and pulled me aside.

"I understand you were instrumental in getting the Mass started here at the stadium?" he asked, putting out his hand to shake mine. "I can't thank you enough, Brian. Billy DeLury and I always had to go downtown to St. Vincent's Hospital for their 4:00 p.m. Saturday Mass, and I would usually miss the TV production meeting. Now, I can attend Mass, receive the Holy Eucharist, and resume my clubhouse visits for additional game research. Thank you so much!"

In March 2016, the day after the death of his former neighbor Nancy Reagan, Vin recorded his incomparable Rosary CD for CAC. I was blessed to be part of the chorus saying the second half of each prayer, much like the Pips to Vin's Gladys Knight.

During a break to check recording levels, Vin asked, "Brian, this isn't blasphemous, is it? I mean, *me* leading anyone in prayer?"

I said that through this recording, he would lead us all back to the devotion of the Rosary, and the Blessed Mother would take care of the rest, which she has.

Vin's final day in the broadcast booth at Dodger Stadium in September 2016 began with Mass in the press conference room attended by more than fifty players, coaches, reporters, ushers, and stadium workers. He was presented with a framed official portrait of Pope Francis by the pontiff's photographer. It sat next to Mrs. Sandi Scully on the second level of the broadcast booth behind Vin that afternoon.

With the Dodgers trailing the Colorado Rockies 2–1 entering the bottom of the ninth inning, Mrs. Scully turned to the papal portrait placed next to her. "Holy Father, you don't want God's devout servant to go home disappointed on his last day, do you?" she asked sheepishly. "Could you please bless—" The crack of Cory Seager's game-tying home run interrupted.

In the last of the tenth, she fidgeted. "Oh, what the heck, I promise I'll never ask again," she said to her papal seatmate. "Could you please bless Vin once more?" Two pitches later, Charlie Culbertson provided the happy ending with a game-winning, walk-off home run, clinching the Dodgers fourth-consecutive National League West title.

I called Vin the following day. He would rejoin the club in San Francisco for the final series of the season and his final broadcast. I asked if he would like to have a family Mass at the stadium in San Francisco on Sunday.

"Gee, Brian, do you think that would be possible?" he asked with his spiritual humility. CAC had been trying to establish a Mass at AT&T Park (now Oracle Park) in San Francisco for years with no success. Thanks to the herculean efforts of Giants vice president of broadcasting Maria Jacinto, we had Mass for forty-three people, including all four generations of the Scully family, on October 2, 2016. It has become one of CAC's pillar Mass ministries. San Francisco archbishop Salvatore Cordileone himself has celebrated the Mass there three different times already. "You brought Catholicism back to China Basin," I told Vin.

There would be one more even more amazing phone call. Through a family connection, I have been blessed to know Donald Cardinal Wuerl, the cardinal archbishop emeritus of Washington DC. I sent him a Vin Scully Rosary CD to listen to and also asked if he might take one with him for His Holiness, with Vin's compliments.

A few months later, a letter arrived from Cardinal Wuerl. Inside was a letter from Vatican City with the seal of the Vatican secretary of state. Cardinal Wuerl had given the CD to Pope Francis. I read, then reread, the letter with mounting shock and awe. It was a thank-you note from the 266th successor of St. Peter. Pope Francis thanked Cardinal Wuerl for the gift and commended the work of CAC to "use sports to spread the Gospel."

His Holiness especially thanked Mr. Scully for his incomparable voice that deepened the devotion of the Rosary. He also thanked Vin for enhancing his fledgling understanding of English, something the young Mr. Scully had heard from thousands of immigrants for whom Brooklyn Dodgers broadcasts had become English lessons seven decades earlier.

I told Vin I would overnight the letter to him. But I said, "I wanted you to hear what it said first. What do you think?"

Nearly a minute passed without a word. I thought I had lost the connection. Baseball's poet laureate, the Tennyson of the airwaves, was speechless. There were no words, which was the most perfect way to describe Vin Scully's faith.

Fr. Willy Raymond
President of Holy Cross Family Ministries

We had a Palm Sunday vigil Mass at Dodger Stadium one year, and it called for the narrator to read the whole Lord's Passion. I knew Vin was going to broadcast the game right after this Mass, so I said, "Mr. Scully, you know, this Mass has St. Matthew's Gospel, and the narration is pretty long. I was wondering if you could do it, but I don't want to—"

And he said, "Oh, yes, I can do that." And he did it, with that incredible voice.

The Pittsburgh Pirates were in town to play the Dodgers that weekend, and after the Mass, some of the players and coaches came up. One of them said, "I have never listened to the Gospel as attentively as I did when Vin Scully read it."

He was one from that generation, such a gentleman who was humble and kind. You will meet few people in life with that quality. I knew he went to Fordham and was very dedicated to his Catholic faith. I think he not only would have made a good priest but also could have been a monsignor—or more.

I know that because, if we happened to be walking around Dodger Stadium together before Mass, as all the people were arriving to do their work—the vendors, the cooks, the ushers—it was like being with the pope. He knew everyone. I remember two elderly Jewish women who were sisters, I think both unmarried, and Vin introduced me to them. Vin knew them all, even though they weren't players, and they loved him. It didn't matter if it was the owner of the team or one of these wonderful Jewish sisters; Vin would spend time with them.

As I kept in touch with him, I knew he made several donations to Holy Cross Family Ministries because he loved Fr. Patrick Peyton and his philosophy that the family that prays together stays together.

Søren Kierkegaard, a theologian and philosopher from Denmark, talked about the three levels of development: Level one is the aesthetic side, driven by the pursuit of power, honor, pleasure, and fame. Level two is the ethical side, which is about following all the rules, doing good and avoiding evil.

The third and highest level he called religious. That is characterized by a leap of faith into a profound relationship with God. Pope Francis said it is an ongoing conversion through encountering Christ. I believe Vin Scully lived his faith on that third level. He was so trustworthy about his faith, not just following the rules but also doing so out of love because he genuinely believed in it.

Tim Klosterman
Chaplain, Mercy General Hospital in Sacramento, California

When we had the last Mass for Vin Scully at Dodger Stadium in September 2016, that whole day felt like a magical, mystical time. So much spirit and energy in Los Angeles was with us, all the way through the end of that game with Charlie Culberson's walk-off home run. The roar of the crowd that day after the home run seemed like a profound tribute to Vin. It was a sound Vin loved to hear and feel.

The day actually started out challenging and difficult. Earlier that morning, the Miami Marlins pitcher from Cuba, José Fernández, died in a boating accident. Brother Vin felt compassion and concern for him and his family. He had been in the Dodgers locker room before Mass talking to players about how Fernández was trying to take care of his family.

Vin didn't like the spotlight, especially at Mass. He was there to worship God and be present. I was hesitant to include him in the homily I prepared for that final Mass, but I felt so moved by the Gospel reading—Luke 16:19—because it was about how Jesus wants us to respect the story of each person. It happened to fit perfectly. It struck me how Vin was so generous in respecting and caring about everyone's story, everyone's humanity. He was always interested in story. It's said that God created humanity because of God's love of a good story. Vin was able to able to capture that greatest creation of God, and he didn't keep it to himself. We were blessed he shared it with us.

Vin highlighted redemption stories, which inspired me. Blessed are those who can tell and share a story. When Brother Vin was our reader at Sunday Mass, he brought those stories to life. He was also able to share the stories

10. Fr. Steve Davoren, *left*, and Fr. Tim Klosterman speak with Vin Scully, holding a portrait of Pope Francis, after the final Mass at Dodger Stadium for the 2016 season. Courtesy of Tom Hoffarth.

of the players and the fans. They were not just distant athletes on the field. He made us all feel special.

I am personally connected with how Vin and Sandi Scully met a half century ago. My uncle Don Klosterman was the general manager of the Los Angeles Rams, and Sandi was his secretary. Vin came to the Rams' office in Century City one day in the early 1970s as part of his work, and he met her there.

When I came to celebrate Mass for the Dodgers starting in 2008, I was a little starstruck. The Dodgers-Angels freeway series was happening, and there was Joe Torre and Mike Scioscia. And I was introduced to Vin. My uncle Don, still one of my heroes, had passed away in 2000. He and Vin were close friends, and the first thing Vin talked to me about was that commonality. He was so welcoming and kind.

What a beautiful, storied life Vin lived.

Lisa Nehus Saxon
Journalist

There was a day in 1984 when the improbable happened. Vin Scully asked if he might pull up a chair and spend some time with me. The brief conversation took place less than twenty-four hours after I'd been carried out of a clubhouse and endured the wrath of an angry MLB public relations director, who chastised me in front of my colleagues. It came a few hours after my own editor at the *Daily News* of Los Angeles refused to go to bat for me, explaining the access problems I endured were mine to solve.

I was seriously considering letting go of my childhood dream of showing the world that women could indeed cover Major League Baseball. Vin, who knew me well, sensed that was the case. And he wasn't about to let it happen. He spoke with the twenty-four-year-old woman who sat aside him during Mass at Corpus Christi Parish in Pacific Palisades, not to the kid he'd tutored for more than a dozen years. Yep, we go way back.

He was whispering in my ear back when I sat in a sixth-grade class at St. John Baptist de la Salle School in Granada Hills, California. I assure you the static radio broadcast of a World Series game I'd tuned in was much more interesting than anything *Warriner's English Grammar and Composition*—the complete course—had to offer. With the radio in my pocket and the earphone tucked beneath my unruly mane of brown hair, I tuned out compound-complex sentences to focus what mattered most: baseball. I knew full well the nun teaching the class would raise her eyebrow and a critical question: What kind of writer are you going to become? Unaware of the social implications of my aspirations, I blurted that I would cover Major League Baseball. The nun laughed. So did my mother—and my high school teachers.

Vin never laughed. He was my constant companion who seemed to take great joy in teaching me—heck, teaching all of us—about baseball, all while dropping metaphors and similes, alliterations and allusions. That twelve-year-old tomboy wanted to learn more about some heavy hitters named Shakespeare, Keats, and Sondheim.

I fell in love with the game he so sweetly described. Vin whispered in my ear, telling me that I belonged.

11. Lisa Nehus Saxon with Vin Scully. Courtesy of Lisa Nehus Saxon.

I doubt Vin ever revisited that chat we had on the team bus ride from the hotel to Riverfront Stadium during the first week of August 1984. I'll never forget it. I was one of only two women assigned to cover Major League Baseball at the time. At the All-Star Break, I became the only woman assigned to a team in the National League. With great trepidation I moved from the California Angels to the Los Angeles Dodgers beat. Back then, every team decided whether women with press credentials would be allowed into clubhouses. In the American League, all the doors were open. In the National League, all the doors were open—except when they were closed.

Always accommodating, the Dodgers honored my press pass and handed each player a wrap-around towel embroidered with his uniform number.

Other teams issued me a press pass—and an obstacle course, telling me where I could go and where I couldn't. I'd do interviews outside the clubhouse, on the dugout steps, or alongside the team bus. I took what I could get.

One August evening in Cincinnati, I took a calculated risk. When a rainstorm cancelled batting practice and my chance to grab an interview with Mario Soto on the field, I high-stepped it toward the Reds' clubhouse and disarmed the portly security guard who tried to stop me. He put up his arm. I showed him the pass that proclaimed "admit bearer." Left speechless, he dropped his arm. I strutted across the red carpet of the clubhouse that no other woman—aside from a cleaning lady and maybe then minority team owner Marge Schott—likely had entered.

Just a few minutes into an interview with a bemused Soto, word came that I had to leave—immediately. The messenger carried me out the door. If anyone in the press box did not know what had happened, he or she became aware when the Reds' PR director chastised me during a five-minute monologue. He assigned an intern to follow me for the rest of the series.

The next day I called my sports editor, told him what had happened, and asked for his help. He replied, "You're a big girl. Take care of it."

Although it was only a few blocks from the team hotel to old Riverfront Stadium, I decided to take the team bus to the game. The load I was carrying that day seemed heavier than usual.

I was among the first to board. Players and writers walked by. No one said a word. I felt invisible until Vin passed the seat he usually occupied and asked if he could sit alongside me.

Vin asked me this simple question: "If you could be anyone in the world, who would you chose to be?" I wanted to be one of the guys who could walk into a clubhouse without causing a stir. I told Vin that I wanted to be like Gordie Verrell, the affable Dodgers beat reporter who seemed to make everyone smile wherever he went.

"I'm sorry to hear that, Lisa," Vin said, adding that in trying to be someone else, I was unwittingly limiting myself. "Who knows? The best version of Lisa Nehus might be better than anyone."

Vin was far from finished. "What you are doing is remarkable, Lisa," he said, putting his left hand on top of my right hand in a comforting, validating way. "Never lose sight of that. Just strive to be the best version of yourself every day."

I covered the game that night, filing four stories, all with that intern on my heels—and a decided bounce in my step.

Thank you, Vin Scully.

Outside the ballpark, I'd often see Vin at Sunday Mass. One day he asked if I would sit by his side. I thanked Vin for his kind gesture and explained I simply wanted to give him space he needed to pray.

"Why, Lisa, if you sit alongside me, it will make it even easier for me to pray," Vin countered.

Even after I stopped covering sports in 2001, Vin made a point of seeking me out whenever he saw me in town. I accepted an award on his behalf when the Baseball Reliquary inducted him into the Shrine of the Eternals in 2017.

During his last season in the Dodgers' broadcast booth in 2016, like everyone, I sought out Vin. Claire Smith, who started covering the New York Yankees for the *Hartford Courant* the year before I took over the Angeles beat in 1983, came to town to work a Dodgers Sunday Night ESPN telecast. When I picked her up at the airport, she asked if we could go to the stadium early and snag a selfie with Vin. We found Vin alone in his booth and chatted for twenty minutes. Vin told us about his first Dodgers broadcast in 1950, a game Don Newcombe started. Lowing his voice as if he were sharing a secret, Vin confided that earlier in the week he and Newcombe were down on the field at the same time. Their eyes locked. Scully said, "All I could think is this: 'Can you believe we are still here?'

"God has been so very good to me," Vin said.

Me too, Vin. Me too.

Dale Marini
Retired Loyola Marymount University administrator

You may have seen this photo (figure 12). It was taken on October 2, 2016, Vin Scully's last day as a broadcaster. One publication included a caption that read, "Retiring Dodgers broadcaster Vin Scully, with his wife Sandi, waves to a fan at AT&T Park."

To me, that one fan represented all fans, an "every fan" waving thanks and showing appreciation for what Vin Scully has meant to all of us. What makes the photo even more meaningful is that it is a Loyola Marymount University alumnus wearing an LMU ice hockey sweatshirt.

That the photo was twenty-one years in the making.

I was associate director of admission at Loyola Marymount University until I retired in 2014. In 1995 Vin Scully called to arrange an appointment for himself and his daughter Catherine to come to my office. Catherine was looking into the possibility of transferring to LMU, and I often met with prospective students.

My one regret is I did not save the voice message he left on my phone. I had admired him and his work for decades, and while he did not actually play for the Dodgers, I felt that he was the team's MVP (Most Valuable Person).

The three of us eventually met, and he exceeded my expectations of him as a person. I was so impressed that he was such a loving and caring parent.

After taking care of Catherine and answering her questions and concerns—and she did matriculate—I turned to her father and said, "Mr. Scully, I just have to take this opportunity to say that I am a great fan of yours!"

His response? "Please, call me Vin, and thank you."

We discussed baseball and his career, and I asked if he would ever consider writing a book, adding I would be first in line to buy it since I loved all his stories. He's been often asked to write a book, he said, but would not, as he would rather use any extra time to be with his family.

Vin then asked if I would like to hear a story. Of course I would!

After World War II Walter O'Malley, then owner of the Brooklyn Dodgers, was playing golf with a friend. He asked if Mr. O'Malley would be

interested in selling the Dodgers. It seems the friend's son had recently returned from the war and was having a difficult time finding something to occupy himself. The friend was hoping that his son could become involved in running the Dodgers.

Mr. O'Malley politely said no, and they continued with their round of golf. Although that in itself is not a very interesting story, Vin, with a twinkle in his eye, leaned forward and asked if I knew who that friend was. When I said I didn't, he said it was Joe Kennedy. The possibility that his son, Jack Kennedy, might have never gone into politics makes for a wonderful story, but what makes it my favorite Vin Scully story is Vin's personal touch.

As he and Catherine were departing, Vin invited me to stop by the press box before Dodgers games if I ever wished. That was an offer that I couldn't refuse. On one occasion I introduced him to my son, Matt, and on another, to my brother, Denny. Vin noticed the resemblance between Denny and me, laughingly saying, "Yes, I can see that you are brothers!"

Later, in October 2016, two friends, Gary and Nona Rafferty, hosted me and my son at Vin's last game in San Francisco. We were at AT&T Park when the gates opened and went to our seats just four rows below Vin's broadcast booth. Vin was intently working as he prepared for the game. Then he took a break, stood up, and faced the field.

I waved my Dodgers cap to get his attention, and I reminded him of our meeting at LMU with his daughter. He smiled and declared that Catherine was at the game. Then his wife Sandi, also in attendance, said all of their children were there too.

I reminded Vin he once met my son, pointing to Matt, a few feet to my right. They waved to each other. That's when the photo was taken. Vin went back to work for one final day.

Vin Scully has said God blessed him by allowing him to have a career that he loved for sixty-seven years. Thank you, Vin, for being with us all those years, and thank you, God, for blessing us with Vin.

12. (*opposite*) Vin Scully, with his wife Sandi, waves to Matt Marini before Scully's final game at AT&T Park in San Francisco on Sunday, October 2, 2016. Photo by AP Photo/ Tony Avelar.

Pablo Kay

Editor-in-chief, *Angelus News*

The first clue was the caller ID. It was just before noon on January 15, 2020. As the office phone rang, the name "Sandra Scully" appeared on the screen. It can't be, I thought.

"Hello. Is this Pablo?" It was Vin Scully's voice, saying *my* name, talking to *me*.

More than three years had passed since Vin had retired from the broadcast booth. A few months earlier, *Angelus News*, the magazine I work for as editor-in-chief, had run a cover story about Vin Scully's Catholic faith. Through the article's author, Tom Hoffarth, I had a box of copies sent to Vin at his request.

But Vin wasn't calling to thank me for the copies, although he eventually got around to that too. I had included something else in the box: a printed image of Our Lady of Guadalupe that had been touched to the miraculous *tilma*, or cactus-fiber cloak, involved in her appearance. It was one of a few such prints I had been given during a trip to Mexico City the year before.

Vin started by explaining that he had been given *Angelus*'s main phone number, had tracked down my extension, and was calling to thank me for the Guadalupe print. He told me he planned to hang it in his office. "I'm deeply grateful for it," he said. "Thank you a million times."

Vin Scully wasn't just talking to *me*. He was thanking *me*—as if I had something of value to offer the greatest sports announcer of all time.

I responded with what must have been an incoherent jumble of words. I remember trying to make the point that never could I have imagined three years ago when I started this job that I'd be talking to someone like him. God is full of surprises, I said.

"You deserve everything you get," he told me. "I can't thank you enough."

He didn't want to tie me up but just wanted to thank me, he said. "No, thank you, Vin," I tried telling him.

That short conversation left me in a state of dazed euphoria for the rest of the day. This was the same sweet voice that had spoken to four generations of my family on my dad's side.

Tocada por la portentosa Imagen Original de Sta. María de Guadalupe el viernes 16 de febrero del 2018

13. A replica of the printed image of Our Lady of Guadalupe, touched to the miraculous tilma, given to Vin Scully by Pablo Kay. Courtesy of Pablo Kay.

My great-grandfather Winston was born in Wisconsin at the turn of the century to Irish immigrants. He moved to LA, became an electrician, got married, and raised six children in South Los Angeles. Whether tinkering in his garage or sitting in the stands at Chavez Ravine, he found in Vin (in the form of his handheld radio) a faithful companion on game days.

I grew up moving around the United States as part of an itinerant family that did missionary work for the Catholic Church. But summers were always spent in LA, and watching the Dodgers (sometimes on channel 5, other times, 11 or 13) during evening visits to my grandparents' house was where Dodger blue began to flow through my veins.

And so, in a life spent moving between so many new places and faces, schools, teachers, and accents, Vin truly made LA home for me. Being a transplant from the East Coast himself, he must have done the same for my great-grandfather too.

It was thanks to Vin, I'd like to think, that generations of Angelenos came to make the Dodgers our own. In my case, I'll always have the memory of a phone call to prove it.

THIRD INNING

"That's the Story, Morning Glory"

The Voice of a Storyteller

I called Vin Scully one day to track down his new home address, to mail something to him. He recently moved to the Hidden Hills area of the San Fernando Valley.

After giving me his house number, he said he was now living on Jim Bridger Road. And he continued, "You know, Jim Bridger was actually a frontiersman, really known as a trailblazer, and from what I read, he was one of the most famous men in the fur trade back in the old West with Kit Carson."

Of course, Vin knew the story behind the name of his street. That story reminded me of those who claimed he could recite a phone book or a grocery list and make it sound as if Walt Whitman authored it.

By his very name, Vin Scully had to carry on the legacy of a scholarly storyteller. The Irish surname Scully is an Anglicized version of an old Gaelic name, Mac Scholaidhe, or O'Scolaidhe. The *O* signifies a male descendant.

Scully also refers to a descendant of a *scholaide*, or town crier. After the twelfth-century English invasion of Ireland, families were driven to parts of Tipperary and needed the town crier to inform them of important events. Clan members were interred at the famous Rock of Cashel and have a memorial there, called Scully's Cross.

Another version of the scholaide is *scolaire*, meaning "student" or "scholar."

Scully is also a derivation of Skelly, which means the descendant of a storyteller, a regular official at the courts of the old Irish kings. Scully goes back to the twelfth century in the ancient records of Westmeath County Archives in Ireland. It can go by variant spellings that include Scally, O'Scully, Sculley, Skulley, and even Sullivan.

Vincent, meanwhile, is a biblical first name derived from the Latin *vincens*, meaning "winning" or "victorious." It is associated with the Christian concept of conquering the sins of the world.

The Vin Scully story, as he tells it, starts with him predicting his future at age eight, when he wrote an essay for the nuns in grammar school about what he wanted to be when he grew up. "The boys were all about being policemen and firemen, doctors and lawyers, while the girls were about nursing or ballet dancers or becoming mothers," he recalled in 2013, on his eighty-sixth birthday. "There was no sports on TV then, just a few things on the radio, maybe a Saturday afternoon football game between Ohio State and Notre Dame. So, when I said I wanted to be a sports announcer, well, that was way out in left field.

"When I eventually got that job with the Dodgers, it really was the fulfillment of a dream just fourteen years later. That's rather remarkable in itself."

Scully admitted that since sports broadcasting was "somewhere in never-never land. . . . I figured when I went off to high school, I would be a writer."

His column for the high-school paper was called Looking Them Over. He eventually worked as a copyboy for the *New York Times* and experienced the newsroom buzz of breaking stories.

The media exposure likely helped Scully have an appreciation for telling stories, not just as an orator but also as a scribe. His own process was much like Hemmingway: short, effective sentences, not too much in between the subject, verb, and period. Each word served its purpose.

But what yarns could he spin in and around the action of a baseball game? Pretty much anything.

In the Society for American Baseball Research's biography project, writer Greg King explained Scully's storytelling range this way:

> On one occasion he might have discussed the connection between Wrigley Field and Mexican General Santa Anna of the Battle of the Alamo—hint: gum. On another he could describe outfielders climbing the terrace at Cincinnati's Crosley Field or the Gashouse Gang rolling around in the dirt in old Sportsman's Park in St. Louis. He might discuss a current book he was reading, such as David Maraniss's biography

of Roberto Clemente, or ask whether listeners were familiar with the writer James Lee Burke and his descriptions of New Orleans, as a player hailing from Bayou Country made an appearance on the mound. He could dust off a Winston Churchill quote in World War II speaking of Europe's "soft underbelly" and smoothly transition to say, "Well, the 'soft underbelly' for Colorado is its pitching." Miss this story or that observation expressed in a creative fashion—and told within the context of a particular game—and one might never have had the opportunity to hear it again. . . . Regardless, it never seemed forced when the story Scully unfolded over the air involved players or other references from earlier eras.

John Millen, CEO and founder of the Reputation Group, helps leaders develop effective communication skills. When teaching storytelling, Millen recommends his clients consider using the Power of 3 technique. Basically, a story should have a clear beginning, middle, and end—a setting, some conflict, and a resolution. That makes the story clear, understandable, and memorable.

Using Scully as an example, Millen explained how that could be taken to another dimension—masterfully weaving any sort of story between the beats of the first, second, and third outs of an inning. "Vin Scully had every talent of an effective storyteller, employing the classic storytelling arc that's used in every medium, including movies, TV shows, and novels," said Millen, who grew up in Southern California. Millen, a Dodgers fan who didn't listen much to sports broadcasting, could appreciate hearing Scully based on his engaging voice and storytelling ability.

"More important than his understanding of this tool, Vin's greatest talent was his ability to flex this format in and out of the game's action and expand and contract the story on the fly to perfectly fit the time available," Millen said.

As an example, Millen found a clip on the MLB's YouTube channel in which Scully explained the origins of the Dodgers-Giants rivalry. It was a TV telecast from San Francisco, as the Dodgers' Kenta Maeda pitched to the Giants' Brandon Crawford and Ángel Pagán to get the last two outs of the bottom of the first inning. Millen noted how during that time Scully set up the story, talked about an inciting incident, described rising action in the season, explained the climactic final two games, and recounted the success of the Dodgers in winning, the failure of the Giants in losing, and their ultimate failure with the Cardinals winning the pennant. It was all brought together as the inning ended.

"In a minute and thirty-four seconds, he has taken you on a journey, while updating you on the game in between—how'd he do that?" Millen marveled. "It's just phenomenal."

The kicker is that Millen didn't realize the video he referenced for Scully's storytelling excellence came from the very last game of his career on October 2, 2016, a few weeks shy of his eighty-ninth birthday—amazing to the end.

One of my last conversations with Scully in the summer of 2021 was another opportunity to hear him tell more stories. One was his new enjoyment of watching soccer and the exploits of English star "'arry Kane," he joked, purposefully leaving off the *H* as the British broadcasters do. Scully also talked about his concerns of the world then, the state of the country, and more current events.

At one point, he circled back to the story of his life, as it was winding down for him on Jim Bridger Road. "I'm very happy the way I'm living, peaceful. . . . That's more than enough for anybody," he said. "I still can't believe I have a phone book, and a lot of the names are people who are gone, and I can't call them. That's part of this stage of life. I think I can hear the next stop." He paused. "So that's the story, morning glory," he concluded.

Joe Davis

Los Angeles Dodgers broadcaster (2016 to present)
Fox Sports lead MLB broadcaster (2022 to present)

Fans expect that stories are part of the baseball broadcast because Vin Scully made it that way from the moment the Dodgers came to Los Angeles. He did it at the highest level; it's all the fans have ever known.

When I was in the Minor Leagues, I had heard him do games over the years on the MLB app. I could flip those games on after I did my games and was doing all those postgame side duties you have as a Minor League broadcaster.

But during the 2016 season, I started with the Dodgers just doing road games, still living in Michigan. I listened to Vin do every home game. It was a nightly crash course. But I found myself listening as a fan: *Man, this is cool hearing these stories.*

Loving stories is part of the human condition—we are a storytelling species. Listeners like having players humanized by their stories. I could appreciate, firsthand, why those stories were meaningful for a broadcast with Vin telling them.

I started to incorporate stories into my own broadcast—poorly, but I felt I was getting better all the time. When I listened to my broadcast and critiqued myself—which I still do often to this day—my ears perked up when I heard myself tell a story. It was interesting how I wanted to lock in and listen to the story, even a bad one. And it's a heck of a lot more interesting than hearing about a guy's OPS or what positions he has played over the last week.

I have studied storytelling and tried to get better at it, recognizing that fans expect it, that it makes for a better listen, and that I had a lot of work to do. It all goes back to Vin setting that example and making that a standard.

In today's broadcast, the play-by-play announcer tries to tee up the analyst. Vin, the last of that breed, did it all solo. He had the blank slate of an inning that he could do whatever he wanted. The modern broadcast, and even broadcasts during Vin's last thirty to fifty years, is a back and forth. All that said, being a storyteller necessitates fitting stories within the confines of a baseball game, within the context of an inning.

Vin was blessed by the baseball gods to have a lot of the innings play along with whatever story he was ready to tell. The inning would follow along with the pace. If he needed an extra beat, he would get another foul ball. And if his story was wrapping up, it seemed like the guy grounded into the double play on cue to end the inning. It was part of his magic.

I view a game through the lens of how many times a team goes through its batting order. The first time through, we tend to establish the headlines for a player. Sometimes, we tell a story, but usually we discuss what he's doing on a basic level and who he is. During the second time through, we start to dive a little deeper and humanize him more. Whereas later on, the third- and fourth-time through the order, it's back to the game. (As a series goes on, we follow that structure, but deeper.) When the broadcast booth has two people, we don't always have the room to tell a story efficiently, and we don't want to get in the way of the crunch time late in the game.

Some speculate about how the new pitch-clock rule will affect broadcasts. I can count on one hand how many times I've wished I had more time in a game between pitches and between hitters. Besides Vin Scully, broadcasters probably haven't wanted more time. Broadcasters probably are not going to have that perfect thread through an entire inning. The pitch clock has only been positive for me, certainly, and for most broadcasters. The game has a nice pace and rhythm. We feel better about the broadcasts now because of how the action rules.

My first interaction with Vin was the night before the team announced I had the Dodgers' job; he called me and left a voice mail, welcoming me to the team. My wife got me a stuffed teddy bear wearing a Dodger jersey. It has a speaker inside, so it talks after it is squeezed. My wife took that voice mail recording and put it inside the bear—pretty cool.

For my twenty-ninth birthday in December 2016, my parents gave me a framed photograph of me with Vin Scully, which we took at the end of his last season. On the photo, Scully wrote, "To Joe: My prayers for you to have a great career."

Had I looked at the job like I was the one replacing Vin Scully, it probably wouldn't have gone well. From the start, I looked at it like it was a responsibility. That continues to define the job. It's an ongoing responsibility to be the guy who followed the best ever to do it and a responsibility to broadcast for a fan base that has only ever had the best ever to do it. Any attempt by me to try to mimic Vin would not have been successful. I learned from Vin and to this day carry the responsibility of the guy who followed him. That is our connection.

We couldn't really prepare for the night when we had to tell Dodgers viewers that Vin had passed away. For about a month before that, we only knew Vin wasn't doing well. We were mindful it could happen at some point.

Between the second and third inning on that night, Mike Levy, our producer, told me Vin just passed away. The team would announce it in conjunction with the family after the third inning, so we had maybe one inning to gather our thoughts.

My first thought was that being responsible for announcing to Dodgers fans, many who considered him a family member, that Vin had passed away, I would be the first to do any kind of public eulogy.

I tried to do justice to who he was a broadcaster and as a person and what he meant to the team and to baseball. I was trying to do it with kind of a smile. Ultimately, my job is to bring joy to people through baseball. As tough as a night that was for people, I still felt I could call the game and tell stories about Vin and make it more a happy remembrance. And, with all that, I was also trying to do him proud by doing the game justice, telling a story but also respecting each pitch—because nobody did that better than him.

Chris Erskine

Los Angeles Times columnist (1990 to 2020)

Breathe deep in this old ballyard. What do you smell, taste, and see? Each year, Dodger Stadium looks more and more like a barber shop in a schmaltzy Broadway musical.

We show up here every April, this shoeless order of nuns traipsing across the parking lot, victims of our own faith. The walk through the lots can be as entertaining as the Dodgers games themselves—the families, the thugs, the couples on first dates. It's perhaps the one place where LA mingles and mostly gets along.

I've seen the most brazen, awful things at this stadium, and kindnesses that you would not believe. One game, the stranger sitting next to my young son went to the gift shop and bought him a souvenir. A couple years later, a foul ball twirled our way, bounced this way and that—*thwack, clunk, ping.* When it was done, it landed in the lap of the guy behind us, who leaned over and handed it to my six-year-old son.

Baseball is a blessing. Doesn't take a nun to figure that out.

As much as anything, a town's sportscasters define the fan experience. Chicago had Jack Brickhouse, then Harry Caray. Saint Louis had Jack Buck. Pittsburgh, Bob Prince. Detroit, Ernie Harwell. Milwaukee, Bob Uecker. New York, Red Barber.

Just as Koufax defined Dodger class, so did Vin Scully, who, in his heart of hearts, would've preferred to sing Harold Arlen ballads but settled for a sixty-seven-year run with the Dodgers, first in Brooklyn, then in LA.

Pretty sure he was five when he started.

You know, some idiots actually urged old man O'Malley to switch gears when he brought the team west, to sub out Scully with someone more laid back than the rat-a-tat-tat New Yorker, someone who might fit in better with the soothing ocean breezes, someone who could capture the cool coastal oeuvre.

Then Scully—a masterful storyteller, a sagacious wit—did exactly that. Scully and LA were the best fit in sports since Knute Rockne laced up his leather cleats (size 10½, if you're curious).

Nearly everyone has a Scully story about his kindness, his humor, his graciousness. He was famous for his handwritten notes and, as he got older, HIS EMAILS IN ALL-CAPS (which I've saved).

Indeed, Vinny went through his day—his life—making ordinary people feel very special with words that wrapped them like a quilt.

What a legacy.

I was obsessed with The Voice. In 2016 I did a cover piece for the *Los Angeles Times* on the musicality of Scully's delivery, roping in a couple of USC music profs to explain the cadences, the chord changes, the way the broadcaster would tinker with the notes. The takeaway—tonally, Scully was an Irish tenor. Spiritually, Frank Sinatra.

"It's swinging," Chris Sampson explained of Scully's voice. "In every instance that I've heard, he's always had swing to it."

"He's not only giving color analysis, he's giving a concert," added voice professor Jeffrey Allen. Allen explained Scully's famous purr this way: "The chords compress the air in a very natural fashion. . . . There's no muscling of the instrument. It's just organic. It just flows through him.

"You're dealing with a virtuoso instrument."

Sampson dug deep into old audio clips, which included a home run that preserved a Fernando Valenzuela victory during the height of Fernandomania.

"It's gone, Fernando, it's gone," Scully says as the crowd roars, a phrasing Sampson says came in three-quarter time, like a waltz: 1-2-3, 1-2-3, 1-2-3.

Sampson discovered how Scully would start with a dominant chord, and the dominant chord would inherently have some tension to it that's leading to a resolution. "And so, this tension is leading up to something big," he said.

More than anything, the two music professors marveled at how Scully could anticipate a game's pivot point and at the way he used his voice, like the swell of an orchestra, to make the moment cinematic. "I think Vin has an instinct to know that something's about to happen . . . so he uses his musicality to build toward that moment," Allen said. "He almost kicks it into gear."

In his typically humble fashion, Scully scoffed at any thought that there was anything special to his craft. "Good grief," he told me, "I must be the only [person] who is off-key while speaking." Yeah, hardly.

RIP, you Irish tenor. This old ballyard will never be the same.

Ross Porter

Los Angeles Dodgers broadcaster (1977 to 2004)

In 2022 I posted on my Ross Porter Sports Videos YouTube channel an interview I did with Vin Scully several years earlier. It was one of my favorites and one of the best I had ever done.

Here is how Vin addressed these subjects:

Faith: "The course of my strength is my faith. It helped me in personal tragedies. The two worst things you can think of are the loss of a wife and a child. The pain never goes away, but while [I was] in despair, God gave me a chance to find a wonderful wife, eighteen grandchildren, plus the fact he's allowed me to do what I love to do."

Success: "Success is momentary. One moment you felt you were able to do the job. Next moment, you weren't. Napoleon's biggest problem was he never knew when to stop. One success, another success."

Humility: "Everything I have is a gift from God. I don't see how ego can get far. I didn't do anything to deserve the gifts. I'm eternally grateful."

Laughter and humor: "Laughter is the basic art of my life for sure. I don't know what I would do if I didn't find things in this world humorous. I really think I've been given a very good sense of humor. I have so many shortcomings that I've really loved to laugh. I find it very easy to laugh at myself. On the golf course, I don't get mad if I make a bad shot. Maybe the next one will be much better. One day on a par three, I hit my tee shot out of bounds. The next shot went in the hole. I got a par—big deal. On to the next hole."

Kindness: "I love people. I enjoy doing the games, but I really enjoy all of the surroundings that go with it. When I walk into the ballpark, I say hello to Marie on the elevator and ask her about her family. I walk into the press room and talk to David, the chef. There is Maria and Martina, the ladies who work in the back. I go out, and all the writers are throwing arrows at each other, laughing and having fun. I go into the booth, and the fellows I work with every day laugh and joke. All of that is as important to me as actually doing the game. It really is. I have been truly blessed with a good relationship, I think, with almost everyone."

A sports hero: "First, de-emphasize the word *sports*. The fact he's a fine athlete gives him a major opportunity to be a real hero. The real hero, to me, is one who truly does something wonderful but doesn't believe he's a hero. The soldier in the battlefield who wants to protect his buddy."

Here are a few more stories about Vin:

- I never saw Vin rude to one person in the twenty-eight years I worked with him.
- The Dodgers had Vin listen to two audition tapes when they decided on their third announcer in December of 1976. Vin chose mine.
- Vin and I had the same birthdate—November 29—and always talked to each other on the phone that day. Jerry Doggett was eleven years older than Vin. And Vin was eleven years older than me.
- At Candlestick Park in San Francisco one cold weekend, in the visitors' broadcast booth, we couldn't close the window and shivered. Vin went to Spec Richardson, the Giants general manager, and told him. The next time the Dodgers went to Candlestick, that window was repaired.
- Vin's favorite food was applesauce.
- Vin was once invited to lunch by the state chairman of one of the political parties in California, who told Vin that the party wanted him to be its gubernatorial candidate. Vin told me he could have told the man right then that he was flattered and thanked him but he was not interested. But he wanted to show respect, so he said he would like twenty-four hours to think about the offer. The next day, Vin politely declined. He laughingly said to me, "The chairman didn't know I was in the other political party."
- One Sunday at Mass, Vin learned of two teenaged brothers stricken with Batten disease, a fatal disease of the nervous system that typically

Happy Birthday!

14. Vin Scully and Ross Porter as they celebrate the same birthday of November 29. Courtesy of Ross Porter.

begins between five and ten years of age. Those affected have mental impairment, seizures, and progressive loss of sight. When Vin was told the facts, he requested the family's phone number, called the father, and invited the family to a Dodgers game. After the family arrived, Vin took the boys to the Dodgers clubhouse and introduced them to the players. They watched batting practice on the field and came to his press box booth. Dinner and the game followed, and from the back of the TV booth they briefly watched him work. It was more than a one-night experience for the two high-schoolers. Vin visited them at their home and invited the pair to a game five times. The older brother died when he was twenty-four. The younger sibling is still alive at twenty-eight.

After Vin retired in 2016, I called him every two weeks. We could talk fifteen minutes, but very little about baseball—mostly about politics, world affairs, our families, stories we had read or heard. One time, I set up a lunch with a couple of mutual friends and planned it for a restaurant one mile from Vin's home. I decided to invite him. He said, "I like all those guys, but Ross, the last thing I want to talk about is baseball."

In the closing months of his life, his daughters made sure he had twenty-four/seven care. The last time I chatted with Vin was exactly one week before he died. He said, "I'm so tired. I don't go downstairs anymore and look at my computer. Much of the time I stay in bed, reading a book, watching television, or taking a nap." As we wound up our conversation, his last words were the same as they always were: "Give my love to Lin."

Ben Platt
Dodgers.com website creator

When I think of Vin, I think of pure happiness because he loved what he did. He loved telling stories. That was never a burden for him. I was fortunate to help him do that.

In 1993 I was an entertainment story producer at CNN. Growing up in Hollywood, I was a big Dodgers fan, with two sets of grandparents who were season-ticket holders. I idolized Vin since I was a small boy. The routine I had with my brother Marc was to go to bed at nine o'clock and, from our bunkbeds, listen to Vin Scully and Jerry Doggett on the radio.

I started doing freelance stories for the team's *Big Blue Review* and got to know a group of writers who worked there. That led to having access to the press box and knowing players and team executives. Mark Langill and Brent Shyer in the front office knew I was into the internet as far back as 1987. The Dodgers and their marketing department wanted to try this thing called a website, and I helped them figure it all out flying by the seat of my pants. The site was new territory, and Peter O'Malley supported it. *USA Today* eventually named it the best sports site in the country, long before MLB.com came around.

In 1996 Vin told me his son-in-law bought him a new computer, but it was still in the box at his house. He didn't know what to do with it. He asked if I could come over and figure it out for him. I could sense he was overwhelmed by this new thing—just remember, he was in his midsixties and had always worked hard to prepare for games.

On Opening Day 1997 he stopped by my office to see what I was up to. He said he was ready with the homework he did on the Philadelphia

15. Ben Platt and Vin Scully together at Platt's wedding. Courtesy of Ben Platt.

Phillies and went to his booth. Deciding to see what I could find online, I had twenty-seven pages on the Phillies within ten minutes. It took me longer to print it out on the dot matrix printer. I brought it to him about twenty minutes before the game, when I saw all his newspaper clippings and handwritten notes. I showed him the pages I printed out and circled with yellow Sharpie. "This must have taken you hours," Vin said. For the first four or five innings, I listened to his broadcast; he hit on everything I got for him. The next day he called me to thank me for all that material. "Yesterday's day was a dream," he said. "All those things you found were manna from heaven."

He now earnestly wanted to research on his computer. I went to his home three days a week for a few hours at a time to get him up to speed, covering what to search, what to bookmark—including the *American Journalism Review*, which had all sorts of resources. I just asked him to have an open mind, understand that the internet is brand new for him, and be patient. We would get it. I would make sure.

He was always looking for that little nugget to wrap around a fifteen-minute story. He was a poet and wanted to tell his stories. I was able to

16. A view from Vin Scully's press box seat as a ceremony for his retirement takes place on the field at Dodger Stadium, 2016. Courtesy of Ben Platt.

show him new places to find information. That all seemed to reinvigorate him after that 1994–95 baseball labor issue.

Something between Vinny and me clicked, and we became great friends. I got to go with him to Atlanta in 1999 when MLB had the All-Century Team announced during the World Series, and Vin introduced them all—and he introduced me to every one of them. That was the power of Vinny. Everyone loved him. Then he had me join him flying back to LA on a private plane.

He asked me what my childhood name was—it was Benjie. So that's what he called me. People with the Dodgers told me that when he started calling you by your childhood name, he was your friend.

I grew up in Beverly Hills around famous people my entire life. Vin never saw himself a celebrity. He was just lucky to be out of Red Barber's shadow. I think he just fell into broadcasting; Red Barber took him, and he moved up the ranks. And, of course, he was brilliant at it. As much as he was the poet laureate of baseball, what he really wanted to be was a song-and-dance man. He idolized Gene Kelly and wanted to do his own version of "Singin' in the Rain."

The coolest day of my life was December 31, 1999—the last day of the millennium. I was home with no plans and got a call from Vin at about ten o'clock. "What are you doing today?"

"Not much."

"Want to hang out with me?"

"Sure. What do you want to do?"

He had a voice-over job, then went shopping, picked up some things, and had lunch at a deli out in the Valley—just us two friends. I told him, "You know, Vinny, I'll never forget this day. I got to hang out with one of my best friends. That was great."

When anyone asked me about Vin, I just said he was a gentleman's gentleman, a sweet man who cared a lot.

Dan Durbin

USC journalism professor

During a long-forgotten broadcast in an unremembered year, the Los Angeles Dodgers were inching through the tail end of an interminably long game against the Arizona Diamondbacks. After four hours of nonaction, the director and the camera crew, desperate to show anything of interest to a dwindling cable TV audience, scanned the outfield until they landed on an aged groundskeeper.

Like the game, the bent and bearded old man seemed to be wheezing his last as he ever so slowly pushed a small corner of tarp off the field. Just as the camera fell on this hoary reminder of time passing, a lilting tenor rang out from the television set.

"When this game began, that gentleman was a young unshaven lad."

I smiled and thought, *That is Vin Scully. That one line encapsulates his art.*

Scully was a master, perhaps *the* master, of the descriptive art of baseball broadcasting. His ability to capture a moment in a brief brilliantly apt phrase was the stuff of legend. Describing the game, keeping listeners informed about what was going on, was the least of Scully's skills.

At the nadir of a meaningless game in a meaningless series between two teams that would never see the postseason, Scully captured your thoughts and gave them expression with a grace and humor you wish you had shown. In a moment of mutual fatigue, with the television audience feeling like that tired old man, holding on despite the futility of the endless contest, Scully perfectly described the groundskeeper, the audience's feelings, the game, and the moment in eleven graceful, slightly archaic words.

Soon after that game, a long-forgotten article by an unremembered journalist appeared in one of the Los Angeles papers. The reporter commented on Scully's mild joke. He, too, noted that it was an illustration of Scully's art, a skill at bringing eloquence and grace into even the least of sports moments. That journalist and I were only two of the thousands who must have felt Scully spoke for them, and that was only one moment out of tens of thousands over sixty-seven years of broadcasting.

We all knew what we had in Vin Scully. None of us wanted to take that for granted. Should you ever take an artist, even an artist of the spoken word, for granted? Inevitably, of course, we did. Scully was there too often, spinning out stories, descriptive prose and poignant insights by the dozen nearly every night of the summer months. Much as we didn't want to, we acted as if he would always be there.

Of course, Los Angeles baseball fans weren't the only ones who knew they had something special in Vin Scully. The major networks knew Scully was star material. In the 1970s CBS hired him to call NFL football games. In the 1980s NBC hired him to cover baseball. And in 1969, in a somewhat deranged moment of sixties mania, the executives at NBC decided Scully would be the perfect host for a new game show, *It Takes Two*. With his easy charm and impromptu verbal skills, Scully seemed destined to be a hit in the daytime game-show market. The suits at NBC were so certain Scully would succeed that they commissioned Hasbro to make a bookshelf game based on the show—NBC's only game show to make it into that line of games. You can watch Vin throwing as much energy as he can into the awkward proceedings on YouTube, all to no avail. The show would be gone before the Beatles broke up. It turns out there are some broadcasts even Vin Scully can't save.

But Scully could and did save countless slow moments in sports broadcasting. Scully was famous for filling baseball's perpetually empty air space with beautifully realized stories. In his autobiography and in countless after dinner speeches, Jon Miller, himself an artist of the airwaves, would tell tales (perhaps fairly close to the truth) of hearing Scully weave stories in and around gameplay with preternatural skill.

Scully was also renowned for his objectivity. In a broadcasting model that often catered to homers and colorful characters, Scully's was the one voice that could be relied on to give an unbiased narrative. He would intone lines like, "Throw your sombreros in the air!" marking Fernando Valenzuela's no-hitter, with just enough emotion to show Dodgers fans that he was celebrating with them, not as one of them.

In all the games I heard him broadcast, I only heard Scully betray true emotion once. In one of his most famous calls, one that is sure to be repeated many times in this book, you can hear Scully's voice just begin to crack. If you listen closely to his call of Kirk Gibson's famous walk-off home run in the 1988 World Series, you can hear excitement, thrill, and joy squeeze painfully out of the word *gone* as he calls out, "She is gone!" He tried to hold it in. But you can hear it.

I watched that momentous moment on an old RCA ColorTrak television set that had perpetual problems with its red tint. I didn't plan to watch the Series. I had no intention of watching the hapless Dodgers get bashed and bludgeoned by those (perhaps) artificially enhanced Oakland A's. A group of friends and I planned to freefall into Tower Records on Ventura Boulevard in the southern San Fernando Valley that night. But I made them wait to see the inevitable strikeout of a hobbled Gibson by the American League's best relief pitcher. I wanted that moment to justify my decision to skip the rest of the World Series.

So, as my friends waited impatiently, I followed Scully's epic call of the at bat and was surprised to hear real emotion creep out in his home run call. But, as exciting as all of that was, that wasn't the Vin Scully moment. That came later.

As my friends made motions toward the door and threatened to leave without me, I watched Gibson's home run limp-trot. Scully remained silent.

I watched as the Dodgers rushed the field and celebrated. Scully remained silent. I watched the reaction shots of the A's dugout, players walking out with the assurance that this was only a momentary setback, that they would win tomorrow and the rest of the games. Scully remained silent.

After a lengthy stage wait, finally, Scully spoke.

"In a year that has been so improbable, the impossible has happened."

Now, I've long suspected that many years ago, say in 1952 or 1953, Scully sat bored during a particularly lazy afternoon game at Ebbets Field and wondered, *If I ever call an extraordinary at bat in a World Series in which the underdog team suddenly beats the dominant favorites by a walk-off home run, what can I say that will perfectly sum up the moment?* He then wrote that line down in the endless marginalia that filled his personally produced research for each game. That brilliant line then sat faithfully for three decades before Scully had a chance to use it.

No one comes up with a line like that on the spur of the moment. John Milton, the Puritan poet that Vin Scully, the Catholic broadcaster, most often quoted, particularly regarding those who "only stand and wait" in baseball's ever-lengthening games, would have given his right eye for a line like that. It just doesn't happen off the cuff.

What Vin Scully did, and what no other broadcaster could do as well, was take a moment of your life, a moment of baseball, and transcend it with words. He didn't simply describe that moment; he recreated it into something lasting. He infused it with a rhetorical art.

That is why, when all but the smallest handful of games he called are long-forgotten contests in unremembered seasons, Scully's words will linger on, resonating in the minds and memories of those who heard him.

T. J. Simers

Los Angeles Times sports columnist (1990 to 2013)

It was a plan. Okay, it was my plan: when it came time for the national anthem, I would make sure I was standing at the press box urinal, right next to Vin Scully.

Like you, I'm surprised the guy had to go. But it was the only place where I was pretty sure I could catch Vin Scully alone.

One time he told me a story about Rocky Bridges and the national anthem. Bridges told the player next to him, "Every time they play this song, I have a terrible game."

I laughed and jiggled so hard I had to look down to see if I had tinkled on Scully's shoes. I'm happy to report Scully emerged unscathed, but it wouldn't be the last time I would make the unflappable one nervous.

I asked him to appear on stage with me and John Wooden. The concept was simple. To raise money for children's charities, I would interview the two icons on live TV, with Jerry West delivering a pep talk to the high-priced donors. The show would be at the Nokia Theatre across from Staples Center—I know those two names have been changed, but it's irrelevant.

Wolfgang Puck donated the food to the high rollers, and Scully & Wooden for the Kids made the rounds. Scully pulled me aside to say he didn't want any copies of the event to be made and shown later. More than that, he was nervous.

He had seen Wooden a week earlier at an LA Coliseum event, where Wooden appeared near death. It dawned on Scully that he would share the stage with a near-dead man and a pugnacious jerk who knew nothing about taking TV cues.

We had sold out the more than seven thousand tickets for the event; it was Father's Day, and folks were expecting a show. And Wooden gave them one, with Scully wheeling Wooden in his wheelchair to center stage and visibly taking a step back to allow Wooden to dominate the spotlight— the single most gracious tribute to an icon I have ever witnessed, and most people had no idea. It was Scully's credo—make sure that when folks leave they want more.

But Scully did get the chance to tell my favorite story. He had gone to the Vatican with his pal Ralph Branca and Branca's wife. They were going to get a private audience, and Scully's mother was so thrilled for his son and gave him all kinds of instructions on what to say to Pope Pius XII. As the pope worked his way around a small group, Scully said he was so impressed the pope's gift of gab. When he got to Branca, it was obvious he knew about Bobby Thomson's home run off Branca to win the pennant for the Giants. The pope then exchanged pleasantries with Branca's wife.

Scully said his palms were sweaty as he prepared for his visit with the pope. When the pope turned toward Scully, with Scully trying to remember everything for his mother, the pope said, "I presume you are with them" and then moved on. That's quintessential Scully—looking for humility wherever he could find it.

When the Father's Day show was over, Scully grabbed me before we had left the stage. "I got to have a copy of that," he said. And when Wooden passed away, Scully granted the TV powers permission to show the event again.

The books are now filling up with stories of those who couldn't pull themselves away from Scully to hear one more story.

I used Sandy Koufax Bobblehead Night as my excuse to get more from Scully—revisiting the poetry that was his radio call of Koufax's perfect game. During my discussion, he said he had never listened to that call again. "I almost felt like it was an out-of-body experience. I was so mesmerized," Scully said. "I almost felt everything he did. All of a sudden, I was sweating on the mound. All of a sudden, I was rubbing up the ball. I don't think I've ever come close to that feeling again."

Scully's initial assessment of a skinny Koufax when he first saw him the Dodger clubhouse had been "This guy will never make it." But here, as Scully and Koufax were making history, a dark thought had passed through Scully's head while Koufax was perfect.

Scully had called Don Larsen's perfect World Series game and had watched a little later. He said, "I'm watching myself say, 'Ball one. Foul ball.' Two batters and I went back to watching football."

He was ready for Koufax, though, telling his radio audience, "It is 9:41 p.m. on September the ninth." He said upon reflection, "I was just looking for something to say. So, I thought to myself, *I'll do the only thing that doesn't mean a darn thing. I'll mention the time.*"

When it was time to leave, and much too soon, I asked Scully what he had done after such an incredible night.

"I got on the elevator and went home," he said.

FOURTH INNING

"I'm the Last Person Who Should Ever Complain"

Humility and Sincerity

Golf has a way of revealing so much about one's humility. Vin Scully understood that; it fit his disposition. As a golfer himself, he knew the thrills one moment could be squashed by the agony that came one stroke later.

With some humble pride, Scully once told me about his own golf game—a longtime member at Bel-Air Country Club, he lived in the Pacific Palisades near the famous Riviera Country Club, where he took lessons and learned how to play. At one point he moved to a house on the Sherwood Country Club course in Thousand Oaks, just to the right of the par-three seventeenth hole.

"There's the old chestnut: No one is completely useless; you can always serve as a horrible example," was how he described his game. At one time he had a 12 handicap. He had three holes-in-one, all at Bel-Air. His best round was a 77, and "I was walking on air, and I've never come close to that again."

Scully's twenty-five-year run calling golf on all three major networks started at CBS in 1975, and he was included in the network's prestigious coverage of the Masters. He moved over to NBC to call the Skins Game and the Players Championship, usually paired with Lee Trevino. ABC brought Scully over to redo the Skins Game in 1991 and the Senior Skins Game in '92. He was still on network golf in 2000.

The classic example of Scully's golf broadcasting ability can be found on YouTube and the *Golf Digest* website, a video of when he called the 1981 Heritage Golf Classic on Hilton Head Island in South Carolina. Rik Massengale, a three-time winner on the PGA Tour, found himself stuck in a deep pot bunker on the fourteenth hole at Harbour Town Golf Links. He was shoulder-high to the golf course, locating the nearby green as if he was a human periscope. A stepladder propped up inside the bunker provided the best entry and exit to this steeply enclosed prison.

Massengale would eventually use six desperate swings to get out of that sandy hole and take a quintuple-bogey 8. It made for some of the most excruciating two minutes of TV coverage. Scully's dutiful description, full of empathy and dry humor, invited the viewers in as if it were an episode of *Candid Camera.*

"Now pull up a chair and take a look at the agony of a gentleman who is caught in the pothole at fourteen," Scully began. Massengale took a whack at the ball, only to have it bounce off the side and back at him.

"When you can't take it any longer, why, we'll understand if you leave." Swing, and the ball ricocheted back.

"Fourth shot," Scully reported.

Swing, and the ball ricocheted back.

"And you're too old to laugh or cry . . . well, he took the laugh . . . but that was short-lived, as the poet says," Scully noted.

The picture told the story, but Scully's narration was even more compelling.

"Now it's exasperation . . . desperation . . . Rik now looks at the ladder and says, 'Maybe I could use the ladder. . . . Look out caddie, I'm coming your way.'"

Swing, and the ball ricocheted back.

"All right, I can't go forward . . . once more into the breach," Scully said.

Swing, and the ball clipped the top of the bunker. It bounded toward the green . . . until—

"Huzzah! I cried," Scully exclaimed, referencing an old-time military interjection, credited to revolutionaries involved in the Boston Tea Party.

"And now look out water," Scully noted, as the ball rolled toward the nearby lake, then stopped, and the cameras picked up the playing partners shuffling their feet and trying to look the other way.

Because it all was previously recorded on tape, Scully wrapped it up for the viewers by explaining Massengale took two putts to finish the hole, then the coverage went back to live action. Scully also added that it was "a casualty of what looks like a meteoroid that landed just left of the green at fourteen."

Scully's awareness and sensitivity to go with self-effacing modesty could have developed for him at an early age.

"I remember when I was very young, we lived in a fifth-floor walk-up apartment in New York, not a tenement, but where if you looked out the window, you'd see another window," he told me on the occasion of his ninetieth birthday, explaining why that only reminded him that marking a personal milestone led to some discomfort.

"I knew we didn't have any money. So I always tried to downplay my birthday so that my parents wouldn't feel obligated to spend money they really didn't have. I never thought about the number itself. I just kind of pushed it aside as something no one else should get excited about."

When Scully did some due diligence on becoming a TV gameshow host in the late '60s, he said he tried to read more about pop culture, current events, and movies.

"Sir Laurence Olivier was asked what makes a great actor and he said, 'The humility to prepare and the confidence to pull it off,'" Scully said of how he approached this new career. "Believe me, I'm loaded with the humility to prepare."

In June 1989 Scully was caught in a precarious situation in which he called ten innings of a Cubs-Cardinals Saturday-afternoon, nationally televised game in Saint Louis; flew to Houston to join the Dodgers and then call twenty-two more innings of a game that started Saturday night and bled into early Sunday morning; catch a few hours of sleep; and come back to do a thirteen-inning game on Sunday afternoon.

He called it "really nothing. . . . As a youngster growing up in the Bronx, I had a lot of tough jobs. I washed silverware in a hotel, I shoveled snow, I slotted mail, I was a milkman. A lot of people have it tougher than I do. I love my work and am well paid, so I'm the last person who should ever complain."

In November 2016, when he was trying to get his head around being asked to appear at the White House to accept the Presidential Medal of Freedom from President Obama, Scully was exasperated. "I'm deadly serious—when I've been given a gift of 67 years of broadcasting, and then have to take a bow, I can't think it's something that I actually did. It's really about the 67 years.

"It's very nice and I deeply appreciate it, but when I heard about it, I said something like, 'Are you sure you're calling me?' It's not like I invented penicillin. I can't stand in a spotlight as if I just saved a child from drowning.

"It really came out of the blue. What do I have to do with a presidential award?"

The sincerity reminded me of that previously mentioned 1992 interview I did in the Dodger Stadium dining room. To complete a biographical box on his personal highlights, I asked for his birthday. I had not seen it referenced in any books or media. Was that ever revealed?

Scully not only gave his birthdate—which came as news to some in the Dodgers' own PR department—but also added, "I'm afraid that slowly but surely it's going to be as if I'm the old man in the mountain."

Sports Illustrated writer Steve Rushin, in an August 2022 appreciation piece, noted that Scully's humility was one of the reasons so many loved him. Rushin described an experience that many had: If one happed to be on the receiving end of his phone call, it started with him saying, "Hello, this is Vin Scully."

Well, of course it is.

"I always introduce myself because I never know who knows me," Scully said.

No more explanation is necessary.

Orel Hershiser

Los Angeles Dodgers All-Star pitcher (1983 to 1994, 2000)
Winner of the 1988 National League Cy Young Award
Los Angeles Dodgers TV analyst (2014 to present)

About a year into his retirement, Vin Scully and I did a Q&A appearance at a corporate event. We were the last people to go out on stage, so we had about thirty or forty minutes to sit on a couch in the green room. And we just talked. Not much of it was about baseball. It was about family, health, things going on in the world, some of his memories of Jackie Robinson or Sandy Koufax.

I still think of moments like that, or a competitive round of golf, a bus ride, a meal together, and I realize all of the things he taught all of us just by being an example. He lived his life in front of us as a broadcaster, a Dodger, and an icon. He was one of the most impactful people you will ever meet.

This was an American patriot, a Christian, a deep scholar. He added context to life. He had opinions and enlightened you on almost every subject in the world.

He had integrity. He had a huge heart. He was humble. He taught us how to be gentlemen, how to dress, how to conduct ourselves with fans. He taught us how to exist in the world, hold ourselves up in the highest esteem, and live our life accordingly. He was a role model. Whatever it was we should be, we could find it in Vin Scully.

And still I don't know if Vinny ever knew how big a shadow he cast.

For those of us who played for the Dodgers, Vin was a marker in your life. I remember when I met him in Vero Beach in spring training in 1980. I was in awe. Then he was describing the last out of the 1988 World Series when I was on the mound.

Some fans saw him as a father or a grandfather, yet they may have never met him. Still, he became their friend. That's what he meant to Los Angeles. And that is what he meant to baseball.

I know there is an ongoing narrative that he will live forever. A century from now we will still be talking about Vin Scully.

Eric Karros

Los Angeles Dodgers first baseman (1991 to 2002)

My dad grew up in a Masonic Boys Home in Utica, New York, and our family lived in New Jersey, where I was born, until we moved to San Diego, where my mom grew up. Since my dad grew up a Brooklyn Dodgers fan, our house in San Diego was still all about the Dodgers—even though I grew up a fan of the Cincinnati Reds and Pete Rose. When my dad came home from work as a banker and went into his office, he figured out a way to get the radio reception of the Dodgers' games from LA. When I wanted to spend time with him, it was laying on the floor near his desk, talking to him, and all the while in the background was a Dodgers game and the voice of Vin Scully. That was the ritual.

I got to know Vin on various levels over the years as a player in spring training, at Dodgers alumni events, and in the broadcasting world. And for me, the story that stands out to best represent Vin was the following.

After I retired, a friend of mine, Grant, asked if I could get Vin to call or leave a message for his brother, Kent, who had brain cancer and did not have long to live. He was a huge Dodgers fan and had a wife and four kids, ranging from middle school to high school. Kent had not been responsive to much of anything until then. I emailed Vin with the information, but I never heard back from him.

A week later, Grant called to thank me. He said Vin left a beautiful message for his brother. Vin talked about when he had troubles; he trusted that everything was in God's hands but sometimes didn't understand it. Vin said he would pray for him and his family. Grant said that when Kent heard Vin's voice, his eyelids opened and closed. It made an impact. Kent passed just weeks after hearing Vin's voice mail.

Not long after Grant's call, I had a game to broadcast at Dodger Stadium. I went into Vin's booth and thanked him for making that call to Kent. "What do you mean?" Vin asked. I told him I knew that he must have gotten my message and made the call, because I got to hear the message.

Vin just smiled. He never would take credit for it or want recognition. He just did it. That epitomized who he was.

My memory of that phone call went way beyond baseball. Yes, everyone identifies him from his voice and the role he played in a game. Yes, I have known him as everyone else, as someone who was part of our family, more well-known than any player, always talking to you every night. But what he did with that call is something I will always remember about him.

Derrick Hall

**Arizona Diamondbacks president and CEO (2006 to present)
Los Angeles Dodgers executive (1993 to 2005)**

Vin Scully often took me to play golf at Bel-Air Country Club. One time he stood over a putt that was only about two feet. He pulled it and missed it and said, "Oh dirty name." I responded, "Come on Vin! Just say it once. Let me hear you." He said, "No, no, just dirty name!"

Another time he had flown out to Florida during spring training for a Sunday telecast. We always had drivers who would pick us up in Orlando and drive us to Dodgertown. He wanted us to go to lunch off property when he arrived, so I borrowed one of our rental cars from the complex and waited for him to drop his belongings in his room. We then took off, and as we were driving up A1A and I had one hand on the wheel dangling over the top and was steering more with my wrist, I asked him, "How was your driver this morning?"

He paused and then replied, "Well, he was just okay."

"Why just okay?"

He quickly said, "Well, it was obvious he did not understand the importance of driving in the ten-and-two position."

I then placed both hands on the wheel in accordance!

Here's one more story: One season, broadcaster Ross Porter was going to take an extended leave due to a health issue, and I was considering fill-in options. I asked Vin for his advice and told him of my concerns with the budget, that I could not bring in another talent or pay an existing broadcaster more. Vin suggested I just ask Rick Monday to take all the innings and that he would do it for the good of the company. I agreed but did not have the ability to offer him more pay. Vin offered this advice: "Oh you won't need to pay him more, Sweet Swinger [as he would call me on and off the golf course]. Believe me when I say, tenors love to sing." He was correct, and Mo agreed to pick us up. When I went back to Vin to tell him he was right, he said, "So from now on, just remember, tenors love to sing!"

Boyd Robertson
Dodgers TV booth stage manager (1989 to 2021)

In my twenty-eight years of working in the television booth with Vin, home and road, he would always walk in and ask how we were doing that particular day. We might discuss the news of the day in the United States or greater Los Angeles. On weekends we would from time to time talk about professional golf tournaments or other sporting events going on while we were working baseball games.

In April, when the baseball season was getting underway and the Masters Tournament was going on, we would talk about that. Vin worked the eighteenth tower for CBS. The first time I asked if he had played Augusta National Golf Club, he said, "As soon as the tournament was over and off the air, I head to the airport to catch up with the Dodgers." He was never able to play the course, but to me that showed all of us how dedicated he was to the O'Malley family to not cause any more delays in calling Dodgers games.

From time to time, Vin would have meet-and-greets arranged through the Dodgers organization before a game he worked. I would be given the information by the Dodgers publicity department and talk to Vin about how and when we would make it happen. As you can imagine, people from all walks of life came by to say hello and visit over the years.

I would often tell the visitors before escorting them into the booth that he wanted to be called Vin, not Mr. Scully. I even had a lady tell me her grandfather said to make sure "you call him Mr. Scully." I put her at ease and said he would be pleased with just Vin. She understood and called him Vin.

When someone met Vin in the booth, he would ask the person's name and other questions. Many would say, "I listened to you on my transistor radio in my bed and would go to sleep listening to you."

Vin would come back with, "I put a lot of people to sleep listening on the radio."

Before the guests left, Vin would say goodbye and repeat their first name to them. He always made it special because it would probably be the only time they would get to interact with him.

17. Vin Scully with Boyd Robertson at Dodger Stadium. Courtesy of Boyd Robertson.

He truly cared—I watched it happen. Vin was a gentleman and respectful to all. I was often asked if Vin ever had a bad day. I'm not sure what a bad day was with him. He's always did his homework, was always professional and with energy. Maybe it came from what he said he heard once from an old-time writer in New York: "Only losers beef." And that rubs off on everyone.

You didn't complain around him—after all, what could you complain about?

Tim Mead

National Baseball Hall of Fame president (2019 to 2021)
Los Angeles Angels executive (1999 to 2019)

When we lost Vin Scully in 2022, like so many others, I felt compelled to express my thoughts and feelings on social media about one of the country's last great icons. I closed my eyes, leaned back in the chair, and thought about Vin and the professional and personal kindness he directed my way through my years as a member of Angels baseball. Then I realized my affinity toward Vin was more important to me as a young fan than it was as a professional blessed to interact with him periodically over the course of the seasons.

As an eleven-year-old baseball-is-everything transplant from Arlington, Virginia, listening to his magic voice and storytelling genius via transistor radio was gripping and riveting. I went to school but listened to Vin and the late great Angels broadcaster Dick Enberg for my daily baseball education. Some family members and close friends would debate where my primary focus was directed!

I wanted my grain-of-sand-on-the-beach post to not just reflect the present feelings of a middle-aged MLB employee. Rather, I searched for a description of my own personal baseball journey with Vin, from childhood through adulthood, hoping others might relate, having shared the same course. Within a few moments, with his image and voice uninterrupted at the forefront of my thoughts, I typed the following: "We watched him. We listened to him. We learned from him. We were better because of him. And now we shall miss him"—the summation of how one man unknowingly helped a youngster integrate his passion and love of the game into an eventual career spanning four decades.

In May 2016 the Angels held a special gathering on the broadcast level of Angels Stadium to present gifts and honor this true legend as he celebrated his final season, with Mike Scioscia, Mike Trout, Jered Weaver, Dave Hansen, Mickey Hatcher, Alfredo Griffin, and Ron Roenicke among those participating. Lots of stories, laughter and mutual respect permeated the get-together. It was one of those cherished experiences where you hope your memory plays a never-ending loop.

18. Vin Scully with Tim Mead at Angel Stadium. Courtesy of Tim Mead.

After his passing, I looked for photos our communications staff took with Vin, along with others from that day. Certainly, those photos for each of us reinforced the statement "a picture is worth a thousand words!"

Then I remembered a voice message I had saved from Vin six years earlier because, at fifty-six seconds, it personified the broadcaster I idolized and the man I held in the highest regard:

> Hi, Tim, it's Vin Scully. It's Wednesday October the fifth. I am slowly trying to catch up for all the good things that have occurred to me over the last two weeks and, for that matter, for my entire life. Anyway, you're one of the first calls, and hopefully you're off on a rest, which would be well deserved. I just wanted to thank you and the Angels organization for the picture of me with the players, with Mike, and then having them sign, and then frame it. It's a beautiful addition to my office. I guess I will just be an Angel fan now when the American League is active. Anyway, God bless you, Tim, and everybody in that organization. I wish you only good health and happiness and a lot of success. Thanks.

Without pause, his message was inclusive of humility, appreciation, and respect, a small sampling of the endless attributes applicable to this very special man. May his voice and legacy continue to resonate with the generations ahead!

John Olguin
Los Angeles Dodgers executive (1992 to 2005)

I love something that Vin Scully said all the time about those of us who worked in baseball. He referred to us as having the luxury of working in *the toy department of life*—because even when it was bad, it was still pretty good. I use that line often.

So many times, when you idolize someone in your youth and then ultimately get the opportunity to meet the person, he or she rarely lives up to your idealization. Vin Scully completely counters that idea. As someone who could quote Charles Dickens as easily as he could quote Mickey Hatcher, it seems only appropriate to quote great American literature when speaking of Vin Scully. So, if you subscribe to the Maya Angelou quote "I have learned that people will forget what you said and people will forget what you did but people will never forget how you made them feel," then Vin Scully epitomized it.

I often brought people—dignitaries, friends, VIPs, or anyone else—into Vin Scully's TV booth during games to give them a glimpse at greatness. While there, I just stood quietly in the back to watch and listen to the master at work. At the inning break, Vin would stand up, turn around, and make everyone feel like they were his long-lost family. He would introduce himself, shake everyone's hand, and ask a question or two about who they were or what they did. He would speak to every child and maybe even take a quick photo with the group. The interaction would last for only a few minutes between innings, but the impressions lasted a lifetime. It was truly a thing of beauty to be a part of, even though I might have taken it for granted at the time.

I was recently reminded of the impression he left on people. I met up with some friends I had not spent much time with since high school. One came to see me at a Dodgers game many years before and said the inter-action with Vin was something "me and my family will never forget." He, his wife, and eight-year-old son met Vin, and Vin completely focused on his son (who is over thirty now) as he wore his baseball jersey and cap. Vin asked his name, his jersey number, and the position he played for his team. After the young boy told him all of that, Vin went on to use his on-air voice and introduce him as if he were part of the Dodgers lineup: "Now batting for your Los Angeles Dodgers, number 22, playing second base, Bradley Boles!" In just three minutes, he made that young family feel like they were the most important people in the world.

One other example occurred when I worked later in the racing world. One of our team's IndyCar Series drivers, Charlie Kimball, would throw out the first pitch at a Dodgers game before the Grand Prix of Long Beach. Charlie grew up in Camarillo as a massive Dodgers and Vin Scully fan. That night, he was on the field for batting practice, met countless Dodgers play-ers, and was introduced to the crowd as he wore a Dodgers jersey with his name and his car number 83. It was a storybook evening for a Dodgers fan.

But to this day, every time I see him, Charlie speaks of meeting Vin Scully later that evening. I took him and his wife, Cathleen, to the press box. At the inning break, Vin turned around to say hello and noticed Cath-leen wearing a USC T-shirt. He raised his two fingers in the air and said, "Fight on!" He made the night for Cathleen, a graduate of the University of Southern California. Vin asked Cathleen about USC and asked Charlie about his recent win and the upcoming race. The interaction lasted maybe three minutes, but the memory will last the Kimballs' whole lives.

Just as he did on the air, Vin Scully knew exactly the right thing to say at exactly the right time in life. He was always *on*. He was the same person, whether he was meeting someone for the first time or just chatting with someone on a bus ride or during dinner conversation. He never seemed to have a bad day.

Jill Painter Lopez
Journalist

The only thing better than listening to Vin Scully was watching Vin Scully. Seeing how his smile ignited a smile in others was such a joy. I was lucky to witness so many lovely encounters in the Vin Scully Press Box over fourteen years.

I often dined with Associated Press reporter Beth Harris in the Dodger Stadium press cafeteria. Lucky for us, we were usually done about the same time as Vin, and I can't count the number of times he skipped ahead of us to open the door with a "Hello, Jill. Hello, Beth." We were giddy every single time. It was fun to watch Beth's reaction. Mine was the same. It never got old.

I once took a selfie with him in the press box in 2014, and he talked and I laughed the whole way through it. It was the best selfie I ever took. I swore I'd never take another. I did, but none have been as fun.

During Vin's final season calling Dodgers games in 2016, I saw a steady stream of players and broadcasters who went to his booth to pay their respects. I loved standing in the back watching. He had a long conversation with Bryce Harper, who was then the twenty-three-year-old All-Star with the Washington Nationals—a lot of smiles and laughs. A sixty-something age difference didn't matter. Vin connected with everyone.

In September 2016, on the day of his final home game, I went to Mass that Sunday morning in the Dodgers' press conference room. It was special to watch Vin be honored that day and to start his day with his faith. He could've done without any attention; he was humbled. Later that day, Charlie Culberson hit a walk-off home run, and the Dodgers won the NL West. During the champagne-soaked celebration in the clubhouse, I asked Culberson about having Scully call his homer in his final regular season game.

"I'm excited to be able to hear how Vin called that," Culberson said. "Very emotional."

My husband, Ricardo Lopez, also a sports journalist, and I had a phone call with Scully during the pandemic in September 2020. Ricardo grew up a Dodgers fan in Mexico listening to Jaime Jarrin guide him through

19. Vin Scully with Jill Painter Lopez at Woodland Hills Country Club in California, 2014. Courtesy of Jill Painter Lopez.

Fernandomania. He became a Vin Scully fan too. My husband requested an interview with Scully for the first time. Of course, Vin said yes. Ricardo told him it was an honor, and afterward I interviewed Vin.

Vin told me, "I might not know [Ricardo], but I feel like we're friends now." My husband always treasures that Zoom video. That's how people felt after an experience with Vin—like they were friends or family.

I loved watching Vin's interactions with the late Dave Pearson, the long-time Dodgers press box chef. Pearson offered a smile and delightful greeting of "Sweetie" to everyone. It always worked. He prepared every plate of food with care, but I especially loved to watch when he prepared a meal for Vin. It was always completed with applesauce—Vin's favorite—and Pearson put that dollop on as though it were to be eaten by a king.

Pearson was later diagnosed with cancer and had to retire. His health declined rapidly. I visited him at his San Fernando Valley home one day when he was in hospice and he had a steady morphine drip. As I arrived, I was told that Vin had just called him, his friend, to offer some encouragement. I'd often heard of Vin calling or visiting people or sending a note. If he was told he could make someone's day, he did so with pleasure.

Vin was always cheerful, always smiling. I know he had bad days and went through difficult times. He just never showed them.

FIFTH INNING

"Be Quiet and Eat Your Cookie"

Building Connections

In his 2000 autobiography, *The Other Great Depression: How I'm Overcoming on a Daily Basis at Least a Million Addictions and Dysfunctions and Finding a Spiritual (Sometimes) Life*, comedian Richard Lewis included a chapter simply called "Thanks, Vin." Lewis wrote about the first love in his life, the Brooklyn Dodgers of the 1950s.

"Even more consistent than the Dodgers losing World Series championships to the Yankees was one of their broadcasters, who soon would be their 'voice,' and a heavenly escape for me," Lewis wrote. "Vin Scully's voice and perceptions have sometimes taken up more space in my head than my own thoughts, which has been a great thing when my thoughts are making me miserable."

Lewis's torment moving to Los Angeles included living in what he called was a dump of an apartment "right next to some motel that doubled as a whorehouse." But he recalls one night turning on the radio as he was unpacking and hearing Scully's voice:

> As crisp and eloquent as ever, even . . . biblically sounding. All my fears and doubts and concerns about being in a strange city pursuing my dream were at once washed out of my memories. . . . I floated back in time and started to visualize the Dodgers as I had as a little boy when this same evocative artist painted his word-pictures with such effortless verbal brushstrokes . . .
>
> I put my hands behind my head, lay back, forgot about goals, fears, money, everything, because Vin Scully was back on the radio and that was good enough for me. . . . I forget about everything, if only for a couple of innings. Because even more than the game, I just have to hear someone else's voice in my head. And that would have to be Vin Scully's.

There must be some explanation for the way Scully's voice activated serotonin in the brain, igniting a chemical reaction that connected distant memories to the present. The intoxicating nostalgia of it all brought us back as if it were yesterday, with baseball and with Scully.

The Scully-fan bond was stronger than many family ties, some admit. The connection was only tested over the years by external forces—namely, ownership changes.

Scully's personal connection to the O'Malley family went back to his 1950 hiring. Although team general manager and co-owner Branch Rickey approved Scully's hiring, just three years after the signing of Jackie Robinson, Walter O'Malley became Scully's primary chaperone after Rickey departed to Pittsburgh. When Walter O'Malley died in 1979, his son, Peter, assumed control of the franchise and maintained a bond with Scully that began decades earlier.

The sale of the Dodgers in 1998 took the team off its O'Malley moorings and joined it to the Fox Sports corporate flotilla. Rumbling started that the new ownership group might consider Scully, closing in on age seventy, unfit for the edgy Fox attitude younger-skewed marketing.

That anxiety could have come from an incident not long before that when the Detroit Tigers handed over its president's role to Bo Schembechler, the bombastic former University of Michigan football coach. He declared that beloved broadcaster Ernie Harwell's days on the team's WJR-radio airwaves would be done after the 1991 season, and the firing was "not going to change, no matter how much clamor is made of it."

Clamor was made, Schembechler left the team the next year, and the seventy-two-year-old Harwell, whose departure from the Brooklyn Dodgers to the New York Giants opened the door for Scully to enter in 1950, came back by popular demand.

A Fox spokesman had to finally declare that Scully would be with the Dodgers as long as he wanted to be. Fox only wanted to stick around until 2004 and then sold out to new owner Frank McCourt. More angst ensued. The departure of a few key front-office people in the transition made Scully start his fifty-fifth season with some trepidation.

"No one likes change, and you can see how it can be unsettling to every-one, even on the periphery," Scully explained to me. "I understand the uneasiness, but if I can help by being allowed to do the games, it'll be my honor and pleasure."

In August 2011 that sentiment was reinforced when, in the top of the sixth inning of a Dodgers-Rockies telecast, Scully looked into the camera coming out of a commercial break and held up a cookie.

"Every time this year, a nice lady in Woodland Hills named Mrs. Marti Squyres sends me some chocolate-chip cookies," Scully explained. "This year when she sent them, in the letter she said, 'This is a bribe to get you to come back next year.'

"Well, I don't want to make a big deal out of it. You and I have been friends a long time. But after a lot of soul searching, a few prayers . . . we decided that we will come back with the Dodgers for next year.

"God's been awfully good to me, allowing me to do the things that I've always wanted to do. I asked him for one more year at least. He said, 'Okay, be quiet, and eat your cookie.'"

With a wink, he had a catch in his voice as he added, "Let's go back [to the game]."

There was thick and gooey context to that announcement: Two months earlier, McCourt filed bankruptcy court documents. Scully was listed among forty creditors who held the largest unsecured claims—he was owed more than $150,000. Scully declined comment on the matter, but others spoke up for him. "The fact that Frank McCourt owes money to Vin Scully is like someone forgetting to call their mother on Mother's Day," said David Carter, executive director of the USC Sports Business Institute.

Guggenheim Baseball Management rescued the franchise from McCourt control in 2012. Its first announcement was to Scully—again, he could stay as long as he liked. He did—four more years. But it came with a glitch in the distribution system.

Viewers found it difficult to watch him call games after the new owners created their own Dodgers-centric SportsNet LA regional sports cable channel. It would have all games home and away, so no more over-the-air broadcasts. That started a dragged-out contract dispute with other cable operators over subscriber fees. Some viewers came to feel as if they were caught in an unresolvable hostage situation. A group called Knights of the Road took out a paid advertisement in the *Los Angeles Daily News* under the headline "Who Owns Vin Scully?" It started a social media campaign: #Freevinnie.

"Time Warner's billion-dollar TV package should not buy the rights to keep Vin Scully's voice quiet or break the bond he has established over half a century with the Los Angeles listening audience," the ultimatum read. "The Dodgers do not need to go to arbitration to make the right call. Vin Scully should belong to baseball."

The group had no real or imagined legal recourse, but the message came through. And through it all, Scully stayed true to the games and broadcast, never mentioning the business squabble on the air, and even rarely off air.

Fan loyalty to Scully went back to the O'Malleys endorsing a single voice with a single mic on the game calls. This established a trust, not just for the Dodgers' brand but also for endorsements that paid the bills. Scully became a prized commercial pitchman, especially with product placement during a game or with ads airing between innings.

Who else but Scully could convince Los Angeles that not only was a Farmer John's shank and butt portion edible, but also it was even quite delightful with its easternmost in quality and westernmost in flavor, whatever that actually meant. The same went for pork-mixed hot dogs, braunschweiger, or, maybe worst yet, liverwurst.

Scully started by doing live cigarette and beer spots during the Brooklyn broadcasts, which was common throughout Major League Baseball. Companies soon enlisted him to tout their cars, gasoline, soda, airlines, savings and loans, house paint, hi-fi stereos, and shaving products. He could lead young viewers in a Mr. Rogers sort of way to believe that the latest Danny Goodman $2 souvenir special—basically, Goodman was the head of the team's novelty and trinkets department who had an excess stock to offload—was worth considering breaking open the piggy bank.

Dodgers team historian Mark Langill once wrote how, according to urban legend, the Union Oil Company of California said it would not assure the Dodgers a construction loan in the early 1960s for their new ballpark unless Scully had been signed to a ten-year deal. Union 76, with a gas station planted in the parking lot beyond the center-field fence for customers' convenience, knew the trust and connection he built with the audience could sell their LA-friendly petrol. The Dodgers added more years to Scully's deal. "So Dodger Stadium, in a sense, became 'The House That Vin Built,'" Langill concluded.

Fans were reminded of Scully's staying power with the company in April 2023. The Dodgers had a Vin Scully Jersey giveaway night, sponsored by Union 76. It drew a sellout on an otherwise nondescript Tuesday night at Dodger Stadium.

In the pregame ceremonies, Scully's children and grandchildren were on the field. Looking out at them lined up down the third base line, one saw a perfect example of how their connective DNA reflected the common bond Scully had created with the Dodgers' generations of fans—seven, or more, if you chart it correctly.

Scully's 1927 birthdate aligned him with what is known as the Greatest Generation—those who are patriotic, driven by a strong work ethic, committed, and loyal. They were children of those who grew up and came of age during World War I. The Silent Generation, which some peg as starting in the late 1920s and going up to 1945, upheld the ideals of their parents.

When Scully started with the Dodgers in 1950, he was talking to an audience that included some born in the 1800s. He would eventually connect his own age group with the Baby Boomers (1946–64), Generation X (1965–80), Millennials (1981–96), and Generation Z (1997–2012) by the time he retired. That means his voice could have been an effective conduit to people whose ages spanned more than 150 years. Some of the first Generation Alphas (born in 2013) could have consciously soaked in his melodious syntax.

With the generations of digital natives, Scully's adaptation to social media became endearing. Trying to get on board with Twitter—calling his posts a "twit" and trying to see if he could get something trending—led to him having, at ninety-two years old, his own Twitter, Instagram, and Facebook accounts, at the height of COVID lockdown when he longed for connection.

"I'm not going to have anything to do with any controversy of any kind," Scully said at the time. "It's very friendly, very simple and just a small contribution to whatever is going on." That could have been social media's original mission statement if Scully had any interest in it during its creation.

As a way to explain what he felt his connection was to the viewers, Scully signed off for the last time in San Francisco on October 2, 2016, using words he conjured up during his isolation from the game during the 1994 MLB strike. In late 1994 Scully told Los Angeles radio host Joe McDonnell that the ongoing labor dispute, which canceled the World Series, made him feel lost. When the games resumed in 1995, Scully said he quickly figured out what he would say to the fans upon the game's return—something he would carry through to the end of his run.

"As I was driving to the stadium and getting goosebumps again, I knew I would say this: 'Friends, I need you more than you need me,'" Scully told McDonnell.

Heading into retirement, Scully included this line in his final message: "I'll miss our time together more than I can say."

Peter O'Malley
Los Angeles Dodgers President (1970 to 1998)

My dad, Walter O'Malley, deserves credit for sensing Vin Scully's talent. When my dad became president of the Dodgers in October 1950, Vin was a young man. But they bonded. Vin trusted my dad, my dad trusted Vin, and that was the beginning of their relationship.

Vin was like a brother to me and my sister, Terry. I have all special memories of quality time together. We enjoyed traveling to many places beginning in 1956 for the monthlong Dodgers Goodwill Tour throughout Japan, where we were roommates.

There was spring training in Vero Beach, Florida; Copenhagen, Denmark, to visit the Hans Christian Andersen Museum; Park City, Utah, for skiing with our families; Florence, Italy, to attend a performance conducted by Zubin Mehta; Monterrey, Mexico, in 1991 for the Dodgers exhibition games; Washington DC, as guests of Danny Kaye when he was the recipi-

20. Vin Scully holds an array of balloons during a ceremony as the Brooklyn Dodgers visit Japan in 1956. Courtesy of Peter O'Malley.

ent of Kennedy Center Honors; Taiwan, for the 1993 Dodgers Friendship Series; and Las Vegas.

Vin was a delight to be with and the most genuine friend. He was four-teen karat, as nice a man who was ever put on earth, as good as a friend as he was behind the microphone. His honesty and integrity came through every day. So did his class, the way he described a game: impartially and expertly. That set him apart.

I've always admired Vin's faith. He often gave credit to the nuns from Ireland who taught him and influenced his life, starting in grammar school. At Fordham the Jesuits continued Vin's education. He appreciated his faith and didn't take it for granted. Faith can be lost or enhanced, and in Vin's case it was a constant positive influence on his life.

We owe him a lot, the city of Los Angeles, the Dodgers fans, all sports fans. We owe him for his career. No one means more to the Dodgers than Vin Scully, not just because of all those years behind the microphone but also because of his personality, his reputation, his professionalism.

Al Michaels

Hall of Fame network broadcaster

I am one of the few people in the world that heard Vin Scully's entire career. He was magical. Along with my father, he was a gigantic influence in my life and my career. There's no question about that.

Growing up in Brooklyn, I was a Dodgers fan. Vin's voice was one of the first I heard, with Red Barber and Connie Desmond. I lived ten blocks away from Ebbets Field. My father walked me over there for a weekend afternoon game when I was maybe six or seven. The grass was green. The signage on the outfield wall was in bright colors. And as Vin would say, the Dodgers uniforms were wedding-cake white.

My father pointed to the open-air broadcast booth in front of the upper deck and said that there were the announcers, the ones you hear on the radio and we watch from time to time on TV in New York on channel 9. There was Barber, Desmond, and a young Vin Scully, in his first or second year.

I was enthralled. My first thought was, *What a job—you get in for free?* It was the impetus to be a sportscaster, building a career in baseball.

As a teenager, I was distraught when the Dodgers left Brooklyn in 1958. As it turned out, my father was transferred in his work to Los Angeles. I didn't miss a beat. I probably went to fifty games a year during the Coliseum years and, along with thousands of others, brought the transistor radio. I actually didn't need one because everyone else had one. Los Angeles was new to Major League Baseball, and fans found it wondrous listening to Vinny. He taught everyone so much. He was brilliant.

When I started my baseball broadcasting career in Honolulu, for the Hawaii Islanders of the Pacific Coast League in 1968, I was as nervous as a cat on the plane ride over about what was ahead for me. I kept telling myself over and over, *Just sound like Vin*. It came from listening to him all those years. Early in my career, I very much sounded like his clone. That's how I was able to get through the first couple of weeks in Hawaii. Eventually I was able to develop my own style and rhythm, but there was always a lot of Vin Scully in me when I was on the air.

I first met Vin when he was on vacation in Hawaii. I got word he was in Honolulu during the baseball offseason, when I worked at the local ABC affiliate as a sportscaster. I knew he was at the Kahala Hilton, and I picked up the phone and called his room. I was very nervous. "Hi, Mr. Scully. I'm Al Michaels; I'm on television here. I know you're on vacation; would you mind if I came over with a cameraman for a five-minute interview?"

"Oh, sure," he said. He couldn't have been more gracious. I was giddy just to meet him.

Meanwhile, three years later, in 1971, I was the lead announcer for the Cincinnati Reds. The Reds had Pete Rose, Johnny Bench, and Tony Perez, and Sparky Anderson was the manager—the Big Red Machine. On our first trip to LA, Vinny asked me if I would be his guest on the Dodgers' warmup pregame show, a show I'd heard thousands of times. That provided one of the great thrills imaginable at that time—Vin interviewing me.

We developed a great friendship. We belonged to the same golf club at Bel-Air. We had many meals together. He was extremely complementary if he watched a football game I called. It never ceased to thrill me when I heard his voice on the phone. I think I have four voice mails from him on my old answering machine that will never be erased.

What made Vin Scully so brilliant was this: He was natural. He didn't sound like a guy playing announcer. He was a warmhearted and kind man. His voice was comfortable because of the gentleman he was, embracing and empathetic. That is what you strive for. You don't want to be an annoyance. He was authentic.

The call has to come from your heart. You've just seen something, but the call is what you feel in your bones. He was very fortunate—and I was too—to be there in certain moments where you could make it iconic or you could really screw things up. He put a coda on so many things, like Gibson's home run in 1988 after he hobbled to the plate. The call came from what his eyes saw, transmitted to his heart, then out of his mouth. There's an element of luck involved, but so is a lot of the humanity of the person. He read the room as well as anyone in the history of the business.

He had the ability to transition. Some broadcasters had to do a simul-cast—the same call heard on the radio as well as TV. Vin already did radio brilliantly. He then did TV brilliantly. He worked both mediums. He could use every verb in the dictionary on radio, and he was more than just someone putting captions and ellipses on the TV screen.

He was a teacher. I learned baseball from Vinny, as did millions of listeners of all generations, about the strategy, the players, the history of the game. He wasn't just a great storyteller; his play by play was just as fantastic.

He was prepared. He could take a run-of-the-mill 9–1 game—and God knows he had thousands of them—and could turn it into a great listen. Because he was extremely well read, he brought it every night.

So many times, after driving around LA and hearing Vin on the radio, I would sit in the driveway with the car idling, waiting for him to finish the story. I felt like I was in a time warp. Where am I? Am I in Brooklyn? Am I ten? How could this be?

In 2021 I was honored with the Baseball Hall of Fame's Ford Frick Award. I did an interview on MLB Network in which I said, "I probably learned more from Vin than anybody." From Vin's Twitter account came a post: "Kind of you to say Al. . . . Welcome to the club."

I was honored by the Southern California Sports Broadcasters Association, which asked whom I wanted at the dais to talk about me. One of the organizers said, "What about Vinny?" Of course, but I couldn't ask him. Then they told me Vinny was coming. That was just too much for me. When I grew up with someone who formed who I was in my vocation and all of the sudden he comes over to say a few words about me in a packed room—it has never ceased to thrill me.

I admit my dream once was to someday succeed Vin Scully as the voice of the Dodgers. But then I worried. I am going to retire before he did? No one has a sixty-seven-year career in anything.

There's no question in my mind he was the greatest baseball broadcaster of all time. If broadcasting was a horse race, Vinny would be Secretariat winning by thirty-three lengths at Belmont.

I got a PhD in baseball, but Vinny was my first teacher. I'm forever grateful. What a life this man lived.

Jessica Mendoza
Los Angeles Dodgers TV analyst (2022 to present)
ESPN MLB TV analyst (2015 to present)

Anyone who's been a coach's child knows growing up is twenty-four hours a day of technique and mechanics. I love my dad, who taught me everything about baseball and softball. But to hear Vin Scully call a game was a new connection, always a breath of fresh air. Vin brought something else. He actually opened my eyes up to how it connected to history—even to things like Greek gods. I grew up with a very technical understanding of baseball. But Vin showed me the beauty of it.

We didn't realize when growing up how much Vin's voice was always just there as a narrator to our lives. We had him on every day, not just watching the games but also when we were doing homework or in a family conversation. Looking back on it, I can see how much Vin was a part of our family. He would welcome us on air and thank us when he was done; it just felt like Vin at the head of the dinner table sharing a story with us.

We also had a connection to Jaime Jarrin. My dad's family lived in Orange County, and my grandmother loved listening to Jaime on the Spanish broadcast. Spanish was still a second language for me. I appreciated how much my grandmother enjoyed it because my grandfather played baseball, and they came here from Mexico with baseball was very much part of their integration into this country.

I did get to meet Vin once, but I was always hoping for a more private moment, away from the stadium, just a small five-minute chat to see him as a genuine person. He didn't live far from where I grew up—just ten minutes from my house—and I always felt there was a chance I would run into him at a grocery store. And it seemed as if we would always hear, "Oh, Vin Scully was just here; you just missed him." I wished I could tell him all the things I wanted to tell him—or maybe just listen to him and not have to tell him anything.

In 2015, when I was at Dodger Stadium for the first time doing an ESPN Sunday night game, I had an incredible, overwhelming feeling to sit not just in Vin's broadcast booth—his name and pictures are everywhere—but also in his chair. Workers told me, "This is where Vin sits." And I thought, *What the—*

During that national broadcast, Jake Arrieta threw a no-hitter for the Chicago Cubs against the Dodgers. This was a historic event, but already a big moment for me. That made it surreal. But I felt Vin's presence more than ever that night, and it actually gave me comfort. It kept me in the moment.

As a broadcaster, I think Vin's greatest lesson to us all is to just know when to take a breath. During a replay, there can be such a constant need to talk. He never forced anything. He just felt everything. That's hard to do. I challenge myself that way all the time. It is easy to get an adrenaline rush and have a sudden need to start pointing things out. I'm not necessarily trying to channel Vin, but I definitely want to have his pace and presence always with me when I think about baseball. It's just really allowing the game to breathe.

On the night Vin died, I was in the Dodgers' TV booth with Joe Davis. We had been told for a couple weeks that Vin was sick. That gave me time to think about the moments he meant not just to me while growing up but also to my family. When we were told during the game that Vin was gone, I would likely not have been able to process that emotionally if I hadn't known he was sick. But it was still very hard. Honestly, I was trembling a bit because I didn't want to say the wrong thing. I just wanted to make sure I was authentic. I was also conscious of how many people loved him. I was just wanting to hear from them. Somehow, I tried to channel all our emotions together, because I felt it was a very connecting experience.

I came back to do a game in San Francisco less than a year after that game when he passed away. I stared for about twenty minutes at the plaque in the broadcast booth to mark the place of Vin's last MLB broadcast. I thought about how emotional that was. I had to control the emotions, but I also didn't want to hinder it. I wanted everyone to feel my emotions. That's a fine line. I realized how vulnerable I can be when I allow myself to do that on the air. But I did so because I felt so connected to everyone who was watching the night he died.

Broadcasters are taught to only talk to one person. Just look into that one camera, they are told, so you don't feel overwhelmed. It was the one time I wanted every single person who was watching to share and feel connected to Vin in that moment. It was amazing. It helped me not only be emotional but also feel happy. It felt like Vin was there.

Vin genuinely helped connect us all together. I know that can sound spiritual, but that idea really made me feel connected to everybody who was watching. That was a powerful feeling.

Kevin Fagan
Drabble comic-strip artist (1979 to present)

I was watching a Dodgers game sometime in the 1980s when Vin Scully was talking about how The Wave was gaining momentum in Dodger Stadium.

I was inspired: I did a piece in which Norman and Patrick were trying to get The Wave started in church. They would stand up with arms extended upward and sit back down.

On the night the strip came out, Vin actually read and described my cartoon. It caught me by complete surprise. It was a surreal experience.

When I was a kid, I'd always dreamed of Vin describing my heroics on the baseball field. But this was just as good.

Late in the season, I sent that original "Wave" strip to Vin, addressed to Dodger Stadium. He actually didn't get the package until the start of next season. He still sent me a thank-you note and even apologized!

Over the years, especially during the 2013, '14, and '15 seasons as his career was winding down, I authored several strips about Vin as a tribute. One that caught the attention of many on social media posted on October 5, 2013, right in the middle of the playoffs.

Ralph had just bought a big-screen TV to watch sporting events, but his wife, June, was astounded he turned down the volume and was listening to Vin call the game on the radio instead. Ralph was just doing what many Dodgers fans did when the playoffs rolled around and a national broadcaster took over the TV rights.

21. Kevin Fagan with Vin Scully, displaying a *Drabble* comic strip Fagan created, 2014. Courtesy of Kevin Fagan.

It was the way I had watched Dodgers playoffs games for as long as I can remember. The last time before that, in 2009, I remember how frustrating it got with the delay between him on radio and the network TV video. So, I just turned off the TV. I'd rather listen to him.

I knew all about the pain Dodgers fans felt when they couldn't hear Vin do playoff games.

I thought about when I was growing up in Inglewood in the midsixties, when I was often home alone. My parents were divorced, so my dad was not around as much as I'd have liked, and my mom was a waitress and worked a lot. I went to my first Dodgers game in 1968—I saw Don Drysdale pitch.

I would always listen to Vin broadcast the Dodgers games. Not only did I learn about baseball, but I also learned a lot of life lessons. I can remember when he could paraphrase a reference to the Gettysburg Address—how the world will little note, nor long remember what we say here today—then go look it up for its context.

When watching a Dodgers-Giants telecast from Candlestick Park in the summer of 1969, I heard Vin talk about the events that would happen the next day, when "Messrs. Armstrong, Aldrin, and Collins" were about to partake in the first lunar landing.

When kids were given a free baseball as they entered the stadium on Ball Night, Vin reminded them to actually play with it, not to put it away in a sock drawer. When Mother's Day approached, Vin would remind kids of the importance of it and not to forget it. Vin mentioned that the movie *The Quiet Man* was shown one night with the players in Vero Beach during spring training. I've enjoyed it many times ever since then.

I remember when I was a kid people knew they could leave a game early on a weeknight because they could hear Vin when driving home—and they really weren't missing anything. Nowadays, that doesn't happen. Maybe that's why people stay in the park until the end now?

Vin saw things in a game most others wouldn't notice. An ordinary ground-out to second could actually have been a very important at bat because the hitter moved the runner to third, or maybe he forced the pitcher to throw a lot of pitches. Or he saw the cotton-candy sky or the mountains behind the center-field fence.

On TV, the cameras would find children and families in the crowd. Vin shared warm thoughts about kids eating ice cream or falling asleep on dad's shoulder. Life was important.

I was thinking that the way I do my *Drabble* strips might be similar to how Vin did his job. My job requires a lot of quiet time when I jot down thoughts and doodle and plan out what I'm going to do at the drawing board. I believe Vin also put a lot of preparation into his broadcasts, including making notes of stories and anecdotes he'd like to share. I think he also did a lot of reading. I've always told aspiring cartoonists that the more things you read and know about, the more material you'll have to draw from.

When Vin was to be honored in 2016 with a Lifetime Achievement Award at the LA Sports Awards, one of my strips appeared in the ceremony's program—thanks to Peter O'Malley, former owner of the Dodgers. He bought the actual original strip for Vin. I would have given it to him for free, but he insisted.

I had always thought of Vin as a friend who enriched my life—and that was before ever meeting him. My family and I eventually got an opportunity to meet Vin at the stadium before a game in 2014. I was able to give Vin another strip I had drawn. He couldn't have been more gracious. He asked my sons questions about themselves, told us some stories, and gladly signed a baseball or two.

I thanked him for all of the joy he brought us over the years and for making me a hero to my family that night. Vin invited me to stop by the booth anytime I was at the stadium. When we got to our seats for the game, I remember telling my boys, "Always remember, that's how a gentleman conducts himself."

A few days later, a handwritten thank-you note from Vin arrived. Vin was very good at writing thank-you notes to people, just another example of what a class act he was. We exchanged emails after that. What a dream come true to get to know him!

He made us feel special and appreciated. We felt the same way as just about everyone else who was ever lucky enough to meet him. The ability to uplift others just by being yourself is rare. Vin Scully had that ability.

Sammy Roth

Journalist

During his final months in the broadcast booth, Vin Scully couldn't stop insisting his impending retirement was no big deal. After all, he was just an ordinary guy who'd been lucky enough to do what he loved for sixty-seven years. What he wanted most of all—as he told every journalist who asked—was to be remembered as a good, honest man who lived his values and loved his family.

I was twenty-four years old when Vin called his last Dodgers game, and I'd never known baseball without him. I grew up at Dodger Stadium, showing up early to Sunday afternoon games and begging my dad not to take me home when night games went to extra innings. When I wasn't at the ballpark, I listened to Vin. He was a legend, a fixture in the firmament of my childhood.

When Vin retired, I was sad. When he died, I was devastated. My brother broke the news, texting me as I took an evening walk in my neighborhood. I almost couldn't believe it. Overwhelmed, I plopped down on the sidewalk and just sat with the news. Eventually I did the only thing I could think of, which was to open Twitter and watch the accolades to Vin roll in: his masterful storytelling, his calming voice, his incredible longevity.

And then I thought about José Fernández. It had been six years since the twenty-four-year-old Miami Marlins pitcher died in a boating accident, just hours before Vin's last game at Dodger Stadium. Fernández had been one of the brightest lights in Major League Baseball, a Cuban defector who played with such joy it was impossible not to love watching him, even when he was annihilating your team—like when he started against the Dodgers two weeks before his death, striking out fourteen over seven shutout innings.

Vin handled the tragedy with his usual grace, reading a tweet Fernández had sent the year before: "If you were given a book with the story of your life, would you read the end?"

"He was twenty-three then and already thinking some pretty deep thoughts," Vin said.

22. Sammy Roth, with his parents, at Dodger Stadium on September 25, 2016. Courtesy of Sammy Roth.

It would be too simple to say Fernández's death had put Vin's retirement into perspective. I was still in tears when Vin said his final goodbye over the Dodger Stadium loudspeakers.

But what I learned then—and what came back to me as I sat on the sidewalk a few blocks from my apartment—was that Vin was right about his retirement not being a big deal. The greatness he achieved in the booth paled in comparison to the mark he left as a human being.

I'll always remember Vin's pitch-perfect broadcasts, because of course I will. But more than that, I'll remember the example he set as a human being. I'll remember the kindness he showed to total strangers, like when I asked him for an autograph as a kid and he happily obliged, full of his usual humor and charm. I'll remember how he always said "we," not "I," on the air—an acknowledgment of the behind-the-scenes technicians who helped him do his job.

I'll remember how he quit smoking by replacing the packet of cigarettes in his shirt pocket with a picture of his family—a family he cared for deeply, his wife Sandi becoming his constant companion in the press box near the end of his career. I'll remember the affection he showered on babies and toddlers in the stands at Dodger Stadium, as they laughed and dripped ice cream on themselves and threw foul balls back onto the field.

I'll remember his passion for his work, even after sixty-seven years. One of my favorite moments was during his final season, when he apologized for broadcasting a Dodgers-Nationals game with a sore throat. He knew he should have stayed home, he said, but he badly wanted to see the showdown between Clayton Kershaw and Stephen Strasburg, two of the best pitchers in the game. I hope I can still muster that kind of youthful enthusiasm when I'm eighty-eight.

I'll remember how Vin embraced players of all races and ethnicities, even as baseball struggled with diversity and many Americans grew fearful of immigrants. I loved how he celebrated Yasiel Puig when the Cuban defector took the Dodgers by storm, nicknaming him the "Wild Horse" and marveling at his second career home run: "Que viva Cuba! Viva Puig!"

Most of all, I'll remember Vin's modesty. I'll remember his discomfort with the spotlight, his instinct to shine a light on anyone other than himself. I'll remember how embarrassed he looked during that last game at Dodger Stadium, when fifty thousand of his closest friends—he always said we were friends, not fans—spontaneously chanted his name between innings. I'll remember how he told us, after the game, that he needed us far more than we'd ever needed him.

And I'll never forget how he ended his broadcast a few nights earlier, at the close of Vin Scully Appreciation Day, chuckling, "You've gotta be fed up tired with me, that's for sure." No, Vin. Never.

When I tell my kids and grandkids about him, that's what I'll do my darnedest to make sure they understand—not the voice behind the microphone, but the man behind the voice.

Joe Saltzman
USC communications professor

My parents were from Brooklyn, and I grew up loving the Brooklyn Dodgers. But there was no television when I was young, only a shortwave radio and Dodger broadcaster Red Barber to bring the team to life. But in 1950 Vin Scully joined Barber and took over the announcing duties in 1953 when Barber left. For five years, until the Dodgers came to Los Angeles in 1958, Vin Scully created for me, and thousands of others, a complete world of baseball with its lore, its stories, and the ethos of the game and of life itself.

With little money to go to a game and the black-and-white TV set only giving an approximation of what baseball looked like, Scully fashioned dynamic word-pictures—the vibrations of the air creating a sound that, for me, was nothing but pure magic. Scully formed the basic fiber for my imagination with his larger-than-life images of baseball and the people who watched it, played it, managed it, owned it.

Even when I could afford a color television and buy tickets to go to the game, I, like many, kept a portable radio by my ear so I could hear Scully describe what I was seeing. To anyone who never experienced Scully's unique way of describing a game, taking a radio to the game itself must seem ludicrous. But for me, a baseball game without Scully was a flat black-and-white version of the game. I needed Scully's voice and imagery to turn it into dazzling color.

I was not alone. It was almost surrealistic to go to a Dodger game and hear Scully's voice from hundreds of radios filling the air. It made the game they were watching so much more than nine innings and a field of players.

In between balls and strikes and the occasional hit, Scully would tell us why baseball mattered. It wasn't just an anonymous man standing at the plate. It was a human being whose history mattered. Scully combined physical descriptions of a player with stories about that player's place in history, with the quirks of what made that player matter, with the reasons he might get a hit, or strike out, or score a run. When Kirk Gibson limped to the plate in the 1988 World Series, Scully said, "All year long they looked to him to light the fire, and all year long he answered the demands. [And then came the fateful pitch.] High fly ball into right field. She is gone! [Pause.] In a year that has been so improbable, the impossible has happened."

I watched that happen on television, but until I heard Scully say it, I didn't believe it.

There has never been a sports announcer as erudite and as brimming over with history as Scully. Listen to a typical Scully description: "Football is to baseball as blackjack is to bridge. One is the quick jolt. The other the deliberate, slow-paced game of skill, but never was a sport more ideally suited to television than baseball. It's all there in front of you. It's theater, really. The star is the spotlight on the mound, the supporting cast fanned out around him, the mathematical precision of the game moving with the kind of inevitability of Greek tragedy, with the Greek chorus in the bleachers."

Even our heroes got the Scully trademark descriptions. Many announced that outfielder Robert Clemente had one of the best arms in baseball. But only Scully could put it this way: "Clemente could field the ball in New York and throw out a guy in Pittsburgh." Many announcers told you that Bob Gibson pitched very fast. But only Scully could say, "He pitches as though he's double-parked." Everyone knew base stealer Maury Wills was fast. But Scully told us why: "When he runs, it's all downhill."

When you watch ballgames today on TV or listen to them on radio, usually two people are talking to you—one doing the game and the other doing color. But I usually turn off the sound because their patter is mostly filled with clichés or trivia. It's just boring to listen to them because they add little to the game itself.

We may never hear another Vince Scully again. Like the other great announcers who grew up with radio—Chick Hearn, Red Barber, Dick Enberg, Jack Buck—Scully knew how to tell us not only what was happening but also why it was important. He weaved into his broadcast not only stories about baseball but also stories about human history, and he had an uncanny sense to only do that when these stories were relevant to what was happening in the game. He was never a distraction but always a sane voice amid the noise.

Scully gave meaning to the game. In doing so, he told us all why baseball mattered and how it related to our lives, our past, our present, and our future. Scully's baseball was a lesson in how to get along with others, how to survive in a world of imperfection, how not to let our own mistakes dominate our lives, and how to get over misfortune and tragedy, how to look for a brighter tomorrow because no matter what happened in today's game, there would always be another tomorrow, another chance to make it right.

Emma Amaya
Los Angeles Dodgers fan

I came to this country from Honduras when I was thirteen and did not speak English. No one in my family was a baseball fan, so the first time I remember hearing Vin Scully on the radio was in the car of my first boyfriend. When we parted ways, I became more of a Dodger fan. Definitely, Vin helped me with my English, and I learned baseball terminology from him. Many years later, I started to listen to Jaime Jarrin. The baseball terminology in Spanish sounded funny to me since I was now so used to the English. But how lucky we are that we could still listen to these two maestros.

I also learned more history from Vin. I remember on one Memorial Day, Vin was reciting the poem "In Flanders Fields." From then on, every Memorial Day I wear a poppy flower on top of my head. Some ask me why. I explain it and mention Vin.

He was always teaching us something. I would make notes and follow up to read more about the subject. If I didn't know the meaning of a word, I would look it up. From his narration of the game, the stories in between plays about the rich baseball history, the human stories, the history, and the poetry, he was always pulling us into the narrative. We might not have seen some old-time players, but through his stories he connected us to those past players, to fans before us. He built those bridges that connected us all.

I remember Vin talking during a game about Hilda Chester, how on a quiet day at Ebbets Field in Brooklyn she yelled, "Vin Scully! I *lovvvve youuu!*" Vin said he felt embarrassed and lowered his head. Hilda then said, "Look at me when I am talking to you," and Vin said the crowd went bananas laughing. As Vin told the story, he laughed. I thought it was funny too, so a friend and I started going under Vin's booth during batting practice and

23. Vin Scully with Emma Amaya. Courtesy of Emma Amaya.

yelling "Vin Scully, we love you!" Vin would stand up and wave back. We did that many times and at different stadiums, even at spring training, and also from the top deck of Dodger Stadium looking down as Vin exited. Sometimes we did it after a game and said, "Good night, Vin Scully!" He always acknowledged us by waving or saying, "Good night!" And if it was cold, "Stay warm!" We would leave smiling.

One time we went to see the Dodgers in Arizona, and we spotted Vin. Nervously we approached him and said, "We are the two crazy fans that yell to you from below your press box that we love you!" In that familiar voice that we all knew and loved, he said, "Oh, you are not crazy. What are your names?" We told him, and he repeated our names and said he was glad to meet us. He said, "I love your enthusiasm." We were on cloud nine.

SIXTH INNING

"It Was Trust Well Placed"

Kindness and Friendship

At the end of 2016 I had to justify my choice of Vin Scully as the Southern California News Group's Sports Person of the Year. The annual honor was for someone who generated the most news—good, bad, or otherwise.

All things considered, Vin did have a pretty good year. So, my essay began as follows: "In early October, St. John's Episcopal Church in Corona updated the 'welcome' message on its street corner marquee. In addition to reminding worshipers about the times for the Sunday services, the clip-on letters spelled out a reminder: 'Be Like Vin Scully. . . . Notice and Praise the Good in Everyone.'"

Good call. Acts of kindness, by the way, were anything but random for him.

Handwritten thank-you notes became Scully's most straight-to-the-heart response to anything he felt was worthy of acknowledgment. It was as ordinary as it was extraordinary, cursive artwork suitable for framing. But that was not the intent.

This was his old-school way of texting. This was on permanent record, something that wouldn't disappear into some cloud.

From the half-dozen notes I received over the years—simple, elegant, on high-end card stock—I treasured how Scully knew the right words to express his appreciation. He recognized accuracy and fairness. He embellished on something he learned. He closed with a humorous and friendly signoff—Mr. Manners, indeed.

In spring 2006 he sent a note reacting to something I wrote about him just before the start of the season: "I am fully aware that the wolves are getting closer to my campfire, and a boost at this stage of my life is extremely important."

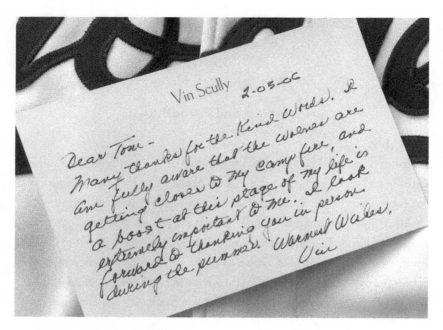

24. A note card from Vin Scully, 2006. Courtesy of Tom Hoffarth.

In late 2013 Scully gave me a cheery Q&A interview as he prepared to be the grand marshal at the upcoming Rose Parade in Pasadena, California. With tongue in cheek, I asked if he now looked at the world through rose-colored glasses. He laughed but then revealed that he had some concerns over upcoming laser eye surgery to correct his vision. He had been wearing extra-thick glasses to help with distance viewing. Whenever he did a live TV shot, the glasses came off. Scully asked that I not write about any of that for the moment, concerned that if word got out about the pending procedure, too many might worry about him.

The surgery was a success. You can find photos of Scully working the rest of his career without the need of any glasses. After the Q&A was printed, he sent along another handwritten note: "It was trust well placed. Many thanks. Vin."

Now it can be told? I think so. He trusted us, which is something special coming from someone who, in a *Los Angeles Times Magazine* 1998 profile, was referred to in the headline "The Most Trusted Man in LA."

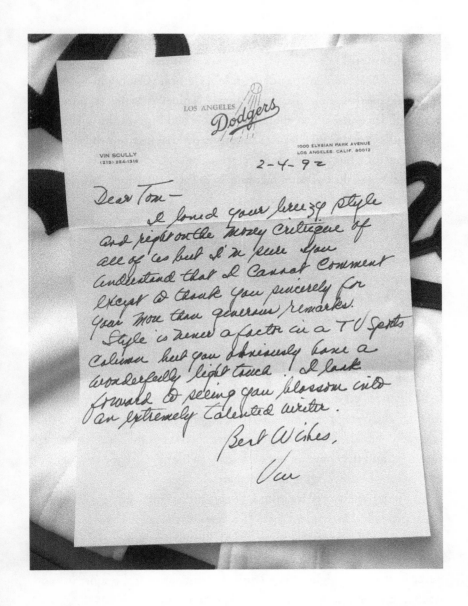

25. A note card from Vin Scully, 1992. Courtesy of Tom Hoffarth.

Aside from the notes, Scully was more than willing to call anyone in need of comfort.

Fr. Steve Davoren, the pastor at St. Mel Catholic Church in Woodland Hills, told me that one of his parishioners—"a ninety-seven-year-old woman who still drives herself to church"—approached him on the Wednesday after Scully's passing. She wanted him to know that not only did she know Vin knew him, but also she and Vin were "now good friends."

"The thing is, she has never met him," said Father Davoren. "She said that after her husband of sixty-five years passed away, she was feeling lonely, and one day her phone rang. It was Vin. Someone had contacted him on her behalf. For a half-hour they spoke. It was just what Vin did—like Christ did—making us all feel like we matter."

Scully spread warmth and good cheer no matter what holiday season.

In 1995 he made the annual cross-country trek to Florida to call the Dodgers' Grapefruit League exhibition games back to Los Angeles. But the circumstances weren't normal. MLB was gearing up to start the season with so-called replacement players, as a strike that started late in 1994 continued on.

Scully stressed the integrity of the game was not going to be compromised. "These are professional baseball players, not truck drivers and shoe salesmen," he said. "These are professional players in the Dodgers organization . . . and they have an opportunity of a lifetime. Major Leaguers are only Minor Leaguers who have been seen."

To these players now wearing Dodgers uniforms, Scully gave a locker-room pep talk. He thanked them "for keeping the game alive."

Petie Roach, a twenty-four-year-old pitcher, first baseman, and outfielder who would end up at the Dodgers' Single-A affiliate that season, might never have gotten higher than Triple-A before leaving the sport in 1999. At that moment, he appreciated Scully's kind words.

"You don't know how people are going to perceive minor leaguers playing in these games," Roach said at the '95 camp. "So when somebody like that says they're proud of you, it makes you feel like you're doing something worthwhile."

Scully told everyone late in the 2013 season he would return for his sixty-fifth season. He explained to the media gathered around him in the press box why he felt a pull to come back. He singled out Maria Hartmark, the Dodger Stadium press dining room manager who always managed to remember his love of applesauce and deliver it when needed. And there was James Mims, the security officer at the entrance to what was then known as the Vin Scully Press Box; he became part of the vetting process for guests to enter and exit his booth. And there was also Dave Pearson, the stadium chef.

Even if Scully didn't know he helped someone by showing compassion or concern, others never forgot it.

"Vin Scully's Kind Gesture Toward a Kentucky Wildcats Sports Icon" was the headline in the *Lexington Herald-Leader*, a story about Scully's passing in 2022.

Claude Sullivan started calling Cincinnati Reds games in 1964. When the team stopped in LA on a road trip, he had a persistent cough. Scully noticed and arranged for Sullivan to see the Dodgers' trainer, which led to an urgent suggestion that Sullivan visit the Mayo Clinic in Minnesota. He was soon diagnosed with a rare, aggressive form of throat cancer. Sullivan died from the disease within three years, at age forty-two. When Sullivan's son, Alan, wrote a book about his father years later, he wanted Scully to know he appreciated the kind gesture.

"Dad probably wouldn't have lasted six months [without the immediate treatment]. So we were grateful as a family that, through Vin, the Dodgers trainer got him to go to Minnesota," Alan Sullivan told the newspaper.

During my newspaper career, I came to know a young man named Roberto Baly. It was hard to miss him in the Los Angeles media circles, as he posted regularly on his website VinScullyIsMyHomeboy.com. We traded social-media correspondence, shared story ideas, and linked to each other's posts. He once posted that he was in the hospital battling an infection caused by chronic granulomatous disease (CGD)—a genetic disorder in which the white blood cells aren't able to kill off bacteria. Roberto went to the hospital another time when CGD lumps went to his lungs and he needed oxygen to breathe. I reached out to Vin to see if he could connect with Roberto. I knew it happened when I saw Roberto feeling better as he posted an updated photo of himself and young son Andrew standing along with Vin at a game. Roberto fed off his love of Vin and the Dodgers. But as the illness progressed, Roberto wasn't able to attend games for five years. I was deeply saddened to see a post on his Facebook page from his brother announcing Roberto's passing on August 29, 2022—less than a month after Vin died. A GoFundMe page had been set up to help cover funeral costs. Knowing that Vin and Roberto connected and corresponded is comforting—home boys together.

Doug McIntyre, a well-known LA radio personality, recalled when he ran into Scully in the parking lot outside a Gelson's supermarket. They had just a brief conversation, but it made an impression on McIntyre when he wrote a tribute piece about Scully in 2022: "Vinny wasn't a celebrity god on Mt. Olympus like Michael Jackson or Sinatra or Kobe. He was family; the avuncular jacket-and-tie clad gentleman who had a good word to say about everyone, even Leo Durocher. He wasn't just 'old school,' he was his own school, polite and well-mannered to the very end. As America grew angrier and crasser, Scully's relentless politeness was a nine-inning reminder it doesn't have to be this way. Sadly, manners are too frequently interpreted as weakness. For Vincent Edward Scully they were the source of his strength."

Jaime Jarrin
Los Angeles Dodgers broadcaster (1959 to 2022)

I was very blessed to be close to Vin for practically all my sixty-four years of broadcasting life. After we met in 1959, we were always somewhere together at the ballpark. We traveled and sat on the plane together. He would pull out his restaurant guide and take me to the best places on the road.

I never tried to imitate him as an announcer. But I did as a person.

I don't know how I became such a good friend. He took me under his wing. I was so green and so young and had some problems with the language. I wish I could command English like Spanish. But he would help me.

I never got Vin to learn Spanish—he said he once tried—but he often came into our booth during a game asking, "How do you pronounce this Latino player's name?" He wanted to be right. Sometimes you hear Perez or Gomez pronounced one way and then another. Vin especially wanted to know about Peña, which was often said differently than the correct "Pen-ya."

When I was first doing the Spanish broadcasts, Vin knew how difficult my job was. He saw how we translated what he said, not like how some Spanish broadcasters tried to take information off the teletype machine and were sometimes one inning behind the game. We didn't have that. Vin was so nice to give me information before the broadcast: it's a windy day, it might rain, we are seeing clouds.

One time his microphone was left open between innings, and I could hear him with Jerry Doggett. Jerry asked him, "Why do you give so much information like that?"

Vin said, "Jaime needs it to do his job, and I know how difficult it is for him to do the games."

He was the pinnacle of our profession. He didn't like to give advice to everyone, but to me he said, "One, don't think you know everything. Two, you have to do your homework before every game." Also, he said, "Don't get too close to the ballplayers because it will affect your work. Be diplomatic, but not too close." And I followed that. Even when I was with Fernando Valenzuela for so much of his rookie season in 1981 as a translator, I could

26. Vin Scully with Jaime Jarrin. Courtesy of Jaime Jarrin.

still keep a distance that Vin talked to me about. If you remember, it was really Fernando who never allowed anyone to get close to him.

Vin was unique in many regards, no question. He didn't like television much, and he was always reading. He recommended books to me about U.S. generals, biographies of Lincoln and Marco Polo, and anything by Louis L'Amour.

He was very kind when he introduced me to so many people in Hollywood. In the 1960s the stars used to come to games more than they do nowadays. Before a game, I would hear Vin in the hallway: "Jaime, come out here! I want to introduce you to someone." So, there was Gregory Peck, Charlton Heston, Chuck Connors, or James Garner. Vin said James was his favorite golf partner, especially in the last few years. I think the closest friend of them all was Danny Kaye. He came almost every day as part owner of the Seattle team. That was an excuse to be there. Vin seemed to go to Danny's house almost every week because Danny became a great chef of Chinese food.

His most impressive act of kindness was when my wife Blanca passed away in 2019. Vin called me right away in Arizona, and he talked to me for about thirty minutes. I just listened. Whatever it was—his command of the language, his intonation, his voice—the call was beautiful. Sometimes I close my eyes and play it back in my memory.

27. Vin Scully with Fred Claire. Courtesy of Fred Claire.

Fred Claire
Los Angeles Dodgers general manager (1987 to 1998)

In reflecting on my life, other than my immediate family, I know of no one who was more of an inspirational person than Vin. Vin always seemed to be present when most needed. When I was fired by the Dodgers, a letter from Vin was one of the most uplifting experiences of my professional life. When I was battling cancer, a message from Vin was uplifting; it is the one message that never will be removed from my telephone. Vin apologizing for saying it took him two weeks to write again reflected who Vin was, trying to say the right thing.

As a world-famous broadcaster, Vin had incredible talent, but more important was his character. Always present in every way were humility, compassion, friendship, and faith.

Vin handled his enormous fame better than anyone I have ever known. For Vin, he treated all of those he encountered with equality and respect.

I spent a great deal of time with Vin at Dodger Stadium, Dodgertown, public events, and an area he accepted but didn't particularly care for—road trips. Being away from his family was an obligation but never a true joy. Family, faith, and friends were the foundation of Vin's life.

VIN SCULLY

7-6-98

Dear Fred –

    I am sure that you will understand how difficult this letter is for me to write — And no doubt difficult for you to read.

    I have tried to compose it many times and each time I kept drifting off in so many different directions that I wound up feeling totally frustrated. The result of all my labors is to keep it very simple.

    I thoroughly enjoyed our many years together and I am saddened to say goodbye. You have my total respect as a decent human being and as a diligent and knowledgeable baseball man as well as my deep admiration and loyalty as a friend. We all are fully aware that nothing lasts forever including ourselves and with that in mind, I pray God will shower you and Sheryl with all His blessings for all the years to come.

        Your friend,

        Vin

28. A note card from Vin Scully to Fred Claire in 1998. Courtesy of Fred Claire.

It was Vin's faith that always provided the path to a life of kindness and a desire to serve others in any way he could. At his funeral Mass, a prayer card was given out with the Prayer of Saint Francis. I remember the words: "Lord, make me an instrument of your peace. . . . Where there is doubt, faith; where there is despair, hope; where there is sadness, joy." That was Vin, each one of those things. I saw each of them play out in his life.

These are just small examples of the reach of Vin on thousands of lives. Vin's voice will never be forgotten in the history of Dodger baseball. Vin's life made an even greater impact on mankind.

I was blessed to have a friendship of more than fifty years with Vin. I don't think in terms of a beginning to the friendship, and I know there never will be an end. Vin was always consistent.

Ned Colletti
Los Angeles Dodgers general manager (2006 to 2014)

I wonder if Vin Scully ever struggled to come up with the most appropriate words to describe a play, a person, a moment in time. I doubt it. Admittedly, it is a challenge for me to come up with my personal "best of Vin Scully" or "the best of the best." I struggle to know where to begin. How can I ever do justice to him or our friendship?

Do I start with the story of him wanting to do something for my only daughter Jenna's wedding in Chicago? Two thousand miles away, he kindly tape-recorded the introduction of the wedding party.

Do I start at the beginning—May 28, 1982? It was just my fifth month in baseball and, after a Friday afternoon game at Wrigley Field, he came over to introduce himself and asked me if I could help find him a cab. He would be inducted into the Baseball Hall of Fame in less than seventy days—and he's introducing himself to me?

It was special then to talk to him, and that never changed through forty years.

I worked on the NBC national telecast of the 1986 and 1988 World Series and was stationed in the network booth, providing him information as some of the most historic finishes in baseball history played out:

"Little roller up along first . . . behind the bag . . . it gets through Buckner.
Here comes Knight, and the Mets win it!"
"High fly ball, into right field—she is gone!"

Through the years, the conversations just got better and deeper. Among the best came during my nine-year run as the general manager of the Dodgers.

There were the Dodgers chartered flights with him sitting in the first seat, first row next to his longtime compadre, the wonderful Billy DeLury—his friend and the former Dodgers executive who worked with the club from September 1, 1950, until his death just days before opening day in 2015. No matter the day, no matter where we were, I knew where I could find both Vin and Billy each Sunday morning on the road: in church.

I was walking to the hotel elevator in Phoenix to head over to Chase Field in 2012. Vin and Billy were having a cup of tea, and I stopped to say hello. After sitting down, I listened to each of them describe in fine detail October 3, 1951: The Dodgers-Giants 1951 playoff game when Bobby Thomson hit the famous homer. Both Vin and Billy explained moment-by-moment what they saw, what they heard, and what they felt on that historic day for baseball in New York City.

How do I chronicle all the dinners on the road—mostly at the ballparks but also in town on the rare road off night? Or the late-night wind-down meetings on the concierge floor of the team hotels, where Vin and Billy waited for me to return before calling it a night? Back in Los Angeles, all the dinners in the Dodgers press dining room with DeLury, Charley Steiner, and Rick Monday? Like clockwork, there Vin would be.

Honestly, there were too many moments to list, too many fond memories of not only the best baseball broadcaster I have ever heard but perhaps also the best person I have ever known—aside from my parents.

There's the conversation we had when I left the general manager's job. It was so beautiful and classy—I started writing it down as he spoke because it brought me near tears.

I called him every year on his birthday, November 29th. I didn't want to take his time, but he would end up saying, "Are you in a hurry?" And we would talk some more.

The last three conversations we had, as his life wound down, come to mind:

He came on a Dodgers SportsNet LA show and talked about auctioning off his personal baseball artifacts. It was time, he said. He was asked what the hardest artifact was to put on the auction truck. He didn't hesitate. "My golf clubs," he said. "I shed a tear knowing where we had been together—all over the globe—and that I would never play again."

Within a few days, I called the auction house and told them I wanted to bid on the clubs, and they agreed they would keep me current. I bid and bid and then bid some more.

I ended up with the clubs—two sets.

A couple of days later, I called Vin to ask how the auction went and if he was feeling any better about the golf clubs.

"Not really," he said. "It was sad because it was a symbol of my stage of life too."

I asked if he felt better knowing who had them.

"I don't know," he replied.

"Well, I have them."

"You have them? Well, that is terrific. Now I'm glad I auctioned them off."

I told him they would be in my family for generations to come. He liked that a lot.

Out of the blue he called me in 2021 to tell me I had overstated his importance in the book I wrote, *The Big Chair*. Vin said, "I read it when it came out. And now I read it again. Are you sure you have the right guy in your description?"

Am I sure? I am positive.

Then there was the final conversation a few months before August 2, 2022. "I am tired," he confided. "I am just waiting my turn."

Bruce Froemming

Major League Baseball umpire (1971 to 2007)

It was in the early 1980s when our crew was coming into Houston, and the Dodgers were also coming in to start a series against the Astros. And as always happened, once I checked in, I went down to the bar and had a beer or whatever. This was the Shamrock Hilton.

I saw Vin Scully a seat or two away from me. We knew each other from years before. I grew up in the Minor League camps at Dodgertown in Vero Beach for years. My first year was in the Minor Leagues there in 1963, seven years before I would go to the big leagues, and that's when I got to know Vin better.

But we never personally had a chance to engage in any long talks. So, I moved over a couple seats. Soon, small talk led to bigger talk.

Vin related that he really liked umpires and respected their work. But he had issues when the umpires didn't clearly signal balls or strikes that he could read easily. He said, "I'm on the radio, and whatever the umpire does, I'm telling the audience. So, if I am getting a delayed strike call, it makes it tough on me." I was struck by how he explained it and what that meant to him.

I gathered that he was such a professional and a friend of the umpires, never looking for problems, never wanting to beat them up during a broadcast. He just saw it as something to bring up. It made so much sense. I had never thought about that before. I was always a guy who would scream, "Strike!" right away. I enjoyed being emotional behind the plate with my calls.

As the years went by and I got to know Vin more, I wanted to salute him—before a game, we umpires would wave our caps to him. That's how much respect we had for him.

Years later, in the last few years I was in the big leagues, I remember Gordie Verrell, one of the beat writers covering the team, came down and asked, "What's with the salute to Scully?" I knew Vin's son was killed in a helicopter crash. He worked as a batboy and was a terrific kid. But over the years, I never—and *never* is a big word—heard him say a bad word about an umpire. Nor did anyone tell me he said a bad thing about umpires. It's unusual to me to have someone in that position all those years and not take a shot at an umpire.

I was at Vin's last game in San Francisco with one my best friends, Eddie Montague, a fellow umpire. I was working then as a supervisor for umpires, and the playoffs were about to start after that final game. We went to the press box, and he treated me and Eddie like we were family—and he already had a lot of family there. To me, it was exciting just to be in his presence for that. He made us feel so at home, so sincere in his reception for us. The press box before that game was so full of well-wishers. But he made time for us. I'll never forget it as an example of how to treat other people. He could not have been nicer.

Vin was one of the nicest people I've ever met. I'm not just saying that to be polite. The quality of his respect, whether toward a janitor or an umpire, that he showed was sincere. It made you really feel good. Before a game, he would always ask, "How are you doing, Bruce?" before I could even sit down to eat. And he was always at a table full of people because everyone wanted to be around him. Just the way he said hello made people feel so different. I can't explain it.

He was the king of the mic, for sure. When you think of a World Series, a big game, he was always there. He put life into the game. But I was glad and blessed I was with him all those years. He was that good of a guy. He was the best.

Bob Miller

Los Angeles Kings broadcaster (1973 to 2017)
Hockey Hall of Fame

Born and raised in Chicago, I had the pleasure of hearing many of the Chicago radio and TV play-by-play announcers—Jack Brickhouse with the White Sox, Cubs, and Bears; Vince Lloyd with the Cubs; Bob Elson with the White Sox; Lloyd Pettit with the White Sox, Cubs, and Blackhawks; Jack Quinlan with the Cubs; and Jim West with the Blackhawks. All were outstanding and inspired me to want a career in radio and TV play-by-play.

I had spent my entire life in the Midwest, so I never had the pleasure of hearing Vin Scully until I was hired by the LA Kings and moved to Los Angeles in August 1973. Soon after I arrived for a meeting in downtown LA, I realized that everywhere I went, I heard Dodgers baseball on transistor radios, with Vin doing the play by play. I thought to myself, *I hope someday fans will tune in to hear me doing the Kings broadcasts.*

I was fortunate to eventually meet Vin in person more than once, and each time it was a thrill. Vin set the standard for every play-by-play announcer, not only in LA but also throughout the country.

He had a pleasing voice and, in addition to calling balls and strikes, the knack of telling stories as if he were speaking directly to you. You didn't want to miss a minute. When you would listen to other baseball announcers, many times the game seemed dull, but with Vin you wanted to hear his knowledge of the game's history and vibrant play-by-play.

The late sportswriter Alan Malamud first introduced me to Vin in 1973, when I quickly realized how gracious Vin was to visitors to his booth. He immediately made me feel welcome and said he was anxious to hear my play-by-play of Kings hockey. I learned from him in that first meeting how to speak with fans in a friendly manner and to ask about their interests and experiences, which enhanced my relationship with Kings fans.

Vin showed it's so easy to be friendly and nice rather than rude and abrupt. Every time I saw Vin, I felt he was genuinely happy to see me, and I went away feeling wonderful. Vin had that down-to-earth personality with everyone.

As the years went on, I had several other opportunities to join Vin at various sports activities. I was surprised and thrilled as the Kings held an on-ice ceremony for my twenty-fifth anniversary with the team in 1998. Vin spoke at the ceremony as did the extremely popular basketball voice of the LA Lakers, Chick Hearn, who got me the job with the Kings.

In 2001 I was asked to be on a television panel discussion with Vin and Chick. At one point I said, "Look at the rings on those guys' fingers." Vin held up his ring from the Dodgers' World Series title in 1988. Chick held up his hand and said, "This is the Lakers NBA championship ring, 1987." Now, the Kings had not won any championships at that time, so when the camera panned over to me, I held up my hand and said, "This is my wedding ring, 1963."

In 2012 the Kings won their first Stanley Cup. I was afraid I would retire and they would win the cup the next year. The morning after that victory, I was asked to appear in person on the John Ireland and Steve Mason radio show on ESPN in LA. While being driven to the studio, I received a phone call from none other than Vin Scully. He congratulated me and the Kings and had some very nice comments. That was another thrill, and I found out the phone call was arranged by John Ireland, the sports talk-show host and Lakers broadcaster.

On January 25, 2014, the first ever outdoor regular-season NHL game in California was held, between the Kings and the Anaheim Ducks. Vin and I were together in person again on the field at Dodger Stadium to welcome 54,099 fans, the largest crowd ever for a Kings home game. Kings fans went home disappointed, as the Ducks shut out the Kings, 3–0.

In September 2016 Vin retired after sixty-seven years. The Kings made up a jersey with number 67 and Vin's name on the back and asked if I would present it to him. I went to Dodger Stadium with a video crew from Fox Sports West. When I presented the jersey, I said, "Vin, when you started announcing, a high number like 67 probably meant you were a prospect, you hadn't yet made the team."

Vin laughed and replied, "I'm trying my best," and we both had a laugh over that.

29. Bob Miller presents a Kings jersey to Vin Scully at Dodger Stadium, 2016. Courtesy of Bob Miller.

For years, Vin would open his broadcast with familiar words: "It's time for Dodger baseball." After Vin's death, the Dodgers continued his legacy by asking numerous personalities to stand at home plate and repeat on the stadium public address and on TV those famous words. I was asked to participate and readily agreed. As I stood at home plate waiting for my TV cue, I was a little nervous, not wanting to mess up the words of a famous icon!

I'm thankful to Vin for showing me how to greet fans with respect and find out a little about their lives and work, how to have humility, and how to pay attention to the fundamentals of presenting an accurate and exciting broadcast. He was the best ever at capturing the moment with exactly the right words and phrases.

Dennis Gilbert

Agent

The first time I met Vin Scully, I was eighteen years old, parking cars at Hillcrest Country Club in West LA. When he pulled up, I addressed him as "Mr. Scully." He, of course, said, "Call me Vin."

I grew up in Gardena and had heard him calling Dodgers games since the team moved to LA in 1958. I told him I had just signed a Minor League contract and in two weeks I would leave for Waterloo, Iowa, to start playing Class-A ball. For the next ten minutes, he told me all about the Midwest League and the baseball played there.

Sometime in the late seventies, we reunited as I was pitching batting practice for the Dodgers to their backup players; when I saw Vin on the field, we talked about the day that we had met years earlier and had a good laugh.

Somehow, for the last ten years of Vin's life, I was fortunate to serve as his agent and I spoke with him frequently, almost every day. Every time I went to a game when he was still working, I would look up to him from my seat during the seventh inning stretch, he would look at me, and we'd just wave to acknowledge we were thinking of each other. When my wife was with me, Vin would blow her a kiss.

The one thing people may not appreciate about Vin was that, hours before every game, he studied the backgrounds of the opposing players to make them more human, not just looking for more statistics. He made notes, notes, and more notes. I asked him what he was doing. "Working on my ad-libs," he would say. And he kept everything.

We often went to Beverly Hills for lunch at the Grill on the Alley; afterward, we would go for a walk. He was the most approachable fellow in the world. Hollywood stars could take a lesson from that. He was always a gentleman, even when it hurt.

We had a dinner once with Jerry Reinsdorf, the owner of the Chicago White Sox. I wanted them to meet each other, as I am his special assistant. That dinner was one of the most memorable I was ever a part of. As much as I like to talk, I just enjoyed listening to the two of them. They barely talked about baseball. It was all about politics, the world, and Brooklyn, where Jerry grew up—nothing of what I expected.

30. Dennis and Cynthia Gilbert share a birthday dinner with Sandi and Vin Scully, November 2015. Courtesy of Dennis Gilbert.

I frequently took clients to games, who would all want to meet Vin. He was the most generous person in the world with his time. I think he needed that connection with people. That was so important in his life.

After I got out of the agent business, ballplayers who came to town to visit wanted to meet Vin. The one I remember most was Bret Saberhagen, who grew up in the San Fernando Valley loving the guy. Bret even pitched a high school championship game on the Dodger Stadium mound. I was happy to connect them, and it was amazing how much Vin knew about Bret's career, as it was mostly in the American League.

Vin always wanted to stay connected with the fans, so in his retirement, we talked about projects that would do that. Starting on Twitter was the best way. We had someone working with him, and not a week went by when he didn't post another wonderful story. He was quite the historian and, of course, the best storyteller.

I was lucky enough to be his agent and his friend at the same time. We could see him at one of his Christmas parties—he not only knew all the songs, but he also sang them to everyone—such a great voice.

He loved the game. He loved life. There were so many things I learned from him about being gracious and humble. If you didn't like Vin, you didn't like life.

Steve Dilbeck
Journalist

Not a chance, not in a million lifetimes—there's an axiom old as the Pacific: meet your heroes and it's Disappointment City—pin to the balloon. I spent forty years covering sports and was fortunate to meet many a childhood hero. Some were jerks, most decent, and a few what you'd hope. But only one was more than I dare to dream, only one exceeded every possible expectation: Vin Scully.

I was just one of a zillion kids growing up in Los Angeles suburbia listening to the melodic tones of everyone's favorite redhead, his wit and storytelling wafting through our home, garage, pool, seemingly everywhere. Scully was indelible, a part of our family. He taught me to love baseball.

When I first started covering the Dodgers in 1985, Scully had already been inducted to the Hall of Fame. Initially, I mostly kept my distance from the icon, as if undeserving.

That changed one afternoon on a road trip to Atlanta. The Dodgers had a bus to take players and media from their hotel to Fulton County Stadium. It was a regular old bus; nothing about it seemed special—until I stepped in and looked up to see Scully sitting in the second row.

A voracious reader, he was halfway into Elmore Leonard's latest. A fan of Leonard, I asked about his new one, and that simple question begat a conversation that never really ended. He told me Leonard began his career writing Westerns. Vin highly recommended several, the icon sitting on a bus, his magical voice directed only at me.

Scully read everything—novels, nonfiction, magazines, newspapers. We would share favorite reads for years. I think I recommended to him—though it easily could have been the other way around—Michael Shaara's Pulitzer Prize–winning historical novel about Gettysburg, *The Killer Angels*. We both cherished that book, but it wasn't until years later I wondered why I'd never pursued any of Shaara's other works. I looked up what else he'd written, and discovered *For Love of the Game*, a baseball novel turned into a 1999 movie that featured Scully as the announcer. Scully never knew about that book until I told him.

31. Vin Scully with Steve Dilbeck. Courtesy of Steve Dilbeck.

Scully had been allowed to improvise his movie lines about forty-year-old pitcher Billy Chapel, played by Kevin Costner, pitching a perfect game in Yankee Stadium in his final start. Said Scully, "The cathedral that is Yankee Stadium belongs to a Chapel" and later, "He's pitching against the future, against age, and, even when you think about his career, against ending. And tonight, I think he might be able to use that aching old arm one more time to push the sun back up in the sky and give us one more day of summer."

Scully could not help being Scully. He'd said, "My thermometer for my baseball fever is still a goose bump," and you never doubted it. He was as affable and genuinely friendly as anyone I've ever known, always downplaying his celebrity. They had a special room in the press dining area for broadcasters, which everyone knew was built so he could eat his meal in peace. Still, he would emerge from his dinner and enviably find a table I was sitting at with peers and pull up a chair to chat. He'd share his wealth of history or current events and, of course, baseball.

One night he shared this story about former Dodger Don Zimmer when he managed the Cubs: "One year we're in Chicago to play the Cubs, and for some reason, we're not broadcasting the game. And Tommy [Lasorda] asks me if I've ever sat in the dugout for a game. I tell him, 'No,' and he says, 'You have to try it.'

"I said as long as it's cleared by the umpires beforehand. I don't want them throwing me out. So, I put on a uniform—spring training tryout number 76, but not for Union—and waited until almost before the game starts and walk through the Wrigley hallway, sit in the dugout, and pull my cap down all the way to my eyes. I don't want anyone to even notice me.

"After the Dodgers are retired in the top of the first, [first base coach] John Vukovich yells over at me, 'Hey, Scully!' And he throws me a baseball. I catch the ball and written on it is, 'If a fight breaks out, I want you.' And it was signed Don Zimmer. All the Cubs are in their dugout, laying down laughing."

During all those years we pulled up a chair, I can't remember him ever telling a bad story. He had more than his share of hardships but was the most consistently upbeat person imaginable. When he said, "As long as you live, keep smiling because it brightens everybody's day," they weren't just words but were how he lived his life.

His warmth always felt genuine. He was renowned for his handwritten thank-you notes. My wife, Darla, heard me sing his praises so long she felt she knew him, so she baked him cookies to thank him for his years of kindness. He responded with a note.

Once, longtime Associated Press stringer Joe Resnick disappeared from the press box. He had terminal colon cancer, but few knew. When I told Vin, he asked for his phone number. His call brought tears of joy to Resnick, who died a few days later.

Vin had an unforced presence. The room was always brighter when he walked in. I can't remember him without a sparkle in his eye and a warm greeting, not just to me but to everyone.

He knew the names of the elevator operator at Dodger Stadium, the press box attendant, scribes from big and small newspapers, fellow broadcasters, producers, and, if the Dodgers had a restroom attendant, he would have

LOS ANGELES DODGERS
5-11-12

Dear Mrs. DilBECK —

I am so greatly appreciative of your Kindness and thoughtfulness in sending me the marvelous Cookies! I have tried a couple and they are great and the grandchildren will make short shrift of them in no time. I look forward to thanking you in person, and don't tell him, but I think the world of your husband!!

Sincerely,
Vin Scully

VIN SCULLY

32. A note card from Vin Scully to Darla Dilbeck, 2012. Courtesy of Steve Dilbeck.

known his name and probably the names of those in his family. He'd greet them all as if it was another fine Irish mist of a day.

Vin Scully, one in a million.

Brent Shyer
Los Angeles Dodgers executive (1988 to 2001)

The first time I met Vin Scully he was wearing his pajamas. It was at Dodgertown in Vero Beach, Florida; I was recently hired as the team's director of publications and assistant publicity director. Vin arrived on a Saturday for the telecast that Sunday. As I learned, his usual routine was to attend Mass at St. Helen Catholic Church in Vero Beach, have dinner, and quietly go back to his room to do his homework.

I was to present some press information to him on Saturday night at his villa. Readying for a good night's sleep, he opened the door in his pajamas and welcomed me like a best friend with his magical voice. "It's great to meet you, and congratulations on the job!" he said.

I told him, "If there is anything I can do for you, please just let me know." And that is how our decades of friendship began.

I had to pinch myself that night as I, like so many thousands of other kids, had grown up in the Los Angeles area listening to Vin and the Dodgers on a transistor radio. Vin once told me, "No other place on earth holds as many memories for me as Dodgertown." He first arrived in the spring of 1950. Dodgertown brought everyone together to stay, dine, and have recreational activities right on base. In 1948 the former U.S. Naval Air Station during World War II was transformed to become an all-inclusive, integrated site for Dodgers Major and Minor League players, managers, coaches, executives, medical personnel, team broadcasters, and sportswriters. In those intimate surroundings, Vin was able to get to know everyone in the organization.

One aspect of Vin that largely goes unspoken was his game preparation. Because of his amazing recall and innate ability to connect a current situation to history, many believed he was just speaking off the cuff. He diligently spent hours upon hours studying baseball media guides and publications, reading about history, watching news, culling through a multitude of news-

33. Vin and Sandi Scully with Brent Shyer. Courtesy of Brent Shyer.

papers, chatting with visiting media and scouts, highlighting Dodger and opponent press notes, and making his own written comments. He essentially kept a book for each opponent the Dodgers would face. Vin was progressive, making active use of the internet for his game research.

For a Dodger game, he was at his seat at least three and a half hours prior to first pitch. Prior to each game, he would excuse himself and call his beautiful wife Sandi at home. He never failed to check in with her before going on air. He and Sandi were perfect for each other. He understood the sacrifice she made to raise their children and handle all home obligations while he was on the road for weeks at a time.

After one night game at Dodger Stadium, she must have been surprised when he came home with duct tape wrapped around his slacks. It so happens the material had disintegrated and the bottom separated away, causing a concern before he went on TV. Assistant producer Boyd Robertson and booth camera operator Rob Menschel jumped into action to wrap Vin up and hold his pants together for the rest of the night!

When the Dodgers added director of broadcasting responsibilities for me, my time with Vin increased to nearly daily phone calls, but our conversations would likely turn to world and national events, books Vin was reading, or how family members were doing. Vin was fascinating, conversant on any topic. He put perspective on what was happening in the world, plus talked about life and faith. Constant dinner mate Billy DeLury, the Dodgers' longtime traveling secretary, and I were only too happy to be in his company.

Once, I asked Vin if he ever got nervous. He recounted the time in December 1984 when he was a presenter for his friend, entertainer Danny Kaye, at the televised Kennedy Center Honors celebration in Washington DC. At a rehearsal, Vin walked alone to a microphone at the front of the massive empty stage and practiced a few words. He asked the producers if a podium could be placed in front of him for the actual event so he could lean on something. But he said that there were so many actors, celebrities, and politicians around that he was a "mess." He wanted to do his best for Danny. Vin had never seen his performance on TV; years later, I found a copy and provided him with a DVD. For the record, his speech was spectacular.

Vin was always in demand. Organizing personal appearances, facilitating various Dodger department needs, coordinating local and national media interviews, handling broadcast-rights-holder requests, and sponsoring voiceovers, meet-and-greets, charitable events, and countless honors for Vin all went with the territory. I also saw the pressure on his time with fan mail. In many cases, he personally responded to a request by encouraging a student on a career path, phoning someone with an illness to brighten his or her day, or congratulating another with a milestone birthday or anniversary. He oversaw the mailing of a handsome photo card to fans who wrote to him.

If there was one person fans and acquaintances inquired about when they found I worked for the Dodgers, it was Vin. I assured them, what you saw during the broadcasts was the same Vin—genuine, joyous, erudite, good-natured, warm, and punctual. I told them that air conditioning in hotel rooms and buses was the bane of his existence, as it affected his voice. Vin loved listening and singing along to CDs of Broadway shows on his way to work, including his favorite—Meredith Willson's *The Music Man*.

Once in Chicago in 1999, we were walking back to the hotel from dinner along Michigan Avenue when Vin was stopped for a moment by an autograph seeker who told him he had listened to his broadcasts for years. Vin said with a smile, "Oh, you ought to get a medal!" That's the essence of Vin. He made you feel as if you were the most important person in the world when you met him.

One Sunday at Dodgertown in the late 1990s, Vin completed a spring telecast and had to make his way to Orlando International Airport. He invited me to join him in his white Cadillac rental car conveniently parked alongside Dodgertown's iconic Holman Stadium back to the villas across a bridge. It was a short ride, but I was thrilled and got in the front passenger seat. He made a quick turn toward the bridge, but it was blocked by a nice woman security guard who put her hand out.

Vin rolled down the driver's side window. She told him, "You can't cross here," oblivious to who was driving.

Vin politely responded, "Oh, it's okay. I have permission." Puzzled, she let him pass not knowing he was driving on a road named Vin Scully Way in 1982. She was just doing her job.

On another occasion, I had the privilege of being invited by Vin to help with the 1999 baseball-themed movie *For Love of the Game*, starring Kevin Costner. As broadcast technical advisor for two days on the Universal Studios lot, I was hired by the producers to write some background about the fictitious players in the script for Vin's game broadcast in the movie, as well as authenticate the workings of the baseball broadcast booth. On the set, director Sam Raimi invited me to be in the movie as part of Vin's broadcast booth, to simulate a real-life interaction. While some of Vin's lines in the script were by the screenwriter, his smooth and brilliant descriptions throughout the movie are largely him describing the game as it unfolded to him for the first time on a TV monitor while the cameras were rolling.

Vin often said, "Time is so precious," but unselfishly he took time to send handwritten notes and make phone calls that were always welcomed and cherished. In 2001 he wrote a note of thanks to me when the Vin Scully Press Box was named at Dodger Stadium. His spirituality always shined through.

When Vin was just a teenager, one of his first jobs was in the Silver Room at Manhattan's Hotel Pennsylvania. He envisioned a maître d' job in the "prestigious" Silver Room but quickly realized he had been hired to work in a small walk-in closet in the bowels of the hotel where scalding hot water was dispensed to clean silver of all types. He also polished silverware and became physically overwhelmed from the heat and smell of old food on the silver. How ironic that he would rise from there to become the gold standard of sports broadcasters.

Doug Mann

Radio-TV sports statistician

I was incredibly blessed to work with Vin for several years, but even more fortunate to develop a dear friendship with him over the last four years of his life. Our frequent talks on the phone were never once about the Dodgers, or any sports, for that matter.

In the booth, I served as the statistician on Dodgers telecasts at Dodger Stadium. I was an observer to not only what was taking place on the field but also what would play a major role in shaping me in the latter years of my life. I was able to focus on how he handled himself in certain situations and marveled at how he dealt with adversity, tragedy, and loss of a personal nature.

I never heard him raise his voice to any of us in the booth—not to stage manager Boyd Robertson, not to camera operator and lighting director Rob Menshel, not to me. He was always cordial and courteous and treated us with the utmost respect.

One of the things I will always treasure are the stories he would tell us three-to-four hours before a game. He would use the same style and approach for those tales as he did for those on the air.

Vin had his priorities. His faith was number one, unquestionably. Number two was his love, devotion, and admiration for Sandi, his wife. Number three was his children, grandchildren, and great grandchildren. At the bottom was whatever he accomplished in baseball and his profession.

Vin and Sandi Scully exemplified the greatest love story I ever witnessed. There was a certain twinkle in their eyes whenever Sandi visited Vin in the booth. I would glance at them in the booth as they occasionally gazed at one another. I noticed Vin had a ritual every forty-five minutes before each game. He would get out his cell phone and step into the hallway and call the same person every time—Sandi. When I brought it up, he politely told me that he just wanted to ask her how her day was going.

I once noticed Vin wore the same watch for all but one game I worked with him. I asked him if there was a special meaning to that watch. He said, "Doug, I would never spend that kind of money on a watch, but it was a gift from Sandi to me." I can only speculate that when he wore it, he would look at it and think of who gave it to him: a wife who loved him as dearly as he did her.

In 2020 he mentioned that he and Sandi "had stopped asking God 'Why?'" He was referring to Sandi's diagnosis of Lou Gehrig's disease. They had come to terms with the news, and because of their faith they were at peace with it. They decided to enjoy whatever time they had left as a couple, simply being in one another's company.

Vin, a devout Catholic, would never curse. When Fox Sports came up with promos for him to read for *The Best Damn Sports Show Period*, he wouldn't say *damn* on the air. He never wavered on that.

One time during a game, Vin mentioned something about a player at bat, but the producer informed him that what he said was incorrect. At first, Vin thought I gave him that information. Stage manager Boyd Robertson informed him, "Vin, it wasn't Doug. You went on your own."

When the player came to bat the next time, Vin brought up the information from earlier, made the correction, and then added: "Scully, you dummy, you!"

There was no need for him to apologize to anyone. Vin was not afraid to make the extra effort to make it right. I remember Vin once telling me, "Doug, I want you to correct me; you have my permission."

During another game, Vin mentioned how numbers first appeared on the back of players' uniforms. I had been unaware he played on the Fordham baseball team in college. I began to do some research and contacted the Sports Information office at Fordham. It kept no records of numbers assigned to players at the time Vin played there.

34. Vin Scully with a replica of a Fordham University baseball jersey, presented by Doug Mann and Mark Langill at Dodger Stadium. Courtesy of Doug Mann.

Mark Langill, the Dodgers team historian, and I cornered Vin outside the TV booth. I reminded him of the story he related about the uniform numbers and wondered what number he wore. Vin replied, "It didn't matter to me what number I wore; that was not important. What was important was that I was getting to play baseball at Fordham."

After several minutes of back-and-forth conversation, Vin finally said, "I wore number 17, but as I stated earlier, it was not important to me."

I went back to the Fordham sports information director, and we got a replica of the jersey Vin wore for the Rams. Mark graciously offered to have it framed. We surprised Vin with the jersey wrapped up in butcher paper before a game. As he slowly tore the paper from the top, he was speechless. I included a note with it that read, "I wanted to reunite you with an old friend. It has been many years since you have seen one another, and your appearances have changed over the years." Vin later related that he thought we had one of his old friends waiting outside the booth. If truth be told, it was indeed.

I am grateful we became what felt like old friends.

When we stopped working together, Vin gave me his cell number, but we would go some twelve years without much communication. I appreciated that offer but knew how much he valued his privacy. His response: "Doug, I want you to call me. I consider you a friend."

I sent Vin and Sandi gifts over the years, including several CDs of songs and artists that I hoped they would enjoy. I sent bottles of wine—Vin's favorite was chardonnay and Sandi's was cabernet. Vin left me voice messages thanking me for not only the gifts but also the thought behind them. In one message he said, "Just knowing you, Doug, has been a lesson of your modest behavior, not an ounce of ego in you. It's incredible."

Vin taught me to be humble and modest and how to be a friend. He allowed me to observe how he dealt with those who would come into the booth to visit him before a game. When people fawned over him, Vin would turn the conversation around and focus on the visitor. I believe Vin took that approach because he genuinely cared.

In one of our last conversations, Vin mentioned two things that will never leave my memory: "Doug, I should have spent more time with you" and "Doug, I consider you a dear friend."

I was able to tell him, "Vin, you taught me more about life, but you also gave me one of the greatest gifts that I have ever received. You gave me something that cannot be bought or sold. It can only be freely given. It has been the gift of your friendship, and I consider that the greatest honor and gift that I have ever received."

Vin was a mentor to me. I sat totally in awe of him, about whom I can clearly say was the greatest man I ever knew. I simply cannot envision what my life would have been like had our paths not crossed. I do know my life was far richer for that happening. I didn't realize that until the last four years of his life.

SEVENTH INNING

"God Bless Us in Our Effort, God Bless America"

History and Patriotism

When Major League Baseball returned following the tragic events of September 11, 2001, Vin Scully came on the air for the first Dodgers' TV broadcast, on Monday night, September 17. Before the Dodgers took the field at Dodger Stadium to play the San Diego Padres, Scully looked into the camera and delivered these words, almost as if he were speaking from the Oval Office:

"Good evening and welcome to Dodger Stadium.

"All of us have experienced a litany of emotions, whether it would be shock, disbelief, and horror, followed by grief, mourning and anger. All of us indeed have lost a lot. We've lost thousands of lives. We've lost some self-confidence. We have lost some of our freedom, and certainly we have lost a way of life.

"The president of the United States has said it's time to go back to work. And so, with a heavy heart, baseball gets up out of the dirt, brushes itself off, and will follow his command, hoping in some small way to inspire the nation to do the same.

"All the ballplayers in the Major Leagues are wearing the American flag. Out of patriotism, yes. Out of love of country, yes. But more so, out of duty and of courage and to pronounce a national firmness of will.

"God bless us in our effort. God bless America."

My interview with him days later focused on where the inspiration came for those words. I knew there was a personal connection to this event: His nephew, Dan McLaughlin, worked as an attorney on the fifty-second floor of one of New York City's Twin Towers. He would have been at his desk at 8:30 a.m. that Tuesday but was out voting in the state's primary election.

"I'm just a very ordinary person asked to say something at a very difficult time," Scully said of his thought process behind what he said that day. "I'm not making some great proclamation. After doing some soul searching, I just said what I felt and what was in my heart. If it helps to bridge a nightmare into some normalcy, I'm pleased to serve as that bridge.

"After a week of watching all the awful things happen, we needed something after all the self-confidence we lost. This is a country that defeated the German army and air corps, the Italian army, and the Japanese armies and air corps in our time. But nineteen people brought us to our knees. . . . I guess America's strength is resilient, and baseball has been helping the inspiring Americas to play again."

Scully could draw upon all sorts of moments in his life—professional and personal—to explain why patriotism and so many different periods of history resonated with him.

Every June 6 was a recognition of D-Day, and Scully's incorporation of that into the game's broadcast was second nature. Fans even came to look forward to those telecasts. What happened when the Allies stormed the beach at Normandy in 1944 during Operation Overlord seemed to have shaped his views on the world permanently. He might never have said it publicly, but that event likely inspired him to join the navy months later, right out of high school. He was in that age group drawn to sacrifice their lives for the freedoms they had come to appreciate and cherish.

"It was the largest air, land, and sea operation undertaken. It included over five thousand ships, eleven thousand airplanes, 150,000 servicemen, and it came down to this," Scully recited during a 2015 Dodgers broadcast. "The boat ramp goes down, you jump, swim, run, and crawl to the cliffs. Many of the first young men were not yet twenty years old, and they entered the surf carrying eighty pounds of equipment. Many of them drowned. They faced over two hundred yards of beach before reaching the first natural feature offering any protection at all."

Scully marveled at how a British Army officer nicknamed "Mad Jack" Churchill used only a longbow, a Scottish broadsword, and a bagpipe in capturing more than forty officers at sword point. "Can you imagine charging the beach at Normandy waving a sword?" Scully asked.

He explained how young J. D. Salinger landed on Utah Beach. He was meant to arrive in the first wave of troops but landed with the second after the ocean's current staggered him southward, which may have saved his life. Salinger had been carrying with him the first six chapters of his novel *The Catcher in the Rye* during the invasion of Normandy.

"All I'm trying to do is impress the young people listening how important this day should always be," Scully would say about wanting to include these stories in a baseball broadcast.

The importance of the U.S. flag as a symbol of freedom became the focal point of a game in April 1976. Scully described on radio how Chicago Cubs center fielder Rick Monday swooped in to grab an American flag moments before two men ran on the Dodger Stadium field and tried to set it afire.

"Outside, ball one . . . and wait a minute, there's an animal loose . . . two of 'em, all right. . . . We're not sure what he's doing out there. . . . It looks like he's going to burn a flag . . . and Rick Monday runs and takes it away from him! [Crowd cheers.] . . . I think the guy was going to set fire to the American flag! Can you imagine that? . . . Monday, when he realized what he was going to do, raced over and took the flag away from him."

And Scully took our breath away. What made this important to Scully is what should have also made it important to all of us.

In September 2022 *Wall Street Journal* columnist Peggy Noonan wrote that when Queen Elizabeth II passed away at age ninety-six, it was a critical point in many of our lives, whether we knew it or not. Billions watched her state funeral on TV. Millions more lined the five-mile route. The reason was that the Queen reminded us of our connection to history.

"The history of a country isn't only a history of its fighting, or shouldn't be," Noonan wrote. "And there were all the wars and battles of wicked imperialism, too. The point is to know all the stories, to keep them alive in human memory. It's not all just water under the bridge, it's not just something that happened, it's part of who you are, who you've been, what you imbibed and got inside you. . . . The crowds in London are saying: Respect the past, and respect your own memory. A 70-year reign contains signposts not only of your life but the life of your times."

Scully was our baseball royalty. We saw our own history during his life and times, and he seemed to be the voice attached to much of it.

Here's another one for the history books: It was a swift-moving game on a very warm Wednesday afternoon at Dodger Stadium on August 28, 2013. The Dodgers were coasting with a 4–0 lead against the Chicago Cubs.

The only real ripple of news that day was how Yasiel Puig, the Dodgers' precocious twenty-two-year-old rookie who was hitting leadoff with a .346 average, had been pulled from the game by manager Don Mattingly before the fifth inning started. The player Scully endearingly called the "Wild Horse" was upset at himself for striking out in the third inning, slamming his bat. Back on the field, he got two late jumps on fly balls hit to him in right field in the fourth inning. Mattingly thought this would be a teachable moment.

On the Dodgers' TV broadcast, Scully could only surmise what happened. As the game melted on, Scully cooled everyone down and diverted from speculation. He had his own teachable moments to bring up.

The top of the seventh inning may have lasted three minutes, tops. The Dodgers' Ricky Nolasco needed just eleven pitches to record two strikeouts and a fly out. In that brief window while calling the action, Scully reminded viewers that on this date fifty years ago, Martin Luther King delivered his iconic "I Have a Dream" speech on the steps of the Lincoln Memorial in Washington DC.

Scully explained how renowned college basketball coach George Raveling still owned the original copy of King's speech. The civil rights leader handed it to the young Raveling upon request while leaving the podium. Scully marveled at some of the details—the speech went off-script when gospel singer Mahalia Jackson spontaneously shouted out to King, "Tell 'em about the dream, Martin, tell 'em about the dream!" So, King improvised.

Here's the backstory: A couple hours prior to the game, I dropped by the broadcast booth and left Scully a couple newspapers that included stories I just wrote. One was about the Raveling-King connection. The other was a feature on Sean Burroughs, who twenty years earlier led his team from Long Beach to the Little League World Series and was now attempting a comeback in the Dodgers' Double-A Chattanooga farm team at age thirty-three.

A few minutes prior to the game's first pitch, as I took my seat on press row, a couple of colleagues said Scully came by, asked where I was, and wanted to return the newspapers at my desk. I wasn't sure if that meant he read them. It was still a thoughtful gesture to think I needed the copies back.

When the time presented itself in the seventh inning, Scully recapped the two stories I gave him and gave me credit for writing them. I felt humbled that I could contribute something of importance to a Scully History 101 lesson.

Another very teachable moment happened years later when Scully engaged in a respectful discussion about how history and patriotism can mean different things to different people. After he retired, Scully participated in a Southern California speakers' series event. In November 2017, in front of about three thousand in Pasadena, he declared he would no longer watch NFL games because some players were kneeling during the national anthem in a form of protest. It drew applause in the auditorium.

"I am so disappointed," he said in the moment. "I used to love to watch the NFL on Sunday. And it's not that I'm some great patriot. I was in the navy. Didn't go anywhere. Didn't do anything. But I have overwhelming respect and admiration for anyone who puts on a uniform and goes to war. So the only thing I can do in my little way is not to preach. I will never watch another NFL game."

I circled back with Scully to make sure he knew the context behind the protest that had been started by NFL quarterback Colin Kaepernick. Scully not only stood firm in his opinion but also doubled down.

"I certainly defend their right to protest," he said. "What has bothered me is that this looks like a way to dishonor our veterans. When I turn the TV on, I see flag-covered coffins and warriors returning from the war without arms or legs, or a young widow crying in a cemetery, or children crying for their dad who never comes home. . . . I see suicides of veterans because of postwar stress because of what happens to them.

"When I see players kneeling, it absolutely kills me that anyone dare do that. If they really wanted to do something, instead of taking a knee, they'd get down on both knees and thank God they live in America."

I had also found a quote from Jackie Robinson in his 1972 memoir: "I cannot stand and sing the anthem. I cannot salute the flag; I know that I am a black man in a white world. In 1972, in 1947, at my birth in 1919, I know that I never had it made." I asked Scully if that was different from what is going on today.

"I think I have said enough," Scully responded diplomatically.

When Scully died in 2022, the website military.com proudly posted an obituary with the headline "Navy Vet Vin Scully Was the Greatest Sportscaster Ever." I imagine Scully would have been proud to see the official title in front of his name.

Could we also think of Scully as one of the game's greatest historians? I once asked John Thorn, Major League Baseball's official historian, that question. Did Scully, then about to retire, influence Thorn's own career path?

"I began listening to and watching Scully when I was eight, in 1955, the annus mirabilis of the Brooklyn Dodgers," Thorn said. "It amazes and delights me that he is still crazy about baseball—and curious about the wider world—after all these years, even if, as a player in our national drama, he exits stage right. I hadn't thought that I was modeling my career after Vin's, but maybe all along I was."

Honoring greatness and other thorny matters of the heart, I also ponder this: The National Baseball Hall of Fame honors broadcasters for their lifetime achievement with the Ford C. Frick Award, named after the baseball commissioner who led the game for fourteen years, starting in 1951. Frick's previous seventeen years were as president of the National League. Frick was generally credited with coming up with the idea to even have a Hall of Fame. Frick was also the commissioner who wanted to quantify the 61 home runs that Roger Maris hit in 1961 as the 162-game single-season home run record. That was so Babe Ruth, whom Frick befriended as a ghostwriter, would keep the record of 60 in a 154-game season.

What if the Hall of Fame brought the Frick Award into the twenty-first century and gave it a refresh? The Vin Scully Award for Broadcasting Achievement has a nice ring to it.

The idea for the change has come up at various times over the last few years. "I try not to have opinions about other people's business," Thorn said when I asked about this. "But Frick is an odd namesake for the award."

The Cooperstown-based museum has a few things from Scully in its collection, including the media guide and the game notes he used during his last broadcast in San Francisco. It has his signed scorecard from July 23, 1951, the annual Hall of Fame exhibition game played between the Brooklyn Dodgers and Philadelphia A's.

It is fair to posit that taking someone's name off a long-standing annual award would be brazen. The counter response might be to name the entire section of the Hall of Fame where all the broadcasting plaques are displayed after Scully. It could be the Vin Scully Wing of the Hall of Fame.

It's neither improbable nor impossible that the scenario could happen. I trust history will one day sort this out.

Josh Rawitch
National Baseball Hall of Fame president (2021 to present)
Los Angeles Dodgers executive (1995 to 2010)

Growing up in the San Fernando Valley, I can safely say Vin Scully is one of the main reasons I became a Dodger fan. I have vivid memories of hearing him on the car radio or in bed at night and, as often as we could, on television when the club went on the road. He taught me about my favorite player, Steve Sax, and about a small town in the Dominican Republic, San Pedro de Macorís, that produced shortstops like Mariano Duncan, who swung at everything because Dominican players couldn't "walk their way off the island," as some have put it. Vin once told a fourteen-year-old me that if I had "a sombrero, throw it to the sky."

For my father and grandparents before me, Vin was the soundtrack of our summer. What I could never have known as that young boy were the personal attributes that made him one of the kindest, most humble people I have ever met. I consider my fifteen years working with him at the Dodgers among the greatest professional experiences of a career that has landed us both—for very different reasons—in Cooperstown.

When Vin was honored with the prestigious Ford C. Frick Award for broadcasting excellence by the National Baseball Hall of Fame in 1982, he was not even halfway through a career. As he stood in Cooper Park, his speech lasted just four minutes and nineteen seconds, and he started it with his trademark humility:

"I guess a vital portion of the human existence is when man is visited with misfortune. He invariably will look his eyes to the heavens and say, 'Why me? Why with the millions and millions of people in this world am I asked to carry a cross?' And yet, if I'm to be honest with you and with myself today, I have to ask the same question when good fortune comes my way. Why me?

"Why with the millions and millions of more deserving people would a red-haired kid with a hole in his pants and his shirt tail hanging out, playing stickball in the streets of New York, end up in Cooperstown?

"I don't have the answer to either question, or either situation. But I do know how I feel. I want to sing, I want to dance, I want to laugh, I want to shout, I want to cry, and I'd like to pray. I'd like to pray with humility and great thanksgiving."

Vin and I shared a love of travel; I loved hearing him tell me stories of his globetrotting. After the Dodgers played in Japan in 1956, Vin and his wife, Joan, joined Ralph and Ann Branca in a trip around the globe, stopping in Karachi, London, and Rome. I remember him ending the story: "You know, you go all around the world, and it's nice to see these places, but then you can't wait to come home to America."

Vin loved his country as much as anyone I know, and it was this love that led to the only time I can remember seeing him disappointed, if not downright angry.

On Memorial Day 2010 our organization threw together a simple pre-game ceremony to honor those who made the ultimate sacrifice. Vin called me into his booth between innings early in the game to tell me respectfully, but in no uncertain terms, that we had fallen short of his expectations and that we needed to be better—that we owed it to the men and women who gave their lives to be better. He was right.

Perhaps the only two things more important to him than his country were his faith and his family. If there was one thing you could count on at Dodger Stadium during my years as an executive, it was Vin sitting in the last booth of the press box, calling his beloved Sandi about an hour before first pitch. But it wasn't just his family that he cared about. From the moment he met my wife and daughter, Erin and Emily, he would always ask

35. Josh Rawitch with Vin Scully. Courtesy of Josh Rawitch.

about them by name. It was a genuine curiosity for how they were doing that would start nearly every conversation.

In fact, he actually welcomed my son, Braden, into the world by announcing his birth while we were still in the hospital. As he did with Sandy Koufax's perfect game, he marked the moment with a time and date stamp because he knew that someday the familial value of that clip would mean more than anything.

It should come as no surprise, then, that when I called him to ask his thoughts on interviewing for my current role at the National Baseball Hall of Fame and Museum, his first question was about my family and how they would handle the change. He said, "You know, you and I aren't the same person, but I thought I would be bored in retirement and unhappy, and I couldn't be better. I haven't missed doing it for one second, and I've enjoyed the slower pace of the last couple years." Once again, he was right.

Vin had a relentless curiosity about everything and was as well read as anyone in his generation. Truth be told, there was very little that he had not seen. This much was evident to me back in August 2003, during my first year as the Dodgers' assistant public relations director. It was a tough season, and the team had just lost again to the Astros. We got on the team bus; one player was singing when another told him to "zip it, or I'll zip it for you." The next thing you know, they're screaming at each other. Right there, in his customary first seat on the right-hand side of the bus, the seventy-five-year-old Vinny faced front and sat quietly like the Godfather. The next day, I told him how funny it was to see him completely unfazed. He said, "After five months of losing, a four-game losing streak, and two very different personalities, this was bound to happen."

Big league bus rides are always interesting, and sitting next to Vin was always a treat. I vividly remember a story he told me in 2010 en route from the San Francisco airport to our hotel at Union Square. During his first year of broadcasting, he left Brooklyn's Ebbets Field by the back door, with a raincoat pulled over his head. Fans started to rush toward him, asking for his autograph, so he signed one when someone yelled from the back of the crowd, "Who is that?" The fan looked at his baseball and yelled back, "Vin Scully." The guy behind him said, "He's nobody," and they all turned and walked away. Vin got a big laugh from that.

I asked him how long it took for him to become recognizable. "Oh, a long time, probably three years or so," he told me. "And nowadays, the trouble is that people have the TV package, so it's not just LA where you're noticed." Of course, Vin was a nationally recognized legend long before satellite television came along, but that was classic Vin Scully, as humble as they come.

I wonder if that fan would have thought of how Vin Scully ultimately came to mean to so many. During that 1956 trip that Vin took to Italy, he had an audience with the pope. I remember watching Vin's farewell address to the crowd in Vero Beach in 2008 before the team's final game and thinking that's what he looked like to me—the pope, speaking to his people.

For millions around the world, he carried that same level of admiration. From my standpoint, he deserved every ounce of it.

Gil Hodges Jr.
Son of Dodgers Hall of Fame first baseman Gil Hodges

Dad served in the U.S. Marine Corps during World War II. When I was learning about history in school, I asked him about what he did during the war. He said he just worked behind a desk—that was the end of it. Years later, I took a phone call from a sportswriter who wanted to interview him about the medals he won during the war. That was the first time I learned about what he really did as a soldier. But it was something he did not want to discuss with his son. That time in his life was very private.

Vin admired and honored that also. They were part of the generation that believed when the country needed you, it was your duty. You considered it an honor and a responsibility.

Vin and Dad had parallel careers and lives. All the praise given to one could have been said about the other—and well deserved for each.

So many knew how Vin prayed for years that Dad would get into the Baseball Hall of Fame. Vin never told anyone that he wrote a letter to the Hall on Dad's behalf, but I knew about it. After Dad was voted in with the class of 2022, I called Vin. I told him I could never thank him enough for his contribution. Do you know what Vin said? "What are you talking about? The little that I did had nothing to do with correcting something that should have happened decades ago." That just exemplified what Vin was about—just beyond humble.

As close as Vin was with Dad, many don't know how really close he was with my mother, Joan. They used to joke all the time about who had the best head of red hair. She told me that she and Fern Furillo, Carl Furillo's wife, fell in love with Vin from the first time they met.

Mom told the story about how she was about to deliver my younger sister in August 1956. Mom was in the hospital listening to the Dodgers' Sunday afternoon game in Philadelphia on the radio. She had been sedated through the delivery and was wheeled back into her room. She said she woke up to Vinny's voice saying: "And that, ladies and gentlemen, was a home run hit for Cynthia Hodges, born today at twelve o'clock noon." Mom said that's how she found out she had a baby girl—and then she went back to sleep!

Dad hit a home run in the second inning. He singled in the ninth inning and scored the tying run. The Dodgers won, 3–2.

Vin knew my mom for almost her entire life. After Dad passed, they stayed in close touch. When Vin lost his wife, Mom made the bond even stronger. When I was growing up, I saw that they were committed to their families and to their Catholic faith. I would make road trips with Dad; we went to Mass together on Sundays. When we were on the road, Vin would be there waiting for us at church. They both had that strong religious connection.

I don't think it was a coincidence that after Dad was finally inducted into the Hall of Fame in July 2022, Vin passed away in early August at ninety-four, and Mom passed away the next month in September at ninety-six. I think they willed themselves to stay here to see that induction. It was part of the intestinal drive and fortitude that generation possessed. I wish kids today could have some comprehension of that.

I have one more example of how Vin and the Hodges family always seemed to stay connected. There was a time when visitors to Dodger Stadium could take a tour, and Vin would be part of it—they got to meet him and shake his hand. My son, who lives in San Francisco, was in Los Angeles for business. Without me knowing about it, he took the stadium walkabout. When it came time to meet Vin, he said he was introduced as Gil Hodges III. Vin looked at him at him and couldn't believe he was seeing Gil's grandson. Instead of a handshake, Vin put his arm around him and gave him a hug. My son called me from the stadium to tell me about it all, and my eyes filled up with tears.

Joe Buck

Fox Sports lead MLB broadcaster (1994 to 2021)

During the last few years of Vin Scully's life, I was often asked by reporters if there was a chance Fox Sports might invite him to come into our booth during the All-Star Game or World Series and maybe call an inning. I was always up for that. I reached out to him with a voice mail and email. I even said, "If someone can hypnotize him and make him say yes, I would drive the car or rent the helicopter to make it happen." Scully was the voice of national baseball TV. He knew I felt that, and he continued to say no, unfortunately.

I understood. As someone who was older—and I saw this with my dad and others—being in a foreign situation on national TV is not comfortable. That wouldn't be fair. But with Vin, it was just the thought of having that voice join the broadcast, I would have left and watched from another room.

I was fortunate to know Vin when I was a kid and was aware of the reverence for him even then. I never really got to know him. Over the years when I saw him in the booth, I went over and gave him a hug.

When he died, a lot of the memories of my dad's passing came back. People like Vin and my dad who lived through World War II had a real thirst for knowledge. They wanted to know about the world around them. That gave them an advantage later in life.

And when you consider historic moments, it is interesting to think about how both Vin and my dad called "The Catch" in the 1982 NFC title game, Ozzie Smith's walk-off home run against the Dodgers in the 1985 NLCS, and the Kirk Gibson 1988 World Series Game One homer—one on TV, the other on radio. Their calls are out there to enjoy. They are linked forever.

When the Dodgers won the World Series in Tampa Bay in 2020, I wanted to remind people about Vin and said something at the end of the Game Six telecast, in the ninth inning. There was time to do it.

It was about recognizing history, someone who bridged generations of players. I never tried to be my dad, or to be Vin Scully. I don't measure up, and that's fine with me. Vin was the all-time greatest do to it. My dad would say the same thing.

Michael Green

University of Nevada, Las Vegas
history department chair and professor

As Julio Urías recorded the final outs of the Dodgers' World Series victory in 2020, Joe Buck of Fox Sports said, "I don't think I've ever done a Major League baseball game and not thought of my dad, but it's impossible to not think of the ninety-two-year-old Vin Scully, the greatest to ever do it, started with the Dodgers in 1950, retired four years ago. . . . Sixty-seven years of his life he poured into the Dodger organization, and you know he's watching and rooting."

And I burst into tears. As a Dodger fan since I was eight, I was happy. But as I thought of what Buck said about his father, Jack Buck, a legendary broadcaster in his own right, and Scully, I thought of my father. He had died ten months before, at age eighty-six. His family moved to Los Angeles from the Bronx in 1944, and he followed the Pacific Coast League's Los Angeles Angels and the Hollywood Stars while remaining a New York Yankees fan—until the day the Dodgers moved to Los Angeles.

Six years after they arrived, he married a Brooklyn-born Dodger fan whose family moved to southern California in 1956, and, she said without a trace of sarcasm, the Dodgers then had to move because they could hardly remain back east without her.

I can join the fans who disagreed when Vin Scully told them at his final home game that he always needed them more than we needed him. My mother was dying of cancer in a local hospital while we were listening to the Dodgers. They were televising, so Vin came over to the radio side in the fourth inning and suddenly said, "Frank Sinatra died today. You young people may think you know romance, but until you've heard Frank Sinatra sing *Songs for Young Lovers* with Nelson Riddle conducting, you . . . don't . . . know . . . romance."

My mother glared. She never liked Sinatra, but she loved Vin. He eased the goodbye.

I remember when I first said hello to him. In 1973, when I was eight, I walked into the kitchen of our home in Las Vegas, where my father was listening to a transistor radio. I became mesmerized. That evening, I decided my future: I would become a Dodger broadcaster. I wrote a fan letter to Scully, who responded with a Dodger newsletter, an autographed photo, and a signed letter advising me to major in English.

A year later, we drove to Los Angeles to see my first Major League game. My maternal grandfather lived with us and was head of security at California's Union Bank, a sometime Dodgers sponsor. The board of directors included Dodgers owner Walter O'Malley, who was able to obtain seats on the club level next to the press box, the third tier at Dodger Stadium. After we arrived at the game, my parents informed me they had planned something even more special: they wrote to Scully, and he welcomed me to meet with him.

We waited near the elevator. Vin emerged with his wife, Sandi, who was pregnant with their daughter, Catherine. My grandfather, his hand extended, announced he used to direct traffic at Ebbets Field in Brooklyn. Vin replied, "I remember you!" My grandfather had retired from the NYPD in 1947, three years before Scully's debut with the Dodgers, so I realize now that was untrue, but it underscored what Scully's broadcast partner of twenty-eight years, Ross Porter, once said: "I have never seen Vin Scully rude to one person."

Scully disappeared into the booth. We waited. A security guard leaned out and crooked a finger toward me. My parents nudged me forward. I approached, wearing my Dodger helmet. When I entered the booth, Vin looked down at me and said, "So you're the guy who wants my job!"

I gaped. He brought me down in the booth and introduced me to Jerry Doggett, whom he would go on to work with for more than thirty-one years. I gaped.

He recorded the opening to the pregame show, thanked me for coming in, and guided me to the door. I gaped.

I have said for years that August 1, 1974, was the most special day of my life until my wedding day. My wife, Deborah, understands why, for an additional reason. In the fourth inning, my grandfather leaned over to my mother, sitting behind my father and me, and whispered, "Do you think he could get a foul ball in here?" My mother shook her head. "The roof is too low."

On the next pitch, a 1-0 delivery from Al Downing, Cito Gaston of the Padres hit a foul behind first. It flew into our section. A man reached for it and slapped it. It came down to the first row, hit me on top of the helmet, and landed in my father's lap. It still sits on a bookcase in our living room.

My hope of succeeding Scully dissipated the first time I heard a recording of my voice after it changed. I decided to pursue a newspaper career. (That Scully worked on the Fordham student newspaper and as a stringer for the *New York Times* had nothing to do with it.)

In college I became a history major and decided to pursue a career in that field. That doesn't mean I stopped listening to Vin or to baseball.

Until recently, the Dodgers radio network almost always included Las Vegas. I also could watch at least some of the telecasts, through network affiliates or on cable. Unfortunately, SportsNet LA reached Las Vegas only in 2020. We lost part of that season to COVID, but to fill the time, the network reran old broadcasts. Vin was retired but still working.

In a way, so was I. To this day, when I watch a game, I broadcast it, if only in my mind. For some reason, the voice I hear isn't mine, but Vin's. Occasionally, his voice pops out.

More crucial to my life, he has influenced how I teach my classes and write about the past and present. As a history professor, I have brought to class the baseball from the night I met him and told that story—and that there is more to it. Downing, who threw the ball, also threw the pitch that Henry Aaron hit for his 715th home run, breaking Babe Ruth's record. And Scully called it, pointing out, "A Black man is getting a standing ovation in the Deep South for breaking the record of an all-time baseball idol. What a marvelous moment for baseball. What a marvelous moment for Atlanta and the state of Georgia. What a marvelous moment for the country and the world."

Gaston, who hit the ball, went on to become the first Black manager to win a World Series with the Toronto Blue Jays in 1992 and 1993—and Scully described both victories on CBS Radio.

And before those events, Scully had broadcast games played by his friend, Jackie Robinson, and beat him one day in an ice-skating race. Somehow, I tell students, the strands of the past wind together, sometimes through objects, sometimes through the people who hold or mold them.

As a history professor, I feel Vin's influence in other ways. I eagerly awaited the top of the sixth inning of Dodgers telecasts because the camera would cut to Vin, who would begin, "On this day in Dodger history." What followed might seem mundane, but he often expanded on it as the inning unfolded, putting it into a broader perspective, just as I might show students how just one strand of the past ties into another.

He also could be more profound, as in his annual tributes to those who fought on D-Day, which reminded us that baseball is part of life and history, but not the most important. He also might have offered a discourse on the history of beards or talk about a player's tattoos. This may have just seemed like a way to pass the time or humanize players. But historians know that personal appearance and fashion change through time and mean different things to different people—he just said it more elegantly than we do.

Vin's mentor, Red Barber, had intended to be an English professor and referred to training "young Scully" as his chance to teach. All of us in the teaching profession dream of that level of success.

But indeed, Vin was a teacher. Listening to how he told a story, how he wove together phrases, have helped me to be a better writer and classroom instructor. How he braided generations of Dodger fans is obvious enough—grandparents and grandchildren listened to him. But in doing so, he taught us what brings generations of people and places and times together, all the while bringing us together himself.

And when students tell me or write on an evaluation that I know how to tell a story, I think to myself, *Thank you, Professor Scully*.

Paul Haddad
Author

It's easy to slip into hyperbole when reflecting on the virtuosity of a legend. But if ever there was an artist who painted with words, it was Vin Scully.

His most celebrated exhibits are his calls of Sandy Koufax's 1965 perfect game, Hank Aaron's 715th home run in 1974, and Kirk Gibson's 1988 World Series home run. To this Dodgers fan, however, Vin's depiction of Fernandomania may just be his masterwork.

History abounds with foils and rivals. But let us consider the value of muses. Andy Warhol was famously inspired by Edie Sedgwick, in the same way that Robert Mapplethorpe had Patti Smith and Hitchcock had his "Hitchcock blondes." In Fernando Valenzuela, Vin found the perfect muse.

Improbable (or impossible) as it may seem, the excitement of Fernando's 1981 rookie season propelled "The Voice" to elevate his game to a new level of excellence.

Unlike other iconic Dodger moments that happen in a flash, Valenzuela's historic season unfolded gradually, allowing Vin to fill in his canvas over a full season. On Opening Day at Dodger Stadium, Fernando was a last-minute replacement for injured starter Jerry Reuss. He hurled a five-hit shutout, confounding the Houston Astros with his screwball. Borrowing from scripture, Vin sensed something magical happening. "And a little child shall lead them," he prophesized on air.

Over the next several months, as fans flocked to stadiums across the country to witness the unknown phenom from Etchohuaquila, Mexico, Vin never failed to rise to the occasion. "Is there *anything* this kid can't do?" he marveled along with us after Fernando drove in the only run in a 1–0 win in Houston. "He has turned the Big Apple on its ear!" he exclaimed after El Toro shut out the Mets in New York.

Back in Los Angeles, after it was revealed that scout Mike Brito drove Valenzuela to the stadium each night, Vin remarked, "The way he's been going, he ought to be delivered in a Brinks truck."

During an April 27 home game against the San Francisco Giants, Fernando was one out away from securing his fourth shutout in five starts.

36. Fernando Valenzuela with Paul Haddad. Courtesy of Paul Haddad.

Reminiscent of Harvey Kuenn's at bat that ended Koufax's perfect game, Scully staged a clinic on how to build toward a big moment, deftly blending play-by-play with pithy aphorisms and a date stamp for good measure. As the crowd roared, pinch hitter Jim Wohlford battled Valenzuela for three and a half minutes, giving plenty of space for Vin's verbal brush strokes:

"It has taken almost three hours to get here. But baseball is the one sport that is not measured in time. Nobody cares that the run scored at a certain time. And no hitter has to worry that time is running out. Time doesn't mean a darn thing here tonight.

"Here's the 2-2 pitch . . . fastball, hit foul.

"There is no one in the Giant on-deck circle. It's against the rules. You're supposed to have somebody out there. But the fact that the on-deck circle is empty might sum up the kind of mastery and spell that Valenzuela has cast so far tonight. . . .

"And the crowd is begging him to make one last pitch and call it a night. What a memorable night, huh? Just one game, April the 27th, but what a game to remember.

"Valenzuela's 2-2 pitch . . . fastball got him swinging!"

A more famous call occurred during the May 14 game against the Montreal Expos. After Fernando gave up a game-tying home run to Andre Dawson in the top of the ninth, deflating the home crowd, Pedro Guerrero slugged a walk-off homer in the bottom of the inning to preserve Fernando's winning streak. "It's gone, Fernando, it's gone!" Vin cried, the only known instance in which he wove a player's name into a home run call. Fernando's record now stood at 8-0, his ERA a ridiculous 0.50.

As Mexican and Latino fans began to fill up Dodger Stadium, Vin honored them in his broadcasts. "The Spanish phrase, they tell me, is *se quita la gorra*—a tip of the cap," he said one night. "And that's what this crowd wants to give Valenzuela now." One time, after another pitching gem, Vin simply threw up his hands. "I swear, Fernando, you are too much in *any* language."

And only Vinny could come up with the perfect couplet to describe Fernando's gutsy performance in Game Three of the World Series. With the Dodgers down 2–0 to the New York Yankees, Fernando willed his way to a 5–4 complete-game victory despite walking seven and tossing 147 pitches. "Somehow this was not the best Fernando game," Vin announced. "It was his finest." The Dodgers went on to capture the crown, culminating a storybook season.

Scully always appreciated what Valenzuela meant to the team and the city. "I don't think I'll see anything quite like that," he recalled years later to Tom Hoffarth. "Watching the Mexican people come to the ballpark, fathers and mothers, hard-working, relatively poor people taking their tiny children to the park, it was almost—and I don't mean to sound sacrilegious—like going to Lourdes."

To listeners like me, we were collateral beneficiaries. Vin once said he needed the fans more than we needed him. But I would argue that he needed Fernando, too, because greatness depends on great things.

Will Leitch
Author

In a popular culture that is in many ways constructed for us to tear people down the very second we decide that we like them, Vin Scully, perhaps more than any other public figure in my lifetime, was untouchable.

Think about that.

Most broadcasters live in constant fear that they will, on live television with millions of people watching and millions more ready to post any damning video on social media, say something that will end their career.

Sometimes this is a hot-mic moment that reveals an ugliness we hadn't previously seen, à la Thom Brennaman; sometimes it's a verbal slip featuring the worst possible word at the worst possible time, à la Glen Kuiper. Usually, though, whether you deserve it or not, when you screw up, we're gonna take you down. It's nothing personal: we do it just because we can.

But Vin? We'd never take down Vin that way.

This is noteworthy for many reasons, but particularly because Vin Scully should have been the ideal target. He talked on the air constantly, often running entire broadcasts himself with no color man. He was perfectly willing, even eager, to roam off script on a moment's notice: I loved the time he went off a five-minute tangent about the time Jonny Gomes met a wolf, or the time he compared Johnny Damon to Charles Manson. He was an old white man from a past generation who knew John Wayne and Bob Hope and Jimmy Stewart.

His politics, as loathe as he was to talk about them on the air, were exactly the sort of politics that would get you vivisected online; he said, for example, in the wake of the NFL kneeling social-justice protests of 2017, that he would "never watch another NFL game." He also, famously, went on an (undeniably amusing) on-air rant—inspired by a Venezuelan player, Hernan Perez, coming to the plate for the Milwaukee Brewers—that featured the soliloquy, "Socialism failing to work, as it always does, this time in Venezuela. You talk about giving everybody something free and all of a sudden, there's no food to eat. And who do you think is the richest person in Venezuela? The daughter of Hugo Chavez. Hello! Anyway, 0-and-2."

Can you imagine what would have happened if Joe Buck had said that? Or Jim Nantz? It would follow them around the rest of their lives.

But when Vin did it? Everyone just chuckled: *There goes Vin.*

As he got older, like many old men, Scully was more and more open about his politics, which had always leaned right-wing: Public records showed he had given to every Republican since the 2004 election . . . until he abstained from giving money to Donald Trump in 2016, for what it's worth. And Scully did this during a time when people were less open to ignoring public figures' political leanings, no matter how well regarded or how much mastery they had over their chosen fields. Ask Tom Brady if people were up for forgetting one's politics during the Trump era. Scully was perfectly situated for a takedown if anybody ever was—over the decade, people have been eager to kill their idols.

Not Vin, though. Even his 2016 socialism rant got bemused rather than outraged coverage. ("Tell us how you really feel, Vin!" Deadspin shrugged affably.) Most listeners would have been furious had any other announcer said that or railed on the NFL protests; we would all have hungrily filled the content maw with all of the takes.

But the thing about Vin was that we loved him so much—considered him so eternal, so immortal—that throwing him into that abyss wouldn't have just been unfair; it would have been debasing. Not debasing to him, mind you; he surely wouldn't have noticed any of it. (Imagine asking Scully to do a Brennaman-esque on-air apology. I shiver just to think about it.) The debasement of putting Scully in that cultural blender would have been ours.

We would have lowered ourselves into treating Scully like the rest of us—like we hated him like we hate ourselves. But we didn't.

Vin Scully may have been the only figure we loved too much to drag him down to our own level. Vin could have said anything, and we would have never stopped revering him. He was timeless in a way that even transcended our own divisive, ugly time. We let him live in the past. It, in a way, was the best kindness we could give him.

Bud Selig

Major League Baseball Commissioner (1992 to 2015)

I have a theory about the history of baseball that I have talked about thousands of times. We are a social institution, and I can give you myriad examples how and why. Vin Scully fits into that theory as well as anyone in the world both on and off the field.

When I gave him the Commissioner's Historic Achievement Award in 2014, it was not just to recognize what Vin meant to the people in Southern California, who lived to hear him every day. His impact as an announcer was phenomenal. I still get chills listening to his classic description of Sandy Koufax's perfect game in 1965. But it was also for the way he represented Los Angeles and the Dodgers, and how he represented the game of baseball as well as anyone I know in the last one hundred years. It was aberrational that such a great voice belonged to such a great gentleman.

When we were in Atlanta in 1999 to announce the All-Century Team, it was a very meaningful day in baseball's history. We had the greatest players of an era. Why wouldn't you have Vin Scully, the greatest voice in history who knows almost all of those players, be the one who announced them? He fit right in.

Maybe to me one of the most remarkable examples that captures how well known his voice was happened that one day as we were trading phone calls, and he called me at my home in Arizona. My wife saw who it was and picked up the phone. "Hi, Sue, it's Vin Scully," he said. And Sue replied, "You didn't have to say who you are. I knew right away."

A commissioner tries not to get involved in claiming someone is the best of all time. If you grew up like me listening to Jack Brickhouse and Harry Caray, or Bob Prince or Mel Allen, they become an important companion for a listener every single day. In my day, baseball on the radio was my whole world. But there was no doubt in my mind Vin Scully was the greatest baseball announcer in history, without question.

He was baseball at its best. You can't do any better.

EIGHTH INNING

"I'm Not Hollywood"

Celebrity and Fame

Almost forty years before Vin Scully received his own terrazzo star on the Hollywood Walk of Fame in 1982, he recalled when he and a buddy on military leave during World War II found themselves skipping up that same Hollywood Boulevard on a Sunday afternoon, gazing at the sidewalk plaques.

At least that's how we might imagine it, like something out of the Broadway musical *On the Town*, before Gene Kelly and Frank Sinatra revived those roles in the 1949 MGM film.

"I think we were just looking for movie stars," Scully said in recounting the day.

Although he has appeared in a nominal number of movies and TV shows and even fashioned himself once upon a time as a song-and-dance man, Scully's star honors his broadcasting career—complete with the old-fashion microphone, a symbol used often these days for his professional vocation. It is on the 6600 block of Hollywood Boulevard, in front of what was the Vogue Theatre, not far from the famous Musso & Frank Grill. Scully is right there between jazz trombonist and bandleader Tommy Dorsey and country music singer Ferlin Husky.

Scully was in the navy in 1945, stationed in San Francisco, and took a free air transport to LA so he could meet up with his friend, a marine at Camp Pendleton. Scully said his only real interaction with a Hollywood star to that point was meeting Harold Peary, a famous radio personality from the 1940s era show called *The Great Gildersleeve*.

"Right around noon, a girl drove up in a convertible and said, 'Do you have any plans for dinner?'" Scully recalled. "I said, 'Heck no,' so we piled in, and she drove us out to this beautiful home to have dinner with her family. In retrospect, the family was right out of central casting.

37. Vin Scully's star on the Hollywood Walk of Fame. Courtesy of Tom Hoffarth.

"After dinner, she drove us back to Hollywood and Vine. We thanked her, and before she left, I asked, 'Say, where were we?'"

She said they had been in a section of Los Angeles called Brentwood. That stuck in Scully's imagination. Years later, when he and his young bride and their newborn son were looking for a place to live in LA after the Dodgers' relocation, a real estate agent asked where they might want to live.

Brentwood, of course. It turned out to be the same building where the new UCLA basketball coach, John Wooden, had also been living with his wife. The Scullys and Woodens ended up as neighbors in the same complex—so very apropos. Scully said that early during his time there he was approaching the security gate of the building with an armful of groceries when Wooden helped him in. That was their first encounter.

An expanded 1964 *Sports Illustrated* profile on the then-thirty-six-year-old Scully by the esteemed Robert Creamer declared that "in the six years that he has been in California, Scully has become as much a part of the

Los Angeles scene as the freeways and the smog. . . . [He] has become a celebrity. . . . Out-of-town visitors at ballgames in Dodger Stadium have Scully pointed out to them—as though he was the Empire State Building."

LA, apparently, had nothing quite comparable—except, maybe, the Hollywood sign, which one can still see looking west from the elevated third base side of Dodger Stadium.

Despite wanting this new voice for its motion picture business, Hollywood didn't even give him a credit in his first film role: the 1960 movie *Wake Me When It's Over*, which starred Ernie Kovacs, Dick Shawn, and Jack Warden and was directed by Mervyn LeRoy. Scully could find a way to laugh about having to play a rather generic, nameless CBS radio announcer in the screwball comedy.

Scully's most noteworthy of twenty acting credits on his Internet Movie Database bio (or, IMDb.com as it's known in the industry) came when he played a very believable version of himself in, and gave credibility to, the 1999 baseball and romance film *For Love of the Game*, starring Kevin Costner as an end-of-the-line Detroit Tigers pitcher gathering all he could muster for one last chance at glory.

"No one personifies the movie's title more than Vin," Costner said at the time it came out.

Director Sam Raimi said Scully ad-libbed "about 80 percent of his lines" in the film. Raimi said he thought screenwriter Dana Stevens might be upset, "but she thought it was fantastic."

Scully played himself so perfectly that one may not notice he actually had former MLB player Steve Lyons there as his game analyst, who barely needed to say a word. Scully also convinced Raimi to reshoot the final baseball scene that played out the way the Tigers finished off the perfect game. Scully said what he first read felt "too Hollywood. . . . It could have happened, but it's a stretch." Scully told Raimi, "I would hate to see you do a stretch when it's so good up to here."

Asked if he considered taking the night off from the Dodgers' home game when so many of the film's stars were soaking in the spotlight at a red-carpet premiere, Scully admitted, "Nah, 'cause I'm not Hollywood. I'd rather be here."

Costner once explained on a visit to *The Rich Eisen Show* in 2018 that all Scully had to do was watch about six minutes of a prefilmed performance with Costner playing the part of Billy Chapel as he worked his way through the lineup at Yankee Stadium. Then Scully did his own version of method acting. As an actor, call him The Natural.

"He was like a songbird," Costner said of Scully's improvisation. "He got through it, and the director says, 'Want to run it again?' And Vin says, 'Do we need to?' . . . And he looks at me. I shrugged."

The relationship Scully and Costner developed led to the actor being the main guest speaker for the Dodgers' tribute to Scully on September 23, 2016, at Dodger Stadium, before some fifty-two thousand in attendance.

In the ten-minute speech, with the soundtrack of *Field of Dreams* playing in the background, Costner said, "If anyone ever wondered what it might feel like to have Vin Scully call your name, I can tell you for sure that it is something close to heaven. . . . You called my imaginary name and my imaginary perfect game, and no one can ever take that away."

If only Costner had wrapped it up with his famous movie line: "Vin . . . wanna have a catch?"

And now it can be told: On the afternoon after the ceremony, as Scully chatted with reporters in the Dodger Stadium press box, I told him that he really looked moved by what Costner was saying. Scully admitted, "Honestly, I couldn't hear him very well. The feedback from the speakers was delaying what he said. I was right next to him. I could hear him say something, then it would reverberate. . . . I think what you saw was probably a look of confusion on my face as I was trying to figure it out."

Maybe the reason the thespian Scully sounded so authentic is that he actually could channel some specific experiences in his baseball broadcasting career of high-profile no-hitters and perfect games for *For Love of the Game*. He called the conclusion of Don Larsen's perfect game in Game Five of the 1956 World Series at Yankee Stadium. That was a rather unlikely performance from someone considered a journeyman pitcher. Just two years earlier, he lost 21 games with Baltimore. Larsen was also pulled from his World Series Game Two start after giving up 4 runs in less than two innings.

There was a real Detroit Tiger, Jack Morris, whose no-hitter Scully described, pitch-by-pitch, on NBC's *Game of the Week* Saturday-afternoon national telecast in 1984.

Then on July 28, 1991, at Dodger Stadium, was a perfect game that Montreal's Dennis Martinez threw against the Dodgers. Scully, in the moment, not only described the performance but also gave context to the feat of a thirty-six-year-old recovering alcoholic.

"It was a very emotional thing," Scully said of that Martinez game. "It was nice to see a man climb a mountain and get to the top. The crowd added to his adrenaline. It had to come crashing down on him. With forty-seven thousand there that day, it added more than anything I could say. I think that's why he cried. It was beautiful to watch."

Scully's IMDb.com bio doesn't include the occasional times when screenwriters honored him by naming characters after him in their scripts. The most obvious was when Chris Carter, creator of the Fox sci-fi series *The X-Files*, named the lead female character Dana Scully, in Vin's honor.

Network TV execs thought enough of Scully to recruit him as an off-the-cuff afternoon game-show host, which was a whole different beast than calling a sporting event, but it took a lot of the same improvising talents. NBC gave Scully the chance to do *It Takes Two*, which allowed him to banter with celebrity couples as they tried to match answers to his questions. It only made it from March 1969 to January 1970. As it turned out, the husband celebrity contestants were often those Scully golfed with: James Garner, Jack Nicholson, Howard Keel, Mac Davis, Bob Newhart, and Sean Connery.

In 1973 CBS's attempt to compete with the ABC Mike Douglas afternoon talk show was to create *The Vin Scully Show*. That lasted just three months.

There was a time when one might pass by the window at Jack Taylor's custom tailor shop and haberdashery in Beverly Hills and see Scully's signed headshot alongside Jack Lemmon, Charles Bronson, and Danny Thomas promoting French silk ties and European-cut blazers.

Scully had plenty of baseball fans in the Hollywood community, including his own neighbors. When he moved to Hidden Hills in the San Fernando Valley, he ended up across the street from singer and baseball fan

Jennifer Lopez. He would wave at her as she walked the neighborhood with her dog.

When actress Alyssa Milano wrote her 2009 book, *Safe at Home: Confessions of a Baseball Fanatic*, she included the following in the introduction: "Some people need yoga to relax. Others turn to Bach's Goldberg Variations. Painters paint. Chocolate soothes some, knitting—or a glass of wine, or a crossword puzzle—others. What brings me to bliss is a simple sound: The dulcet voice of Vin Scully, calling a Dodgers game. . . . I melt like hot pine tar." He could have that effect.

In a 1999 story that appeared in ESPN *the Magazine*, embedded in a list of the "99 Ways to Live the Life of the Ultimate Fan," number 72 was "Listen to Vin call a ballgame on the radio. He is so smooth, so humble that he brings integrity to, of all places, Los Angeles."

Scully's star on the Hollywood Walk of Fame actually made its own headlines in 2011. Some baseball fans walking on Hollywood Boulevard saw the tarnished block lettering VIN SCULLY peeking out of a soiled red carpet held down by some ratty tape; that led to an investigation.

The LA Department of Water and Power had been doing work at that location, and Scully's star took the brunt of cracks, chips, and water stains. Some Dodgers fans offered to pay for repairs. Scully arranged behind the scenes for it to be taken care of. He thanked them for their concern and hoped the matter wouldn't come up again.

"I have no idea what's going on there," Scully told me in 2011. He added, "I just wish it was a blue carpet."

A new star was eventually poured. But Scully's star had been galvanized years earlier.

Patt Morrison
Journalist

You didn't have to be a baseball fan to be spellbound by the word-weaving enchantments conjured up by Vin Scully. And I wasn't, really. A baseball fan, I mean.

Oh, I'd made my way to Dodger Stadium from time to time, like in 1987, when the pope rounded the warning track in the popemobile, and then in 2012, when I had an audience with Vin.

It was high summer in the year of the Dodgers' ownership tangle, and I was there to talk to him for my Q&A column. Hours before game time, he was right there to meet me, in the café behind the press box at the stadium. His hair was immaculate, still showing the strawberry-blond of the red-headed boy he had been. His folded pocket square was as sharp-angled as the second base turn. And his sport coat was the color of—I wouldn't have said so to him because of his modesty—the ribbon of the Medal of Honor.

Whatever you thought of baseball, and even if you didn't think of it at all, Vin was more than any game he called. His voice was the soundtrack of Los Angeles itself. In the city that makes cinema tales for the world, he was our Scheherazade, the storyteller of a thousand and one night games. He was Vinnypedia. He was Homer and Will Rogers and his old hero Red Barber, and he plaited the threads of sports and history and the simple business of living so fluently, so naturally that you didn't realize what a dazzling high-wire act it really was.

Here's one sample of how he did it. The printed page washes out cadence and tone, but you know his voice well enough to hear it in your head, because he talked with a rhythm of waltzing—smoothly switching direction, moving back again.

It's April 2016. Vin had noticed a lot of players sporting Smith Brothers–sized beards, and decided, as he often did, to find out more, and to let the fans in on it:

"If you've been like the way I have been, looking at players with these big beards, I decided I'm gonna do a little research on beards. . . . There's plenty of them around. I'll tell you a couple of stories as we go through it.

Two down, second inning, no score. . . . First of all, they say way back to the dawn of humanity, beards evolved, number one, because ladies liked them, and number two, it was the idea of frightening off adversaries and wild animals. Here's the one strike pitch, swung on and missed. In fact, it was so serious, if you look it up, there's a divine mandate for beards in Leviticus and Deuteronomy. No balls and two strikes the count."

And on it went, so that by the time you got home from the game, full of Dodger dogs and momentous plays, you also brought with you the story that Vin had told you about beards and the Old Testament and about Alexander the Great, who thought he was too beautiful to cover up his face with a beard, and then men started shaving them off and eventually started growing them back again, all the way down history to the first pitch right there with all the hairy-faced boys in blue at Dodger Stadium.

In 1958, the year Vin came west with the Dodgers, Los Angeles was a punchline town of smog and freeways, with more culture in its health nuts' yogurt than in its civic institutions—not my joke. Its next mayor, the Nebraska-born Sam Yorty, pronounced the city's name to rhyme with "Los *bang* a fleas."

Vin arrived in polyglot LA with his own accent, what ESPN once called the "Fordham drawl," for Vin's alma mater, "the voice of a Northerner who took up residence cowboying in the West, who embraced the relaxed way of life but found the happiest of mediums in his accent."

He came to this Valhalla of human beauty with his Technicolor Irish-red hair and his anything-but-closeup-ready Irish teeth. In 2012 he told *Golf Digest* that he envied golfer Lee Trevino's perfect set, so unlike his own original choppers. If he ever wrote an autobiography, he said, "I would title it, 'My Life in Dentistry.'"

LA flips through its celebrities as fast as the turnstiles at Dodger Stadium. The stars and their impeccable teeth came and went. It chewed through generations of politicians and sports heroes, and Vin soldiered on, nearly seven decades as the essential Angeleno, always with us, always for us, but always above the sordid civic concerns of riots and scandals.

Vin could have hosted *Jeopardy!* and the Oscars. Every Opening Day, the Hollywood sign could have been altered to "Vinnywood." TV shows and movies played his game-calling in the background of the action. The LA Philharmonic asked him to read Abraham Lincoln's words for a Hollywood Bowl performance of Aaron Copland's "Lincoln Portrait." LA kids who had never seen the beach, had never seen the snow, knew Vin's voice as well as they knew their moms'.

I remember the shock I felt when, a year after he retired, Vinny pledged, "I will never watch another NFL game," on account of players' take-a-knee national anthem protests against police brutality. I guess each of us always figured Vinny thought the way we did about things he didn't discuss, and for me and presumably a few million Angelenos to find out otherwise— well, I was naive to be taken aback, but I was. I'd imagined that the man who befriended Jackie and Rachel Robinson and understood the struggles of young players of color would do the same for the anger and angst of young Black football players.

The only criticism of him I ran across in the *Los Angeles Times* was a tongue-in-cheek one. In 1966 a *Times* sportswriter warned readers that he was about to "attack something dearer to your hearts than motherhood and Lawrence Welk, or Disneyland and your freckle-faced nephew. . . . We've come to badmouth Vin Scully and baseball. Scully and the Dodgers are indisputably responsible for many of the social and economic ills of our megalopolis. . . . They have replaced Monday night at the movies, Wednesday night at the malt shop, any night at the library."

He was writing about the seductions of the transistor radio, that formidable gizmo that carried Vin's Dodger-game narrations beyond the stadium, into the streets and stores and schools and no doubt even houses of worship, killing off socializing, as the smartphone can now.

My friend Susan Straight, the Inland Empire novelist, remembered that her mother had listened to Vin for years before he moved to LA. She was a Swiss immigrant, an inch shy of five feet tall, and listening to Vin on her Regency TR-1 transistor radio gave her confidence and shut out the importuning men around her who were no gentlemen, not like Vin. Like millions of other immigrants, including her Mexican neighbors, "I actually learned my English from Vin," Susan's mom told her. "He was such a charming speaker, with smooth delivery, and he interjected other events and history, comments about LA and Orange County. He left me kind of spellbound."

If generations of LA immigrants have wound up speaking English with the "Fordham drawl," what's not to like?

His fans heard the swan-smooth delivery; the fellow broadcaster in me recognized his work below the waterline. All the notes and stats in the world on the desk in front of you can't keep you talking and talking. You can't tell the audience, "Hang on while I look that up." It's got to be there in your brain already, and the next sentences have to come together in your head even as the last ones are coming out of your mouth. And if you stop talking, it had better be for a good reason, such as to let the sound of the play and the noise of the crowd do the talking, as Vin did when Atlanta Braves slugger Hank Aaron broke Babe Ruth's home run record in 1974.

Before my interview, I'd listened to Vin in order to prep. Afterward, I listened to him for the pleasure of it.

He gave me his email address, in case I had any questions. I didn't, but a few years later, I had a favor to ask. I've never done that with an interview subject, but Vinny was a radio person, and I was a radio person, and my friend and KPCC colleague Steve Julian was a radio person, and Steve was batting very low numbers against a brain tumor.

Steve was also a full-hearted Dodgers fan. Every year he and his close friend and colleague Larry Mantle took a road trip to Dodgers spring training.

So, I emailed Vin and asked whether he could perhaps call Steve to say hello. His voice alone, so familiar and so beloved, would mean so much. And he did. A few months before Steve died, Vin left a voice mail that Steve's wife, Felicia Friesema, has saved for all these years. It goes in part like this:

"I just wanted to let you know that I heard that Steve is having some problems, and I'm a firm believer in prayer to either decide the issue but also to give us strength and inner peace. So, Steve, I want you to know you'll be on a prayer list out here, and we will be praying for you and for Felicia, and I know it doesn't sound very good to wish you a happy New Year, but God willing there are always amazing things that happen under the sun, and this could very well be one of them. So, to Steve and his wife Felicia, a verbal hug and a verbal squeeze and a prayer for a good year. God bless you, Steve. God bless you, Felicia. Hopefully we will talk again."

In that interview with Vin in 2012, I had asked him whether the team seemed different after all the ownership upheaval.

"Not really," was his answer. "It's as if we're working on a ship, and I'm down in the boiler room shoveling coal, and up on top, where the captain is, that's the ownership. By and large, ownership doesn't have anything to do with me shoveling coal."

I understood the simile, but I wouldn't have said he was shoveling coal. I'd have said he was pressing it into diamonds.

Bryan Cranston
Emmy– and Tony Award–winning actor

On the day I heard Vin Scully passed away, I was working in New Orleans, which made it difficult to find needed comfort from those who shared my feeling. A couple of my friends in the sports-talk business—Rich Eisen and Dan Patrick—reached out to me the next day to have me on their respective shows. But I couldn't talk.

I was reeling from the loss. So, I wrote them a note that they could read on the air. The following is the note, plus a couple added thoughts in between:

A part of my childhood died yesterday.

That may sound dramatic, and maybe it is, but it is honestly how I'm feeling now that Vin Scully has passed.

What a brilliant life he led, and what an important part of my life he served. From the time I was able to understand what the radio was, I would listen to Dodger baseball games from my Los Angeles suburb home. It was the beginning of a lifelong joy.

Vin was never just about the score of the game. His stories made you feel like you were with him . . . like he was sharing a story just for you. As a child that was often a bedtime story, as I would hide my transistor radio under my pillow to avoid parental detection.

38. Bryan Cranston and Vin Scully walk off the stage at the ESPY Awards in Los Angeles in 2017. Courtesy of ESPN.

When times were tough, Vin was there to ease my insecurity and anxiety with the power of distraction. Because even if it was only for the duration of the game, listening to Vin's voice for the next three hours made me feel safe. Comforted.

I finally got to tell him that when my wife surprised me with a gift—a visit with Vin in his broadcast booth in 2016, his last year calling games, and my sixtieth year of listening to him—yes, I'm counting the years since birth.

I had met him before, in passing, but this time I really got a chance to sit for a while and talk. I'm sure I was too emotional to speak clearly, but he responded to me with such graciousness and warmth, exactly as I expected he would.

I got to hug him. I guess I was trying to somehow convey the lifelong gratitude for what he did for all of us native Angelenos. He was our sanctuary.

I continue with the letter:

> One of my greatest thrills was introducing Vin to my daughter, Taylor, at the ESPYS in 2017 after I presented Vin with the Icon Award. Taylor, an adult and a catcher in her Little League experience, nervously confessed to Vin that she listened to him her whole life, just like her dad.

His natural charm was on full display with her.

After the event was over, we walked away in silence. What is there to say after you've just brushed up against greatness? We savored the moment.

> My mind wandered to his voice, and in the privacy of my thoughts, I heard his signature opening greeting, which remains indelible in my memory: "Hi everybody, and a very pleasant good evening to you wherever you may be."

I'm here, Vin. I'm right here.

Harry Shearer
Actor, author, musician, comedian

I grew up in Los Angeles, which meant, among other things, that the voice of Vin Scully echoed from gas stations and convertibles and beach sand for half the year, every year. Scully was the voice of the Dodgers, wafting out of transistor radios to fill the smoggy, summery air with the mellifluous, melodious sound of the dean of play-by-play broadcasters.

And I didn't even like baseball. Well, in truth, I liked baseball until my age reached double digits. I was part of the largest live crowd in the game's history, as about ninety-three thousand folks paid tribute to catcher Roy Campanella at the LA Coliseum. And about ninety-two thousand of them listened to the event on transistor radios as they sat in the downtown twilight, with Scully as their portable companion.

There had been baseball in LA before the Dodgers. Two Minor League teams from the Pacific Coast League, the Hollywood Stars and the Los Angeles Angels, competed for our affections. But nobody needed their radio voices in the ballpark.

Scully was different, an essential part of the fan experience wherever you were.

As a humor practitioner, I found some of Vin's commercials risible. He personally voiced the pitches for Farmer John's meat products, and I made fun of them. "Easternmost in quality, westernmost in flavor." I still don't know what that means.

He was one of the few exceptions to my general rule—that I only do characterizations of people of whom I have a critique. But with Vin, regardless of my feelings about the game, he remained the same throughout the years—a master broadcaster, a master storyteller. I've known a few of the guys at his level in various sports, and Scully was the gold standard in every way.

I was once invited to participate in a conversation at a Hollywood talent agency with Scully, and it was a master class in storytelling. I'd mention a name—say, Sandy Koufax—and Vin would spin a web of tales about the Dodger pitcher that was flat-out mesmerizing.

And by this time, I really didn't like baseball. But Scully's love for the game, and for the people in it, was both palpable and infectious.

And it wasn't just the words, although Vin had grand ad-lib access to a vocabulary both descriptive and analytical. What made his wordscapes unique was the melody—rhapsodic yet conversational, a song that had room for both drama and humor. I can't prove this, but I strongly suspect his monologues could captivate even people who didn't speak English.

Bill Dwyre

Los Angeles Times **sports editor (1981 to 2006)**

The great *Los Angeles Times* sports columnist Jim Murray died in August 1998. He had traveled to Del Mar, written a column about the greatness in victory of veteran jockey Chris McCarron, gone home, and died.

He had a pig valve in his heart that was the medical approach in those days to solving valve issues. Murray, with an Irish sense of humor possibly matched by only one other in the Los Angeles sports media circles, would often joke about his hope that his pig had been a healthy one. For a while, it was.

When his day finally came, it rested on me, as sports editor of the *Times*, and his widow, Linda McCoy-Murray, to figure out the best and most appropriate way to give him a final sendoff. We landed on an afternoon at Dodger Stadium. It was then up to me to decide who would be invited to speak at the memorial. That, of course, had its own pitfalls. Murray was respected, admired, idolized, and beloved by only ten million or so readers in the Los Angeles area, and also by every other writer and broadcaster who lived—many of them with a high level of fame all their own—plus athletes and team officials everywhere. Linda would speak, of course, and we decided on six more as a good number.

It all came together on September 26, 1998. The public was invited; Dodger Stadium would be, well, Dodger Stadium. The six named speakers had all accepted invitations willingly. To have a speaking part in the big Jim Murray goodbye was both welcome and heartfelt by all six.

But I had a problem. Who would be the anchor? Who would have the last word? Who was best suited to send the large crowd away with tears in their eyes and joy in their hearts for having been there on this day when current greatness celebrated past greatness?

The lineup included Jerry West, Al Davis, Chick Hearn, Vin Scully, Al Michaels, and, fittingly, the subject of his final column, McCarron. Each was good with a microphone in hand. Each would have special stories. Each would have the crowd captivated. But who would be the Kenley Jansen in Dodger Stadium this day? Who would be my closer? I had made my share of stupid decisions in my then seventeen years as *Times* sports editor. I couldn't make one this time.

I thought about it long and hard. There was Scully, the master storyteller, a man whom I once praised in a public speaking forum of some sort by telling him that, when he began one of his stories during a Dodgers broadcast, I always prayed that the count on the batter would go to 3-2, with several foul balls, so I could hear the entire story without the dastardly disruption of game action. He had chuckled.

This was the Scully who had shown up one day for lunch at Bel-Air Country Club just as several of us were teeing off on the downhill par-five first hole. He knew me, and Michaels was in the group, and so Vin decided to walk along for a couple holes. I think the idea was to view the high comedy of our swings and toss out a few verbal jabs. We all loved just the thought of it—Vin Scully walking along and kind of narrating, that golden voice there to intone our misery.

But of all things, I had a good hole: decent long drive, almost to the green in two, a chip to about five feet for a birdie putt. To all in my group, and to Vin, who was a fellow hacker, this was unimaginable. Michaels could play, but most of the clods like us do not start off at Bel-Air with a birdie.

So, Vin narrated all the chunked chips and three-putts, building to my putt, which would certainly be gagged. I remember stepping up, telling myself that if I make it the shot will replace that buzzer-beater jump shot in high school. And if I miss, it will be expected and fun, and Scully will be kind and funny in his play-by-play.

But it went in, and there was a moment of stunned silence before Scully intoned this as "the greatest moment, outside of Gibson's home run, that I have ever seen in sports."

That memory alone made my decision for the cleanup hitter of Murray's memorial easy. It would be Scully. With all respects to the others, how foolish of me to even ponder.

When he stepped to the podium and looked out at a crowd that pretty much filled the lower deck from home plate to first base, the melody of Scully was a gift to all of us. I could picture Murray up there, chuckling and pleased with the whole show—which, of course, was the point.

Scully told stories and brought Murray to life as only he could. They had been contemporaries, friends. Murray was perhaps one of only a handful of people around Los Angeles who was not instantly in awe when Scully was in the room.

But to me, the moment of perfection, the moment I was certain my decision to have him go last was the right one, came when Scully simply identified the day. It was fitting, he said, that we honor his friend Jim Murray on a warm but slightly overcast day.

"The Irish call this a soft day," he said, glancing toward the sky while knowing full well Murray would understand and embrace it.

J. P. Hoornstra
Journalist

When a baseball game pauses so a team can change pitchers or a half inning ends, the Dodger Stadium security staff springs into action. Thirteen black-clad guards emerge in foul territory, standing with immaculate posture, their backs turned toward the field. Their eyes scan the crowd for potential idiots daring to leap out of the stands. Then, when the game resumes, each guard retreats to his station. The ritual repeats every night baseball is played in Chavez Ravine.

The implication is subtle but obvious: baseball players are enviable objects of protection, the nine biggest celebrities in the building—except when they are not.

For most of his sixty-seven years as the Dodgers' play-by-play announcer, Vin Scully possessed a degree of celebrity that transcended all but a handful of the players whose feats he was charged with broadcasting. It is impossible to understate how unique this made him among his peers.

The typical play-by-play man or woman is a local celebrity, a familiar voice to fans in the region where their team's games are broadcast. In rare cases, a broadcaster will achieve enough longevity and respect around baseball to earn a seat calling a national game. Even more rare, the broadcaster will earn a place in the Baseball Hall of Fame, at which point it can be said that person belongs not to a team, but to the game itself.

Scully earned the Hall of Fame's Ford C. Frick Award in 1982. While some wait a lifetime or longer to be honored in Cooperstown, Scully spent the majority of his career as a member of the Baseball Hall of Fame. He belonged not merely to baseball but also to American popular culture writ large.

By 2016—his final season in the press box that carried his name, on a Los Angeles city street that bore his name also—one could measure Scully's celebrity by the volume of security that guarded his path to and from his booth. (Hint: The ratio was greater than thirteen to nine, and by the final game of Scully's career, it was eminently necessary. I watched as he was driven through the bowels of Oracle Park during his final game in San Francisco on a utility cart as fans pushed through to follow him into retirement.)

There are better measures of Scully's fame, beginning with the company he kept in his broadcast booth. Boyd Robertson, Scully's longtime stage manager, needed two hands to count the number of celebrities who found time to drop in: actors like Kevin Costner and Bryan Cranston, musicians like Ray Charles and John Williams, the author Michael Connelly, the astronaut Buzz Aldrin, Marvel mogul Stan Lee. Robertson and Scully began working together in 1989.

A better accounting of Scully's celebrity begins in 1958, the Dodgers' first season in Los Angeles. Scully had been with the team since 1950. His partner, Jerry Doggett, had been with the club since 1956. Both were among the nonuniformed team personnel who migrated west from Brooklyn. Scully thus ensured his status as the voice of the first Major League Baseball club in the celebrity capital of the world, thanks in part to an invention only recently released to the masses: the transistor radio.

In the ninety-three-thousand-seat Los Angeles Coliseum, Scully was suddenly in the ear of more Angelenos—famous and unfamous—than perhaps any broadcaster ever. He had a connection to the entertainment industry's elite (via the Friars Club), which came through Danny Goodman, the Dodgers' marketing guru. And he had a house in Pacific Palisades, a community that combined ritzy and rustic in a way that appealed to other famous folks who Scully counted as neighbors.

In one famous incident, Scully and actor Sylvester Stallone found themselves pitted in court. According to the Associated Press, flooding that originated in Stallone's yard caused $106,407 in damages to Scully's home in 1993. A jury ruled that 65 percent of the blame should be borne by Stallone, who fifteen years earlier had the home's former owner relandscape a hill that separated his house from Scully's. But the wealth of stories associating Scully with the local celebs were heartwarming.

One former colleague recounted the time when Scully received a phone call during a game in San Francisco. The caller wanted to know what Scully was doing after the game and invited him over to his hotel room. It was Nat King Cole, who proceeded to play Scully some cuts from his new album.

By the end of his career, it was more difficult to place Scully in the context of other broadcasters than among Hollywood luminaries who had been at the top of their craft for decades. One was more obviously Scully's peer group than the other, even considering the short-lived *Vin Scully Show* had a longer shelf life on YouTube than on CBS.

During Scully's final season in the booth, visiting players, managers, and broadcasters all rode the elevator to the fifth floor of Dodger Stadium to pay their respects to a man whose voice preceded their arrival to the Major League stage by decades. Bryce Harper, the former and future National League Most Valuable Player, came to visit. So did the Boston Red Sox's World Series hero, David Ortiz. Scully made a point throughout his career to avoid being seen hobnobbing with baseball players. In 2016 the most famous players in the game went out of their way to hobnob with him. By then, Scully was just as comfortable among players as he was with anyone.

Catcher A. J. Ellis was among the Dodgers' players who dropped in. "You've got a new fan," Ellis told Scully. "My son came down to the clubhouse the other day, and he said, 'Dad, who's the guy who talks about the Dodgers during the games?' I said, 'Vin Scully?' He goes, 'Yeah, Vin Scuwwy. He's a nice guy. He gave me a high five in the elevator.' So, you're a nice guy."

Dennis McCarthy

Los Angeles Daily News columnist (1982 to present)

They were between innings at a day game in Ebbets Field with maybe two thousand fans in the ballpark when Hilda Chester started shaking her cowbell and hollered, "Vin Scully, I love you."

"In that cracker box of a ballpark, I could hear her," Vin remembered. "I was embarrassed and lowered my head. Hilda hollered back, 'Look at me when I'm talking to you,' and the crowd roared with laughter."

So did Vin. He knew he'd never duplicate that special intimacy with fans at fifty-thousand-seat, sold-out Dodger Stadium, but he was coming close—real close as the club celebrated its twenty-fifth anniversary in Los Angeles in 1983.

He wasn't the iconic, beloved voice of the Dodgers quite yet, but everybody who knew a ball from a strike in Los Angeles was looking at Vin Scully when he talked to them.

Baseball had given him a platform to share stories of respect and just plain, old-fashioned goodness—on and off the baseball field—and he was using it. He loved looking down from his booth between innings after telling a touching story from the past, and seeing thousands of fans with a transistor radio in their hand stand up from their seats, turn around, and give him a nod of respect and thumbs up.

They had come to see the Dodgers play in person, but they needed to hear Vin on the radio, just like they were home. They didn't want to miss his calls, his stories. That's how important he was to them.

It's impossible now to imagine Los Angeles without Vin and the Dodgers, but there was a time when it came down to a game of liar's poker and a handwritten note on a hot dog napkin as to whether the team and its skinny, redheaded kid announcer would leave Brooklyn and come west.

Scully didn't want to, and neither did team owner Walter O'Malley, but he had no choice. He had bet the team's future on New York City Parks Commissioner Robert Moses blinking when O'Malley threatened to leave Brooklyn unless the city built him a new stadium.

Moses didn't blink. He thought O'Malley was lying, trying to bluff him. He wasn't. His father was a lot of things to a lot of people, Peter O'Malley told me on the twenty-fifth anniversary, but one thing he was not was a bluffer.

His father lit another cigar and went to plan B. "I was sitting in Ebbets Field watching one of the World Series games when an usher came down and handed me a note," said the late Los Angeles County Supervisor Kenneth Hahn, who was on a trip east in 1957 scouting teams that might want to move west. "The note was written on a hot dog napkin in pencil. It said, 'Don't sign with anyone until you see me. I want to come. Walter O'Malley.' Well, I just about fell out of my seat. Here I was trying to woo a last place team, and the owner of a World Series team was telling me he wanted to come."

That's how we got the Dodgers, on a hot dog napkin, thanks to a guy who thought Walter O'Malley was bluffing. Robert Moses should have his own special banner hanging in Dodger Stadium. Without him, we might have gotten the Washington Senators.

Scully wasn't thrilled about the possible move, though. "I was a little upset, in the sense I was a New Yorker. My family, friends, and roots were all there. Plus, I had been with the Dodgers about eight years and had been reasonably successful. But I really didn't have a choice. They asked me to come, and I didn't have a job otherwise."

Vintage Scully—boil the story down to a simple, honest truth everyone understands. He needed the paycheck.

Vin packed his bags and kept his job for another fifty-nine years— becoming the voice of so much more than a baseball game.

In a city named for Angels, Vincent Edward Scully became our number one.

At the end of his final broadcast on September 25, 2016, he once again lowered his head in embarrassment for the last story he would tell his city from the Dodger broadcast booth. "You and I have been friends for a long time, but I know in my heart that I've always needed you more than you needed me," Vin said.

The greatest baseball announcer of all time had missed his last call at home plate. No, Vin, we needed you more—much more. Hilda Chester had it right.

NINTH INNING

"The Tao of Vin"

Inspiration and Influence

Colin Cowherd once told his national Fox Sports TV and radio audience that, before he became one of the most recognized sports talk-show commentators in the country, he was driven to become a baseball radio broadcaster. Moving from just outside Seattle to Las Vegas in his early twenties out of college, Cowherd landed in advertising sales for the San Diego Padres' Triple-A affiliate, the Stars. The team allowed him to call one inning each game.

Some four hundred miles from Los Angeles, Cowherd got his first chance to hear Vin Scully broadcasting Dodgers games on the Las Vegas fifty-thousand-watt affiliate, KDWN-AM.

"He was so gifted, so intelligent, so refined, he was intimidating," Cowherd said on the air, marking the day after Vin Scully's passing. "I had aspirations and the will and confidence and bluster. Scully was so good, it was daunting. He was an expert in everything. . . . [He also] brought more joy to more people more often than anyone in Southern California history."

There was no regret in Cowherd switching career goals, especially considering his present-day success.

When Scully approached his eighty-fifth birthday, I reached out to several dozen broadcasters—some trying to get a foot in the door, others who were veterans in the field—to talk about something I called "the Tao of Vin." The exercise was to have each explain how Scully inspired their calling to this profession, how he continued to influence them as communicators, and if there was practical advice once given by Yogi Berra: "If you can't imitate him, don't copy him."

Lou Riggs, a sportscasting instructor hired as a coach for many up-and-coming broadcasters in Southern California for four decades until his passing in 2015, shed some light on all the ways Scully could win friends and influence broadcasters:

> What Scully brings is class, grace, word economy, knowledge, preparation and a smooth, calming delivery. He never talks down to an audience. He's always under control. He understands the art of layout when the crowd is going bonkers. He brings great sense of humor to the booth. If he makes a mistake (which is rare), he can kid himself about it and move on. He recaps better than anyone in the game, giving the score, and telling us frequently what has happened for late tune-inners. You feel like he's someone you could sit down and talk with and go away feeling good about it.
>
> Unfortunately, there aren't many like Scully—well, no one actually—who understands the basic elements of good broadcasting. If any young person wants to be a real professional, put the video games away and listen, digest how Scully presents a picture.

As CBS's Jim Nantz chimed in, "Mr. Scully represents to me a generation of what the art of sports broadcasting is all about. It's how you conduct yourself and handle situations. I do feel there's always a place for the Vin Scully approach, and it will never go extinct. It's just such a higher plane to reach that standard of excellence that then separates the good from the great ones."

Here is how others explain why and when Scully came into their professional consciousness and became an inspirational instructor and a role model.

Ken Levine

Emmy Award–winning TV writer
MLB play-by-play broadcaster (1991 to 2012)

Every day when I was in the Dodger Stadium press box and Vin Scully would say, "Hi, Kenny," I was taken aback. It's like, "Ohmygod! The prettiest girl in school knows my name!"

I hosted *Dodger Talk* on the radio for eight years, and the highlight was getting to actually work with Vin Scully. Vin Scully was my hero.

I became a baseball announcer because of Vin Scully. (I knew at age eight that if I wanted to make it to the big leagues it would not be as a player.) I also became a writer because of Vin Scully.

More than anything else, he was a storyteller. How many nights did I sit in my car in the driveway mesmerized by Scully describing some dramatic game situation?

Looking back, I think it might've been some stupid midseason inning between the Dodgers and Montreal Expos that ultimately meant nothing, but I sat riveted, enthralled. The man was a master storyteller, Shakespeare brought to you by Farmer John wieners.

His inspiration guided my career choices and, in many ways, shaped my life. I owe him a debt I can never repay. (When we were on the road, I made sure he never carried a bag, but I don't think that was sufficient.)

What made Vin Scully so special? His play calling? Knowledge of the game? Sense of humor? Poetic use of language? Storytelling? Rising to the occasion of big moments? Instant recall of games past? Making spring training sound interesting? All of the above . . . but something else.

There was a game late in the season a few years back. Final day of the year, the Dodgers and another team were battling for the division title. And on this Sunday at Dodger Stadium, they were going head-to-head. The winner took it all, and wouldn't you know—it all came down to the ninth inning. (Doncha love baseball?) If you subscribe to MLB.com, you can go back and listen to any team broadcast from that year. They're all archived. A few days after the game, I thought it would be fun to hear how both broadcasters called it.

39. Vin Scully with Ken Levine in the Dodger Stadium press box. Courtesy of Ken Levine.

The visiting broadcaster is also one of the best in the business and in the Hall of Fame; books will be written about him someday. I listened to him first. With the Dodgers up and a man on base, an easy double-play grounder was hit to the shortstop. But this was a rookie, just called up. For whatever reason, he booted it. The announcer lit into him: "This was a play you need to make in the big leagues." He wasn't wrong. And there's something to be said for objectivity. That proved to be a very costly error.

Then I listened to Scully's call of that inning. Same description of the miscue but a very different reaction. Scully said: "Y'know, your heart has to go out to that young man. Not used to playing in front of fifty thousand people and a national TV audience, just called up from the Minors, being in a pressure situation unlike any he's ever faced, he must feel so terrible."

And it hit me—that's what made Vin Scully so exceptional—his humanity. With everything on the line, Scully's reaction was empathy. His inherent goodness was what made us not just admire him but love him.

He truly did become a member of your family. If only he could've been at our Thanksgiving dinners instead of that weird uncle who always had dandruff in his mustache.

Toward the very end of his career, he and I were flying home from Phoenix, where Scully had called a "momentous" spring training game. By the time we arrived at LAX, it was well after 10:00 p.m. Scully was dog tired; he was in his mideighties by then. We exited the restrictive area to where friends and family awaited passengers. Needless to say, when Vin Scully emerged the twenty-or-so people in the area were beyond thrilled. They swarmed around him asking for photos and autographs.

It would have been so understandable if he said he was exhausted and declined, but instead he stayed for fifteen minutes, signing every autograph, shaking every hand (pre-COVID), taking every selfie—humanity.

And he said hello to me every day. I still can't believe my good fortune.

Matt Vasgersian
Major League Baseball broadcaster (1997 to present)

In April 1998 I was in my second year as the TV voice of the Milwaukee Brewers, working under the impression that after a six-year "apprenticeship" as a Minor League play-by-play guy and one year in the big leagues under my belt, I had handled the dramatic step up in class.

The Brewers had a series at Dodger Stadium, and through the walls of the visiting broadcast booth I could hear the announcers in the home booth. Not long after the top of the first, it struck me—Vin Scully was right next door calling the same event that I was.

What business did I have being there? How could I even attempt to put my crummy (then) thirty-year-old soundtrack on this game when there was a Stradivarius next door nailing every note?

The self-reflection at that moment was real, and it took a while to reconvince myself that I actually belonged in the big leagues. From the day any Minor League broadcaster calls the first pitch, the person is aware he or she will never be as good as Vin. The same is true for those lucky enough

40. Vin Scully with Matt Vasgersian. Courtesy of Matt Vasgersian.

to get to the big leagues. None of us will call a better game, and none of us will last as long or resonate with our fan bases the same way.

Some may try to assign some of that cause to the era in which Vin worked, one where baseball was the country's unchallenged number one sport and radio its main source of distribution. But that argument misses the mark.

Vin's appeal—and the reason why he's still so revered—was simply about Vin. As far as style, much has been written of the man whose work defines an entire industry, so I'll offer this: I can recall an interview in which Vin was asked which broadcasters he listened to or thought influenced his style. While he would respectfully cite some of those who came before him, his response was "nobody." Vin explained that in allowing someone else's style to infiltrate his call, his own voice would be less authentic. In other words, Vin called a game in a manner *he* thought was good, not the way he thought people wanted to hear it.

The standard workflow today for too many broadcasters is to have Twitter open as they call the game so as to constantly monitor what people are thinking of them. Even if social media had existed in Vin's prime, I can't imagine he would have ever celebrated himself as so many current broad-casters feel compelled to do.

Scully never pandered—he simply stayed true to the game and true to the craft. It turns out he was on to something. When the most talented and accomplished member of any professional group is also its kindest and most ingratiating, you have that very rare formula for someone who is beloved.

It always struck me that so many hacky blowhards in this business demand star treatment and like to regale people with unsolicited lists of their own accomplishments. And then there was Vin, the most accomplished of them all who conducted himself with nothing but humility and grace. Just as much as his on-air style, perhaps his greatest legacy was teaching us how to behave.

Tom Leykis
Radio personality

On October 14, 1965, my life changed forever. Instead of being in school on that sunny Thursday afternoon off Fordham Road in the Bronx, I found my nine-year-old self sitting on the floor of my grandmother's fifth-floor apartment. Since I lived in the Bronx, I really had nothing invested in the Twins or Dodgers in this World Series. I hadn't watched the first six games. But, on this fateful day, young, bored me turned on my grandmother's brand-new Sears color TV—and there was the black-and-white coverage of World Series Game Seven.

So many viewers would hear, for the first time, the Twins' Ray Scott. They would also hear the man who did play-by-play for the Los Angeles Dodgers, some guy named Vin Scully.

The day I was born in 1956, Vin was already in his seventh season doing Dodger baseball. Scully was a name I had heard, mostly through the clenched teeth of angry Brooklynites in my mother's Park Slope family who remembered he had been the Brooklyn Dodgers' play-by-play guy before owner Walter O'Malley took "their" Dodgers to Southern California. Very few New York baseball fans seemed to remember if he had been good or bad at his job. My entire childhood experience of baseball play-by-play in New York had been nothing but the southern intonations of the Mets' Lindsey Nelson and the Yankees' Mel Allen and Red Barber.

But that all changed. In a brilliantly pitched game by the amazing Sandy Koufax, Scully and his New York accent was so smooth in ways I had never heard before. Even at nine, I could tell in his style that Vin was conscious of being heard nationally, full of a kind of professionalism, energy, and attention to detail I had never heard before. I was mesmerized.

I knew I wanted to be some type of broadcaster. I went to the public library to learn whatever I could about him. He grew up in the exact neighborhood where I was born, in the Washington Heights section of Manhattan. Like my father, he grew up a New York Giants fan. Once I found out he had attended Fordham University, just walking distance from my grandmother's apartment, I started scheming to go to college there. I became obsessed with wanting to broadcast on WFUV, the Fordham radio station he helped found. At sixteen, I became the youngest student at the time to attend Fordham, majoring in communications.

I found out my mother's sister attended Catholic high school in Brooklyn's Park Slope neighborhood with the son of the Dodgers' owner, Peter O'Malley. This intensified my obsession with the Dodgers even if they were three thousand miles away.

I began to watch TV shows produced in LA, like Steve Allen's syndicated daytime talk show. I regularly watched Bob Barker's old game show, *Truth or Consequences*. Bob Crane of *Hogan's Heroes* was once the morning man on KNX? I learned how to pronounce Van Nuys, Sepulveda, and La Cienega Boulevard by watching *Dragnet*, *Adam-12*, and *Emergency!*

I dreamed of the day when I could visit Los Angeles. The first time was a work assignment in 1978. It took another ten years before I could tune into Vin Scully every single day for six months every year. It really was that important for me.

My new radio gig provided me the opportunity to meet many of the idols I had worshipped. Because I was on the competitor to the Dodgers' radio station, KABC, I simply couldn't ever get an interview with the man who changed my life. In fact, many Dodgers games were in afternoon drive opposite my show, and so Vin Scully was now my radio competitor.

Many years later, I was escorted through the Dodgers' press box by my former radio producer and now the Dodgers' vice president of broadcasting, Erik Braverman. He took me into Vin's booth. I could hardly breathe at the thought. I have to admit, I was awestruck and tongue-tied. The whole thing lasted maybe three minutes.

I could never tell Vin how much he meant to me. And now, as Vin is gone, I never will.

As much as many Dodgers fans detested the changes of ownership—first to News Corporation, then to Frank and Jamie McCourt, and finally to the current ownership—Vin Scully stayed in his lane and never let the frequent turbulence affect what he did. I remembered in 2009 that incredible example in professionalism, when a format change I knew was coming ultimately put me out of a job. I learned from Vin that the audience comes first and my personal issues come last.

For the last three years of Vin's extraordinary career, most of Los Angeles couldn't even see him due to the Dodgers' relationship with Time Warner Cable. Vin was essentially broadcasting into a black hole with a fraction of the audience. Yet, as angry as it made me, a viewer and rabid Dodgers fan, Vin continued to be the consummate professional, never bringing the subject up on a broadcast and in newspaper and magazine interviews. I did all I could to find work-arounds to get those last few years of Dodgers SportsNet LA broadcasts, even if it meant getting the MLB app for Canada and watching games in LA.

Some wouldn't be able to handle being marginalized in reaching such a comparatively small audience. For Vin, it was just another assignment that he took on magnificently. His last three years of work were as good as, or even better than, any he had done.

Vin Scully never disappointed me professionally or as a person. If he ever had an issue with anyone, Vin's audience never knew about that.

The summer after he retired, I practiced living my future life without him. I am not ashamed to say I still miss Vin Scully horribly. Vin Scully was my muse for fifty-plus years, without me ever knowing it, for my career ambitions and virtually every good thing about my life today.

How do you say goodbye to someone like that?

Jim Hill

Los Angeles T V sportscaster (1976 to present)

Vin Scully, to me, was like the North Star. Everybody wants to be a star, but there's only one North Star. It's wonderful knowing that's a goal. You just really can't attain it. But it helps make you a better person just trying to. It keeps you going. It keeps you humble.

Ed Hookstratten, my agent, was also the agent for Elvis Presley, Johnny Carson, . . . and Vin Scully. Hook was the Los Angeles Rams' general council and introduced Vin to his wife Sandi. He was the best man at their wedding.

One day, Hook told me to meet him at The Grill on the Alley in Hollywood for lunch. I had no idea why. I got there, turned around, and there was Vin Scully. Ed brought us together so Vin could give me career advice.

I was right out of playing football and getting into broadcasting. I already knew how lucky I was to be there because of the environment I grew up in. I came from the end of the dead-end street in Texas. If I hadn't played football, I would be dead today. Sports saved me. My family loved the Dodgers because of what Jackie Robinson accomplished. When the Dodgers were in the World Series, our family watched, and Vin Scully called those games.

I was in complete awe now. Vin Scully was telling me, "Jim, one of my favorite sayings is from Dr. Martin Luther King about giving back to your fellow man. Talk to the young kids; show them how it's done. You never know when you're going to influence someone. They're watching you."

He taught me about common courtesy. When people stop to say hello, to ask for a photo or autograph, it takes more time to make up a reason why not to do it. Just do it. Besides, people don't have to say anything. So, when they do, take the time to respond. It means a lot.

He told me, "If you go to a press conference that starts at ten o'clock, be there at nine, sit in the front row, and be the first to raise a hand and ask a question. They'll start acknowledging you more." He also said, "When you're traveling, even if it's in the middle of the night, wear a suit and tie. Always represent yourself, your profession and your race." When I dress today, I call it "The Vin Scully Look." Every time he walked into Dodger Stadium, he looked like a million bucks.

That also reminds me of my most embarrassing moment. I was at the Dodger Stadium dining room and made myself a root-beer float: a scoop of ice cream, poured over with soda. I wasn't paying attention. I turned around and spilled it all over Vin Scully. I was speechless. And in typical Vin Scully fashion—I remember it like it was yesterday—he said, "Oh, Jim, it'll be okay." Eventually everything went back to normal because Vin had that ability to calm down even the most incredible situations. There's no one else on earth who could have done that.

When I started to call NFL games on TV, Vin was there for more advice. The most important thing to know was "names and numbers," he said without hesitating. He explained that on the morning he would call an NFL game, he looked into the mirror while he was shaving and just recited names and numbers.

Sometimes you never know how lucky you were until something is gone. I knew how lucky I was when Vin was around. He was my role model. He helped me in more ways he will ever know. In a world where we all strive to be good, but might not know how, he was as close to perfect as I've ever seen. I know he helped make me a better man.

John Ireland

Los Angeles Lakers radio broadcaster (2011 to present)

I've always told people that for an aspiring sportscaster, growing up in Southern California in the seventies and eighties was like going to a year-round master class. Chick Hearn was the voice of the Lakers, Bob Miller the voice of the Kings, and Dick Enberg was the voice of the Angels. And then there was Vin.

When I was a kid, my dad knew I wanted to be a sportscaster one day. I worshipped Chick, and Dad told me that if I really wanted to do what Chick did for a living, I had to broaden my horizons. We had a conversation that went something like this:

Dad said, "You have to know things other than sports if you really want to do this."

I replied, "No I don't—I just need to know how to describe the games."
Dad countered, "Listen to Vin Scully. He talks about *everything*."

It almost seems insulting to call Vin just a sportscaster, because he spent so much time telling you stories that had nothing to do with sports. If you spent time with Vin during a game, you would learn about history, music, entertainment, and so much more. He was a historian, a professor, and an entertainer all at the same time.

And he was just as great off the air as he was on. He never acted as if he was a big deal, even though everybody knew that he was. I've hosted a sports-radio talk show in Los Angeles for the better part of thirty years. Vin only agreed to come on the show three times. The first was to help one of his friends who was organizing a fundraiser for baseball scouts. The second time was to surprise Bob Miller and publicly congratulate the Kings for winning the Stanley Cup. The third time was the year he retired, when he graciously started the interview by thanking us for being kind to him over the years. The message was clear: Vin would come on to help others but never made it about himself.

He was funny. One year, Vin showed up to accept an award from the Southern California Sports Broadcasters for best TV play-by-play. He got a standing ovation, and when he got to the podium, he said, "Every year, when I receive my ballot for the Southern California Sports Broadcaster awards, I look at *all* of the great names that I have the honor of competing with each year. And then, I vote for myself."

He walked away with a room full of people not only laughing hysterically but also marveling at how he somehow always knew exactly what to say. That, to me, is his legacy. He was a wordsmith who knew exactly how, when, and where to deliver the perfect line.

He was also part of something, along with Chick, Bob, and Dick, that I'm not sure he'll ever get the proper credit for. Those guys left a blueprint for other broadcasters on how to behave and how to treat people. Because they were so kind and friendly, it made it almost impossible for other people to act like a jerk. If Vin Scully treated everybody greatly, anybody who didn't would stick out like a sore thumb. It led to an atmosphere of civility that still exists today.

Finally, I think Vin hit the nail on the head when he was asked what he would tell people who were sad that he was retiring. In typical Scully fashion, he quoted, of all people, Dr. Seuss: "Don't cry because it's over; smile because it happened."

Ken Korach
Oakland Athletics radio broadcaster (1996 to present)

Oakland A's TV producer Mark Wolfson was familiar with my idolatry of Vin and how I grew up in Los Angeles listening to him. So, in 1997 when Mark scheduled a pregame interview with Vin, he asked me to host it. I was doing radio at the time alongside one of Vin's contemporaries, the near-as-legendary Bill King. The two were born in the fall of 1927, and I'm not sure what path my career would have taken without their influences.

The segment with Vin was part of the Dodgers' first regular-season visit to Oakland via interleague play. I had never met Vin, although by then he seemed like a second father. Listening to Vin always reminded me of listening to my dad. Both men are heroes of mine, both with voices that commanded my attention but were soothing at the same time, and both had the kind of sage wisdom I craved as a kid.

Let's be clear—I didn't learn Vin's lessons directly from him; they came via his voice on the radio. As someone who wanted to be a radio broadcaster for as long as I can remember, I suppose it was like a budding musician listening to a great jazz player. There's nothing cognitive; I just absorbed it.

I was nervous as hell. I had done radio pregame shows but never a TV pregame show for the A's. Even with a decent amount of prior experience in front of a camera, TV was never my forte. My sleep the night before was restless at best. The thought of not wanting to mess up began to consume me. Throw in all the clichés you want, like a Catholic having an audience with the pope or having a chance to interview Einstein or Lincoln, maybe even Mozart. We were all in awe, or if you can find a word loftier than *awe*—try *reverence*—substitute it.

Vin hated that kind of talk. It was one of his most endearing and amazing traits. He handled his "Vinnyness" with a sizable amount of grace and

41. Vin Scully with Ken Korach in Oakland, 1992. Photo by Michael Zagaris. Courtesy of Ken Korach.

humility. I shouldn't have been so nervous in front of him because he knew I was and did whatever he could to ease it.

My first question was about the essence of a baseball broadcast: cut right to it, get to the philosophy. His answer was simple: "That you're believable. If everything is always great for your team, it doesn't mean anything when something truly great happens." This goes to Vin's sense of fairness, a trait ingrained by the great Red Barber when Vin was a young Dodgers broadcaster in his twenties.

I asked about Kirk Gibson, a question I'm sure A's fans weren't dying to hear. That's when the whole thing became like an out-of-body experience. I didn't know whether to laugh, cry, pinch myself, or just sit there paralyzed listening to his words. Now it was Vinny telling stories as if it were 1965 and Koufax's perfect-game broadcast, in all its eloquence, was coming out of my radio—except this voice was now less than a foot from me.

"Let me tell you about Kirrrrrk Gibbbbson," he said, and I flashed briefly on my clumsy Vin impressions about "Farrrrmer John." It was incredible.

A few days later, my broadcast partner back in my Pacific Coast League days in Phoenix, Kent Derdivanis, correctly critiqued my questions as long-winded. Well, at least I got the words out.

Fast forward to 2015, the year before Vin retired and the A's were at Dodger Stadium for another interleague series. By then, Vin and I had become friendly, and I looked forward to his pearls of wisdom. The A's were struggling that year. He pointed down the field where the A's were warming up. "Don't get too caught up in what they're doing down there," he said. "You've got a job to do up here."

He had a question for my broadcast partner Vince Cotroneo and me: "Can you tell me about Curt Young and the 1988 World Series?" Curt was the current A's pitching coach. Back then, he threw a scoreless inning in Game Two of the series against the Dodgers.

Vin was nearly ninety and would have had full license to mail in his broadcasts. I chided him a bit: "Vin, you're really hustling today." Then he got very serious, and this was Vin at his finest. "This is what we do. We tie it all together. I would feel terrible if Curt Young went to the mound to talk to one of your young pitchers and I didn't know what he had done on the same mound pitching against the Dodgers in the World Series."

He was kicking our butt in his preparation. And it really hit me after that, just like the comment about the essence of a broadcast and how broadcasters have to be believable and give the opposition its due. I didn't know what Vin was doing to prepare as a kid, but one just knew he was doing it. So much of what I do now was formed by Vin fifty to sixty years ago.

The day the Dodgers celebrated Vin Scully Night a few days before his last home game in 2016, I got in my car in the Bay Area and drove down Interstate 5 to Dodger Stadium. The A's allowed me the game off. I bought a ticket in the loge level, just above the Dodger dugout. I wanted to feel what it felt like when I went to my first games there in the sixties. People were in tears when Sandy Koufax was introduced. It was fifty thousand fans sharing their love.

Then Vin, when he addressed his audience from San Francisco during his final broadcast a few days later said, "I've always felt I needed you more than you needed me."

Quite a few of us would beg to differ.

Brian Wheeler
Portland Trail Blazers broadcaster (1998 to 2019)

The time when I grew up in Los Angeles was great for listening to sports radio announcers. Back then, the Dodgers had maybe twenty-five games available on television, so radio was the way I followed them. That meant Vin Scully was there, as were Chick Hearn for the Lakers, Bob Miller for the Kings, Dick Enberg for the Angels and Rams, and Tom Kelly and Fred Hessler for USC and UCLA.

During these formative years of wanting to be a broadcaster, as an only child in his bedroom listening to games and doing homework, I counted them as my companions. I might not have understood all I was hearing, but I knew it sounded pretty special. They were terrific people to pay attention to. None of them used "we" or "us" or "them."

I thought I was at my best when I understood that my first job is to keep people listening. So, even if the team isn't doing well, I have to think of ways to keep things interesting. That was what Vin did with his pacing and storytelling. I always felt, too, that Vin could appreciate when the players on the other team did well, even if it meant the Dodgers lost the game.

When you were in the stands at Dodger Stadium and could hear the echo of Vin's call through the transistor radio, we understood that he knew that too. I remember when he even gave a definition of a convoluted baseball rule. He paused. Then he said, "Oh, sure, I know you knew that. But what about her sitting over there."

I would go with a friend and his father to games, but they seemed to have wanted to leave early to beat the traffic. At least I could hear Vin call the game on KABC as we were in the car getting lost trying to navigate that circular parking lot. One time, we left a game in the ninth inning with the Dodgers down, 1–0, and I couldn't believe it. Steve Garvey hit a two-run homer in the bottom of the ninth to win it. I know that because I heard Vin describe it as we were confused trying to find the exit.

With Vin, I learned how to make a connection to the audience. I borrowed his way to open and close a broadcast: "A very pleasant good evening to you" and "Wishing you a very pleasant good evening."

Vin also taught me about how to let the crowd tell the story after a big play. A broadcaster always has time to catch the audience up on what just happened after the roar of the crowd. I never could tell if Vin had things scripted to say in big moments, but he always sounded genuine and remarkable—the perfect number of words, right to the heart of the matter.

I understood the amount of work he had to do for solo broadcast. One year I did Blazers games by myself. I couldn't imagine doing baseball every day, every inning for six months. That really made one the voice of a team. Vin was synonymous with the Dodgers. Listeners always thought he would go on forever; I certainly did. But I think that as broadcast roles are shared, those days are passing us by.

In the late-2000s, I finally did get to meet Vin at Dodger Stadium press box through some connections. He was very friendly, but it felt like I was talking to an angelic figure. I told him all about my childhood and how much I respected his abilities as a broadcaster. "Ah, that's so kind of you," he said. I told him that I was passing on some of the lessons I learned from him all those years ago and explained that I was in town to help at a sports-casters' training camp and "trying to mold the broadcasters of tomorrow." And Vin said, "We all have to do that, don't we? I'm sure you do a great job." It felt like I was talking to Mr. Rogers.

Mike Parker

Oregon State University broadcaster (1999 to present)

With apologies to Richard Dreyfuss, of the fine film *Mr. Holland's Opus*, my entrée into what was to become my life occurred when, at the age of seven, I entered Mr. Holland's garage.

It was a Saturday afternoon in the spring of 1966. I was playing with my buddy Stuart, two doors down from my home in Hacienda Heights, California. We wandered into the garage, where Mr. Holland was puttering around while listening to something on the radio.

I had not grown up in a sporting household and did not understand the words coming out of the box. So, I asked, "Mr. Holland, what are you listening to?"

He seemed a bit taken aback by the question but managed to answer, "Oh, that's the Dodgers game."

My next question was even more flabbergasting: "What are the Dodgers?"

He proceeded to answer something like, "Well, that's our baseball team."

I listened a bit more: "The one-two pitch on the way—fastball, low, ball two. Two and two to Ron Fairly."

Aristotle once said that those who wish to succeed must first ask the right preliminary questions. I hadn't yet. But I proved the philosopher correct with my next query: "*Who* is that doing the talking?"

Mr. Holland answered, "Why, that's Vin Scully."

And that was it. I had been drawn in by a voice using diction I did not comprehend but was somehow fascinated by. I called it a day with Stuart, rushed home, and asked my dad if we had a radio. We did! He helped me find the game. I sat and listened.

Vin Scully taught me the game from that day on, and the die was cast. His voice set the course of my life, and that is not hyperbole.

My dad, who passed away at the age of ninety-two in September 2014, such a dear, great, wonderful man, saw that his young, adopted son had an interest in something he knew nothing about. As the superintendent of a construction company in Southern California, he mainly drove the freeways of Los Angeles, from job site to job site, and would listen to the radio all the time so he knew who the Dodgers were. He was not a fan, but he knew how to find the games on the radio.

The world has rightly marveled over Vin's descriptions of some of the great moments in baseball history, but my first connection to the world of sports came through his call of a comparatively nondescript at bat. There was something, something in the voice, the rhythm, the timbre, the cadence that drew me in when the count was 2-2 in April.

I began to look forward to the simple beginnings of Dodgers games on the radio. Jerry Doggett would say, "And now for the play-by-play, here's Vin Scully. Vinnie?"

"Well, thank you, Jerry, hi everybody, and a very pleasant good evening to you wherever you may be."

As Yeats said, "I hear it in my deep heart's core."

As Vin Scully taught me the game and I became a fan—bless my dad's heart, he took me to my first game on June 17, 1966, when McCovey hit a three-run homer off Don Sutton, the Giants won, 4–1, and I cried all the way home—I was riveted by his call of the big moments.

My nine-year-old self did not miss a pitch on the radio of Don Drysdale's consecutive scoreless-innings streak in 1968. Vin's ninth inning call of Big D's fifth straight shutout is as good a half inning of baseball as I have ever heard. He described the action and the controversy, explained rule 6.08 (which failed to satisfy Dick Dietz and Herman Franks), and spoke of the ancient bitterness of the Dodgers-Giants rivalry. As H. L. Mencken had said of the Gettysburg Address, Scully's call was "truly stupendous."

The magic that was radio began with Scully, but it soon led me to Dick Enberg calling the Rams and Chick Hearn with the Lakers. Nothing seemed to really come into my world with the same kind of passion as baseball, football, and basketball. Even as a kid, I knew announcing was what I wanted to do someday. I loved Wilt Chamberlain, Willie Davis, and Roman Gabriel, but the men calling the games were my true heroes. They were my inspiration to seek out the profession.

My family moved to Cottage Grove, Oregon, when I was fourteen. For the last twenty-plus years I have been honored to call all three of those sports in one of the great college towns in America—Corvallis, Oregon, the home of the Oregon State Beavers.

I am forever grateful for Mr. Holland's garage, where I met Vin Scully.

Josh Suchon

Albuquerque Isotopes broadcaster (2013 to present)
Los Angeles Dodgers radio host (2008 to 2011)

The year is 2008, my first year as the cohost of postgame *Dodger Talk* and as the embedded reporter on the Dodgers Radio Network. We're in San Francisco, and I get on the team bus. The only person on the bus is Vin Scully. I never wanted to bother Vin, so I don't sit right next to him, and I don't pester him with questions.

But today, Vin is feeling nostalgic and starts the conversation. He weaves this tale about growing up a New York Giants fan, going to the Polo Grounds as a kid, how a ticket for the bleachers cost 55 cents. He could get five cents for returning a soda bottle, he said, so if he collected eleven bottles, he could go to a baseball game for free. He'd sit in right field because Mel Ott, the right fielder, was his favorite player. Mel was a lefty and Vin was a lefty.

It was the most incredible story. I didn't want anyone else to get on the bus and ruin the moment. It felt like Vin was telling me this secret that he'd never told anyone.

Later that day, I shared the story with someone from our traveling party. It turned out that it wasn't really a secret. Vin told this story to many people over the years, in many interviews, and even told the story on the air a few times. I wasn't disappointed. I was in awe.

This was actually one of Vin's many gifts. He just had this way of making you feel special, making you feel like he was telling a story for the first time, that it was your little secret, even if he had told the story many times before.

It never got old when I brought a visitor to Vin's booth at Dodger Stadium. Vin had a few go-to lines. He'd point to a coat hanger and say, "This is where we dangle our participles." That was always my favorite Vin Scully joke.

Grown men and women, young boys and girls, were in absolute awe, sometimes trembling and stumbling over their words. Vin heard this, every day, multiple times every day, but you'd never know it. His reaction was like it was the first time—heartfelt, genuine. He'd thank *them* for sharing their story. He'd give a hug and say, "Let's take a photo." He'd say, "Take another to make sure" and "Check it to make sure it turned out, or we'll do it again."

The people I'd escort out of the press box felt like they had just experienced a religious awakening. The longer I work in baseball, the more I realize that we're not just in the broadcasting business. We're in the business of making memories.

When I left Los Angeles and became the play-by-play announcer for the Triple-A Albuquerque Isotopes, I took a lot of lessons from Vin with me. Yes, I stole many of his expressions, mostly without even realizing it. (If you haven't stolen from Scully, you're probably not very good at play-by-play announcing.) But more so, I've tried to emulate his humanity and that special feeling he created for others.

None of us have the impact of Scully, especially those of us working in the Minor Leagues. But we can still make a difference in someone's life.

I feel awkward sharing any of these stories because they sound like not-so-humble brags. I hope you don't mind and use them as an inspiration yourself.

Someone emailed me because I was mispronouncing "Hagerstown." I assumed it was *hagg-erstown*. He said it was *hay-gerstown*. That started an email conversation. He is disabled and doesn't leave the house much, but he loves baseball, stumbled upon an Isotopes game one night, and now listens almost every day. We've never met.

One day I got on a tangent—who knows what triggered it—and ended up talking about him on the air. We still trade emails from time to time. It might not be an emotional in-person visit in Vin's booth, but these are the connections that baseball provides to otherwise total strangers.

This year, the Isotopes wanted to celebrate the life of Jackie Robinson to ensure students understand his importance. We created an education initiative. If any student, K–12, wrote an essay or created artwork about Jackie, he or she would receive four free tickets to the Jackie Robinson

Celebration game. (Whenever I think about Jackie Robinson, I usually am reminded of the story Vin Scully told of going ice skating with him.)

One student, admittedly not a baseball fan, wrote a powerful essay about visiting the Negro League Museum recently. He relayed what emotions the tour brought out in him and how it's inspiring his life. We had him throw out the ceremonial first pitch. Four of his high school classmates came to a game a month later. One was really interested in Roberto Clemente's life. I told his teacher to have the student write an essay about Clemente, and I'll use my comp tickets for him in the future. Another was really intrigued by baseball analytics. We had him speak to our video coordinator.

We brought them out to one of our School Day Matinee games. Each student spent a couple innings sitting next to me in the broadcast booth. Everyone asked smart questions: What's it like working solo? When are you quiet and let the crowd fill in the blanks? What's the deal with the sand timer? (It's to remind me to keep saying the score.)

The students shadowed our public relations manager, saw how the pitch timer works, saw how the automated ball-strike system works, and learned the history of baseball in Albuquerque.

I don't know how much impact the day will have on the rest of their baseball lives. Maybe some will pursue a career in sports. Maybe it was just a fun day. But it was a memory, and that's our business.

None of us will ever be the broadcaster Vin Scully was. But we can all strive to be the human being that Vin Scully was.

Paul Vercammen

Journalist

My Belgian immigrant parents often jumbled a couple languages in one terse comment to their four children. They wove English, French, and Flemish. "You can be anything you want, even President van de USA," my mom declared in the early 1970s.

I wanted to be Vin Scully.

Never mind all that uptight blathering from Washington DC and that hound-dog-looking dude, Richard Nixon. Vin Scully announced Dodgers games. In my adolescent brain, that was clearly a much more important job that captivated all of Southern California. Way more people here wore Dodger caps than "Nixon's the One" pins.

I launched a campaign to take every mass media, production, writing, speech, and related class to prepare me for my life in broadcasting. All this happened in Santa Barbara, where my fortunate parents had emigrated from Belgium, lured by a distant relative who wound up there by first kissing and marrying an American soldier.

I picked up a tape recorder and began announcing random amateur baseball games, imitating Vin Scully: "Strike three looking, and he leaves the tying run on third without taking the bat off his shoulder." This chatter horrified random passersby, concerned for an odd teenager with hair over his ears, sitting on top of the dugout talking to himself.

From a beige, plastic, boxy radio perched inches from my bed and head, Scully tutored me on broadcasting. During baseball season, while my restaurant-worker parents put in their evening shifts, Scully's smooth voice helped me ease into sleep.

"It's a high drive to deep left field," he would announce. You knew from the words *high drive to deep left field* that odds were good that you would soon hear "She is gone," indicating a home run. Scully never exaggerated or seemed to get a call wrong or screamed like his red hair was on fire.

Neither of us knew it at the time, but Scully began teaching me how to speak proper English at an early age. My parents were sharpening their

English skills while raising us. Their accents were as thick as my mom's vegetable soup, with leaks, celery, peas, and whatever she tossed in the pot, which would stand up spoons.

They had huge holes in their vocabulary where they did not yet know the English word. Vin Scully's vocabulary spanned the entire *Webster's* dictionary, yet he never sounded stuffy.

In first grade I asked my classmates to hand me the *washandje* in my Catholic school boy's room, and they giggled.

"What are you talking about?"

"The ding there, to clean up," I replied and had a realization. *You do not know some English words*, I thought.

But I had Vin Scully as my teacher. I learned *marvelous* sounded better than *good* and *spine-tingling* replaced *nervous*.

"There's twenty-nine thousand people in the ballpark and a million butterflies," he said during Sandy Koufax's perfect game. A lot more about language was learned there than what well-intended teachers wrote on a chalkboard.

With all this Scully tutelage and the various speech, writing, and media classes, I eventually attended Santa Barbara City College. I got pushed by a drill sergeant of a journalism instructor, took more speech and media classes, and then came to a conclusion: it was time to transfer to a university.

My parents' first jobs in America were coat-check girl and busboy, and then they owned a thriving restaurant and bar where people drank enough to fill a lake. I once counted ten blood relatives working in The Bistro, laughing and chattering in three languages and coming home with fistfuls of cash from tips.

"Dad, I want to go to journalism school at the University of Southern California," I told him.

"*Jounalisme, journalisme*," he said the French way, hanging on the *e*. "But look at everyone in the family doing so good in restaurants. People love the bar, food."

My older siblings, led by my big brother, went to bat for me. The two kids born in Belgium could not become president of the United States. The sibling advocacy worked, and I transferred to USC, right in the shadow of Vin Scully and Dodger Stadium.

After serving as sports editor of the *Daily Trojan*, my passion to announce sports waned. But my adoration for Scully and the Dodgers never faded. I jumped on my one-speed bike that survived a dunking in the pool of my dive apartment building and pedaled to see Scully at the Dodgers' World Series victory celebration at LA City Hall in 1981. I graduated and later became mainly a general assignment reporter and anchor, building a career on trying to be detailed, measured, accurate, and passionate.

In my twenty-six years at CNN, I covered a lot of sports stories that had a foot in general news, pop culture, or human interest. Then in September 2020 I got to interview my unwitting mentor, after he retired.

The country was ablaze in social-justice protests, rallies against racism and white supremacy. I covered the riot at The Grove shopping and entertainment complex in Los Angeles, just announcing what I saw as rubber bullets flew, batons swung, police cars burned, windows broke, stores got looted, people got arrested. I knew Scully would say something poignant about America and social-justice issues:

> PV: I know you're not going to dip your toe into any controversy, but you knew Jackie Robinson. This is a time of great contentiousness in America. What do you think Jackie Robinson would say, to perhaps calm this country when we have so much divisiveness over so many issues?
>
> VS: I'm not dodging the issue, but I'll quote somebody who said something that has had a great deal of meaning for me: "We will remember not the words of our enemies, but the silence of our friends." So there's a lot of people who are not speaking up or not telling the right things. And I hope eventually, I pray, that eventually everyone would start talking together. And maybe we can work this thing out. God help us if we don't. [Robinson] spoke out; he was not a silent friend.

With goose bumps and a nod, I wondered if a more articulate human was on the planet.

When we lost Vin Scully, the memories of that interview, of imitating him as a boy, of listening to him on the radio, unspooled. I got to tell the world through my words and the comments of other faithful admirers why Scully meant so much.

I stood on Vin Scully Avenue in front of a makeshift shrine, a painter's palate of colorful flowers, cards, Dodger mementos. "His words were poetry to some people. Vin Scully could read the Denny's menu, and it would sound fantastic," I reported.

"I cannot imagine anyone more popular in this city," a red-eyed fan told me on camera.

I was inside the Dodger Stadium ceremony for Scully, the first game at home after his death. "On a beautiful breezy night in Los Angeles, the adoration for the late Vin Scully flowed at Dodger Stadium," I said.

I explained how fans took videos in front of the Vin Scully press box. One man wore a shirt featuring a photo of young Vin Scully the announcer. "It's time for Dodgers baseball. When you hear those five words, you get chills," another fan proclaimed.

"It's just iconic, the sounds of LA," a woman in a Dodgers jersey wept.

I closed with a comparison. "For them in a way, Vin Scully was to sports-casting what Van Gogh was to art, or Louis Armstrong to jazz. He was simply the best. They don't want to forget him. And they were glad to say goodbye on this night."

I felt at peace, okay with how I honored my inspiration, my idol, my de facto babysitter. When he serenaded me as a boy from the boxy radio aimed at my head, I would usually drift off before the game ended.

In a half-sleep, radio still crackling, I would hear my mom walk in after her hostess shift, high heels off, tip-toeing in stocking feet. She would flip the dial on the radio to off with a click and kiss me goodnight. Then I slept fully, dreaming of Vin Scully's Dodgers.

Jon Weisman

Creator of DodgerThoughts.com website
Los Angeles Dodgers director of digital and print (2013 to 2017)
and vice president of communications (2023 to present)

On the night of August 2, 2022, I wrote the last words I ever thought I would about Vin Scully. I wrote about how I heard the news of his passing in the middle of a Dodgers broadcast, while driving my son and two of his friends to a sleepover, and how I nearly doubled over at the wheel. I wrote about how I had to somehow hold it together until the kids were out of the car and how I broke down in tears and *screamed* once I was alone. I knew the day of his passing was coming. I thought I was prepared for it. I wasn't.

Vin was a central figure for most of my life. From when I was ten years old and dreaming of becoming his successor with the Dodgers (ha!), to being in my twenties and thirties and forties and fifties and dreaming of becoming his equivalent as a writer, Vin was my inspiration and aspiration, a role model on the most personal level. In all my work, I would push toward him like the paradise he represented, to rise to the moment in all facets, to be thoughtful, articulate, smart, sensitive, masterful, insightful, cheerful, and, above all else, kind.

That's the man I grieve: a teacher, a nurturer, a poet, a North Star. Vin made dreamers of all of us.

When I worked for the Dodgers, Vin and I never became close; as much as I would have liked them to, our paths rarely crossed. It was slightly maddening, mostly saddening, and I can't say it doesn't inspire the un-Scully emotion of jealousy from me toward those in his universe. However, it did mean I could still treasure a singular voice mail from him asking for a quick bit of help, or an email that he would write in his ALL-CAPS STYLE, from that email address that began with "red@."

Of Ted Williams, the author John Updike wrote, "Gods do not answer letters." But this god did.

I met my hero, and he remained my hero.

Vin relentlessly spoke the truth except for when he said at the end of his sixty-seven years of pulling up a chair with Dodger fans, "I have always felt that I needed you more than you needed me." Talk about your disinformation campaigns. Maybe Vin *felt* that way, but those feelings could not have been more removed from reality.

However much he needed us, we needed him much more. From 1950 to 2016, one of us came along every minute. Vin came along once in a lifetime.

Since his departure, nature pushes us to move on, rendering Vin a voice from a time gone by. We can hear that voice in our heads clear as a pleasant afternoon wherever we may be, but it is now Proustian, a remembrance of things past, from Dodger history or our own. How many of us, after all, can recall a moment in our personal lives having nothing to do with baseball for which Vin provided the soundtrack?

But today and tomorrow, even as we remain on our own, I believe we are left with a task to go on living our lives with Vin as an active voice, encouraging us to be observant, to always take the high road, with resilience, determination, gratitude, and joy. Lincoln spoke to "the better angels of our nature." Vin is now one of those better angels, and we will be at our best if we keep listening.

When I think of the tapes of Vin's voice that run in my head, one of them is something I never actually heard him say. A while ago, I came upon a guest column Vin wrote for the *Los Angeles Times* while on a Dodgers road trip in September 1965. (This would have been about a week before Sandy Koufax's perfect game). When I shared this find in one of my sacred email exchanges with him, he appreciated it but said he didn't remember doing it. He might have dictated it, or he might have jotted it down on hotel stationery. We don't know. But every time I read it to myself, I hear it in that Fordham drawl of his, something more artful and poignant than any of us could ever conceive.

Here's how the piece began: "It came up rain, a gray somber rain that put a frown on the careworn face of Pittsburgh. My window was streaked with erratic wet lines that made me think of a small child crying. Rain meant disappointment to thousands of fans—and a doubleheader to broadcast—and it meant that on that wet afternoon, I was face to face with the biggest enemy on the road . . . TIME." The capital letters were his.

Epilogue

A column I wrote in spring 2017, leading into the first season of Los Angeles Dodgers baseball in sixty-seven years without Vin Scully as the team's broadcaster, tried to help everyone face, and perhaps embrace, something I called "Scully separation anxiety" or "postpoet depression."

Dr. Randye J. Semple, a USC mindfulness-based therapist, explained that Scully's retirement and now his absence from our everyday enjoyment of the games was much like a grieving process when a favorite grandfather passes away, someone for whom we held a certain fondness and a connection. She reminded us that "we can control very few things in life, but one thing we do control is how we respond to things." In the summer of 2022 when Vin Scully passed away, the city of Los Angeles seemingly had already been through a mourning period, and the response to this inevitability reopened the whole reality of his departure. So, how would the city honor him justly?

Whenever the people who inhabit this sprawling, disconnected Southern California area decide to pay tribute to a local icon who has left us—be it the basketball star and his daughter who perished tragically in a helicopter crash or a celebrity mountain lion people embraced as their resilient traffic-dodging mascot—I appreciate the innovation, imagination, and resourcefulness that goes into it.

To honor Scully, artistic expression has included someone embossing a new forearm tattoo and another designing a poignant silk-screen T-shirt design. A fresh mural on the side of a grill house or laundromat often just happens. When a Scully image in the Melrose district was vandalized, eventually restored by the artist ZLA, it became a news story. Another stunning mural created by Louie "Sloe" Palsino on the side of an auto-detail shop in Bellflower included Scully with other city icons, but it, too, was

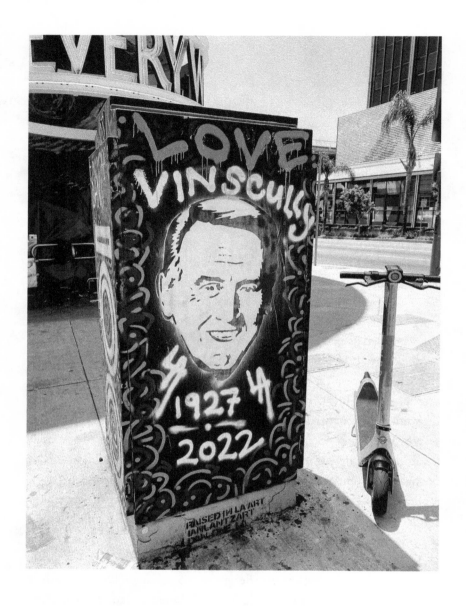

42. On the corner of Sunset Boulevard and Cahuenga Boulevard, just a few blocks from his star on the Hollywood Walk of Fame, a piece of Vin Scully street art covers a utility box. Courtesy of Tom Hoffarth.

newsworthy when it apparently violated city zoning standards. Store owner Robert Cornejo had to write an essay to the city council to keep it intact.

One day I stopped at the intersection of Sunset and Cahuenga in Hollywood and saw a portrait of Scully on the side of an electrical street signal box. The light changed green. I stayed stopped.

Paying tribute can happen through song. A country-western piece by Dan Bern called "The Golden Voice of Vin Scully" is about a West Coast truck driver longing to be within radio range of a Dodgers game. An album release in the summer of 2023 by the group The Baseball Project ends with the track "The Voice of Baseball," written by R.E.M. guitarists Peter Buck and Scott McCaughey. The lyrics included calling Scully "a soul you know you can trust."

Even rapper and hip-hop artist Earl Sweatshirt, who grew up in Santa Monica and lives in LA, used a sample of Scully's voice from his final game, for his August 2023 album *Voir Dire* in collaboration with The Alchemist. They call the song "Vin Skully."

In September 2023 the sixteenth class of the California Hall of Fame in Sacramento included Scully, with Shirley Temple Black, Etta James, Archie Williams, and Carrie Fisher.

On the national stage, the 2023 book *Why We Love Baseball: A History in 50 Moments* by Joe Posnanski includes three extended references to Scully in essays that fit the title's theme.

I expect someday to see Scully's image on a U.S. postage stamp. It would have my stamp of approval.

In late October 2022 the Mexican holiday Día de los Muertos, or Day of the Dead, saw a magnificent traditional *ofrenda* dedicated to Vin Scully in Los Angeles's Grand Park. An ofrenda, or offering, is what a family creates to honor someone who has recently died, welcoming back their souls for a brief reunion. This particular ofrenda had a stunning tiered royal blue and bright white construction with photographs, candles, rosaries, and other artifacts. The sign in front of it read "#VivaVin." When the Dodgers had their September 2023 Día de los Dodgers night, more ofrendas were displayed around the ballpark to honor departed family members, with notecard messages. Many framed images of Scully were included.

I have my own mini ofrenda on a bookshelf in my office. It has a replica of the Vin Scully Ave. street sign, a couple of specially made baseball cards, and a tall prayer candle I found from an Etsy vendor who created it after Vin's 2022 passing. The candle includes a note that says, "Win for Vin" with a smiley face, asking for intercession to help the Dodgers' playoff run that season. There are also bobbleheads, a black-circled patch that Dodgers players wore on their uniform after his passing, a minimalistic lithograph tribute to Scully by Anaheim artist S. Preston, plus and a new cap designed by Travis Chock and the geniuses at Baseballism that includes a "VIN" microphone logo.

My real priceless treasure is a baseball Vin signed, which he had snuck into a batch of fresh balls as he helped me collect items for a charity auction that would support inner-city elementary school scholarships. We were in the broadcast booth hours before a game when Vin signed ball after ball, cradling each in his right hand, then elevating his left arm and curling his wrist so his left hand would not smear the ink. He was almost apologetic as he explained why he was purposefully signing the sweet spot—that horizontal swatch of cowhide uninterrupted by the red stitches—of the baseball: he could then add a message in the space above and below his name.

As he delicately handed all the signed balls back to me, I noticed the last one had an extra inscription. Under his cursive signature were the words TO TOM—GOD BLESS.

Scully had seamlessly found a way to turn a baseball into an act of love and reverence.

The voice of Vin, the signature of Scully, is always close by if I need a reminder of that perfect eloquence.

Acknowledgments

Raise your glasses to Vin Scully. We can uncork and savor vintage Vin in any season.

This project could have included ten times more essays. The quality would have increased exponentially. My deepest gratitude goes to all those who stepped up to the plate to support this, starting with Bob Costas and Peter O'Malley, who not only accepted the invitation but also gave it an immediate surge of momentum and purpose. This wasn't an easy ask for some; it brought up very emotional memories. I understood and tried to shepherd them through that.

The scholarly backing of University of Nebraska Press, a prodigious supporter of baseball-related books over the years, was a key to this execution. Rob Taylor thankfully accepted the book's premise and execution and walked me through the process. More support came from editors Courtney Ochsner, Haley Mendlik, and Ann Baker, copyeditor Joseph Webb, and marketing specialist Rosemary Sekora, with whom I've had a longtime association.

Steve Lowery and David Davis are my gurus of go in the book-writing world. They cultivated my wish list of essayists and smoothed over many rough edges. If I were up to my hips in alligators, they would have the rescue plan. Kevin O'Malley gracefully dove in as well to help shape the content and recruit writers.

I owe my career in journalism to some master Sherpas who have educated me about the high-volume, low-pay work as a critical cog in the paragraph factory. Konnie Krislock's influence remains a blessing all these years after she changed my whole career path in the late 1970s at Hawthorne High, through passion, sharp wit, and no-nonsense execution. It is profound to have her continue with me working on this today—especially because, as

43. Vin Scully with Tom Hoffarth at the premiere of the MLB Network documentary *Only in Hollywood*, in 2018. Courtesy of Tom Hoffarth.

she has pointed out, a Protestant can always educate a Catholic on proper religious titles.

Ed Cray, the late, great USC journalism history professor, set a high bar with authorship of biographies that sit eye level on a nearby bookshelf for inspiration. Joe Jares, another departed and accomplished USC professor and newspaper colleague, would have likely told me to take on this assignment because I was doing something important. I am humbled current USC professors Joe Saltzman and Dan Durbin had the time to act as closers for this project with their academic and personal perspective.

I have two Tom Kellys to acknowledge. The first is the late iconic Los Angeles–based sports broadcaster, who gave me my first book project with

Tales from the USC *Trojans Sideline* in the early 2000s. He and Vin were true golf aficionados. When Tom passed away in the summer of Vin's final season of 2016, Vin remembered him this way: "He fulfilled all the required definitions of a great sports announcer. He was always well prepared, interesting and informative with a wonderful personality. In my mind, he had only one flaw—he was ten times the golfer I was." And on the morning after Scully's passing, Fr. Tom Kelly, recently retired as a military priest who toured the world, shared with the congregation at American Martyrs Catholic Church in Manhattan Beach the importance of Scully's faith. We see a lot of Vin Scully in American Martyrs parish pastor, Msgr. John Barry. These wise Irish gentlemen know a greater reward awaits.

None of this would have happened without Rhonda, a source of strength, faith, and balance as a spouse, so many years after first sharing the same kindergarten classroom with me. Our son and daughter, Andrew and Hannah; their spouses; our grandchildren; our parents; our brothers and sisters, nieces and nephews, and in-laws are the people I never want to disappoint. Vin showed how prioritizing time with family is one thing you'll never regret.

To Vin, I offer a modest prayer of intercession. I only wanted to do this as a way to honor and celebrate what we all saw as right and just. Thank you to the Scully family for its blessings on this.

This finite space to e-Vin-gelize will, I hope, inspire readers to craft many more essays on this project. My wish is for you to visit the website https://vinscullyappreciationbook.com/ to keep paying this forward with *eloquentia perfecta*.

Notes on Sources

Preface

Excerpts are included from the *New York Times'* story "Unlikely Parallels in a Year of Momentous Deaths," by William McDonald, December 29, 2022. I extracted several pieces I wrote for the Southern California News Group, specifically "Why Vin Scully Wants to Be Known as 'a Man Who Lived Up to His Own Beliefs,'" September 25, 2016, and the Internet Baseball Writers Association of America Substack platform "Remembering Vin Scully on What Would Been His 95th Birthday," November 29, 2022. More was added from Tom Verducci's two pieces for *Sports Illustrated*, from May 10, 2016 ("The Voice of Baseball"), and August 3, 2022 ("The Beautiful Life of Vin Scully"). Bob Nightengale's *USA Today* tribute to Scully is "Voice Won't Be Forgotten" (August 3, 2022).

Timeline

Because this book is less a biography and more an oral history, a timeline of events in Vin Scully's life, touchstones that provide context, is valuable for specific facts and figures.

One of the most entertaining Scully interviews in recent years, by *Sports Illustrated*'s Tom Verducci for the print magazine as well as online video, "Vin Scully Reminisces about the 'Brooklyn Bums' and Ebbets Field," was about Vin Scully's final call of the 1955 World Series. Posted on May 6, 2016, it can be found at https://www.si.com/mlb/video/2016/05/06/vin-scully -dodgers-ebbets-field-1955-world-series.

Curt Smith's *Voices of Summer: Ranking Baseball's 101 All-Time Best Announcers* (Carroll & Graf, 2005) includes Scully's ranking of number 1, as well as Scully discussing his move from Brooklyn to Los Angeles. Scully's call of Sandy Koufax's September 9, 1965, perfect game is explained wonderfully as part of the Society of American Baseball Research's Games Project: "September 9, 1965: 'A Million Butterflies' and One Perfect Game for Sandy Koufax," by Mike Huber, https://sabr.org/gamesproj/game/september-9 -1965-a-million-butterflies-and-one-perfect-game-for-sandy-koufax/.

First Inning

My first in-person interview with Vin Scully produced the cover of the April 5, 1992, TV magazine for the *Daily Breeze* (Torrance CA), titled "Vin Scully: The Voice." The next day, April 6, 1992, I had the extended Q&A "One Voice: Scully Still Talkin' Baseball."

Second Inning

Vin Scully gave me several interviews about his faith and family for *Angelus News*, the Catholic news publication of the Archdiocese of Los Angeles. One was from the October 16, 2019, issue, "'The One Thing That Makes It Work': An Exclusive Interview with Vin Scully" (https://angelusnews.com /local/la-catholics/sports-broadcasting-legend-vin-scully-opens-up-about -his-catholic-faith-in-an-exclusive-interview/), and another was a tribute story on him on August 15, 2022: "The Catholic Life of Vin Scully, the Golden Voice Who Talked with God" (https://angelusnews.com/local/la -catholics/remembering-vin-scully/). My October 3, 2013, interview with Scully about the spiritually of the Mickey Mantle home run came from the *Los Angeles Daily News*, October 3, 2013: "Vintage Vin." Interviews are also included from the *Sporting News* (July 21, 1986, "Scully Still Gets—and Gives—Goosebumps"), the *National Catholic Register* (October 3, 2013, "Hunt for a Red October"), *Sports Illustrated* (May 10, 2016, "The Voice of Baseball: Get to Know Vin Scully, the Man Behind the Mic," by Tom Verducci), the *Los Angeles Times* ("Inside Vin Scully," by Bill Plaschke, April, 26, 1998), and Faith Theater Productions (August 5, 2022, "Vin Scully: FTP Remembers Working with the Legendary Sportscaster"). Andre Ethier's recollection of Scully reading the Bible during a ballpark Mass came from a SportsNet LA tribute to Scully on August 3, 2022. Information about Scully's connections to Fordham are from several issues of *Fordham News*, including "Posthumous Gift Comes to Fordham from Sports Broadcasting

Legend Vin Scully," November 10, 2022, and "A Bond of Connection: On the Life and Faith of Vin Scully," March 28, 2023. Scully's return to his alma mater in 2000 is from the St. Thomas High School website story "Beloved Broadcaster Vin Scully: Committed Catholic, a Link to St. Thomas," on August 4, 2022. The full acceptance speech Scully gave for the Gabriel Awards can be found at the award organization's YouTube channel: "Vin Scully and the Pope," https://www.youtube.com/watch?v=SGVEJN7bw7Y.

Third Inning

Genealogy.com and Ancestory.com have research on the origin of the Scully name. The Society for American Baseball Research has a nice Scully biography written by Greg King at https://sabr.org/bioproj/person/vin-scully/#_edn32. My quotes from communications strategist John Millen came from a May 15, 2023, interview. For more context, see https://johnmillen.com.

Fourth Inning

My discussion with Scully about his golf game came from July 19, 2006, for the Southern California News Group: "Teeing Off with . . ." The video of Scully's call at the 1981 Heritage Golf Classic for CBS came via GolfDigest.com: "Vin Scully's Greatest Call May Have Been When This PGA Tour Pro Couldn't Escape a Pot Bunker," by Alex Myers, August 3, 2022, https://www.golfdigest.com/story/vin-scully-greatest-call-may-have-been-pga-tour-pro-couldnt-escape-pot-bunker-video/amp.

The Steve Rushin appreciation piece on Vin Scully was part of "The Smaller Vin Scully Made Himself, the Larger He Became," for *Sports Illustrated* (August 4, 2022). Scully's reaction to the Presidential Medal of Freedom honor came from my interview with him, which was posted on November 16, 2018, for the Southern California News Group.

Fifth Inning

The Other Great Depression: How I'm Overcoming on a Daily Basis at Least a Million Addictions and Dysfunctions and Finding a Spiritual (Sometimes) Life, by Richard Lewis, is available through PublicAffairs Publications, 2000. I used material from pages 76 to 79.

I used quotes from Scully via Southern California News Group from April 2, 2004, "Ah, the Voice of Reassurance"; from August 26, 2011, "A Batch of Chocolate Chip Cookies Was the Deal Breaker"; and from June 28, 2011, "Filing Leaves Us at a Point of Vinsanity." All three articles are in the author's possession.

Dodgers team historian Mark Langill's 2016 piece "Top Dog: Vin Scully Entertained Dodgers Fans—Even between Innings" was from *Dodger Insider* magazine.

Scully's discussion of starting a Twitter account comes from September 1, 2020, *Los Angeles Times*, "Why Is Vin Scully Jumping into Social Media?" by Bill Plaschke.

Sixth Inning

The Southern California News Group Sports Person of the Year ran on December 30, 2016: "An Easy Call: Vin Scully as Sports Person of the Year for SCNG," https://www.dailynews.com/2016/12/30/an-easy-call-vin-scully-as-sports-person-of-the-year-for-scng/.

The story of Petie Roach at Dodgertown in 1995 was from March 14, 1995, "Talkin' Baseball: Game Is Good; Scully Doesn't Care Who's Playing," by Bill Cizek, *Daily Breeze* (Torrance CA). The *Lexington Herald-Leader* published the story about Scully's passing in 2002: "Vin Scully's Kind Gesture toward a Kentucky Sports Icon," by Mark Story, https://www.kentucky.com/sports/spt-columns-blogs/mark-story/article264284096.html.

More on the creator of VinScullyIsMyHomeboy.com, Roberto Baly, can be found from a nice post by Howard Cole on his BaseballSavvy.com site in 2011; it allowed me to sing the praises of Roberto: "Q&A with Vin Scully Is My Homeboy's Roberto Baly," http://www.baseballsavvy.com/ob_Q&AVSIMH.html.

Doug McIntyre's Southern California News Group story about talking to Scully came from August 7, 2022, "Vin Scully's Passing Leaves Us Speechless."

Seventh Inning

The complete speech from Vin Scully on September 17, 2011, is at MLB.com ("Scully's Touching Speech," https://www.mlb.com/video/scully-s-touching-speech-c18652293).

My follow-up interview came on September 21, 2001: "Scully's Words Give Comfort," Southern California News Group. Scully's discussion of D-Day came from June 6, 2019, "Watch: Vin Scully's Stories of D-Day," by Rowan Kavner, Dodgers Mlblogs (https://dodgers.mlblogs.com/watch-vin-scullys-stories-on-d-day-8368f285e773), and June 6, 2021, "This Day in Dodgers History: Vin Scully's Calls on D-Day Anniversary," DodgerBlue.com (https://dodgerblue.com/dodgers-video-vin-scully-quotes-poem-d-day-anniversary/2021/06/06/).

The video of Rick Monday saving the American flag in 1976, with Scully's call, comes from MLB Advanced Media ("Rick Monday Saves American Flag," April 25, 2020, https://www.mlb.com/video/rick-monday-saves-american-flag).

My Southern California News Group stories come from August 2013, "Martin Luther King's Dream Never Dies for George Raveling" and "Sean Burroughs, Long Beach Little League Star, Looks Back at 20 Years of Baseball."

Peggy Noonan of the *Wall Street Journal* wrote on September 15, 2022, "Elizabeth II Was Queen of Our Times" (https://www.wsj.com/articles/elizabeth-ii-was-queen-of-our-times-history-funeral-death-stories-memory-pope-john-paul-sovereign-london-guards-11663279246).

My story on Scully and the NFL came from November 11, 2017, "Hoffarth on the Media: Blowback on Vin Scully's NFL Stance a Reminder about Respecting Opinions," Southern California News Group. John Thorn's comments about Scully came from my September 30, 2016, piece: "Vin Scully Deserves One Last Honor at Cooperstown," Southern California News Group.

Eighth Inning

More background on Scully's Hollywood Walk of Fame can be found at https://walkoffame.com/vin-scully. His story about visiting the Walk of Fame in 1945 came from my interview from April 3, 2008: "Dodgertown for a Day: Vin Scully Recalls Shift to Odd Ballpark," for the Southern California News Group.

The 1964 *Sports Illustrated* piece on Scully on May 4 came from "The Transistor Kid," by Robert Creamer (https://vault.si.com/vault/1964/05

/04/the-transistor-kid). Scully's Internet Movie Database bio is at https://www.imdb.com/name/nm0780303/.

The discussion about Scully's participation in the movie *For Love of the Game* came from September 17, 1999, "Baseball's Ambassador," by Glenn Whipp, Southern California News Group, and September 20, 1999, "It's Really Vin's Game, Onscreen and Off," by Matt Coltrin, *Los Angeles Times*.

Actress Alyssa Milano's book is *Safe at Home: Confessions of a Baseball Fanatic*, 2009, William Morrow.

Ninth Inning

The Tao of Scully series included February 4, 2011, "Media: L.A.'s Best/Worst of Play-by-Play: The Tao of Scully" and April 1, 2011, "Media: More of the Tao of Dodgers Legend Scully" for Southern California News Group.

Epilogue

The interview with USC therapist Dr. Randye J. Semple is from the April 1, 2017, story "How Are Dodgers Fans Coping with Vin Scully Separation Anxiety?" for the Southern California News Group.

The story of a vandalized Scully mural was covered by many Dodgers fans sites, including DodgersNation.com on August 24, 2023, with "Previously Vandalized Vin Scully Mural Restored in Los Angeles" by Noah Camras (https://dodgersnation.com/dodgers-news-previously-vandalized-vin-scully-mural-restored-in-los-angeles/2023/08/24/). The Bellflower mural story was covered on April 28, 2023, by the *Los Angeles Times* in "Big Bellflower Mural with Kobe, Vin, Tupac and Others Is in Danger of Erasure."

The lyrics to the song "The Golden Voice of Vin Scully" by Dan Bern is on his website DanBern.com. The lyrics to the song "The Voice of Baseball" by the Baseball Project is at BaseballProject.net.

The Joe Posnanski book *Why We Love Baseball: A History in 50 Moments* is from Dutton Books (2023). Scully's virtual induction and bio on the California Hall of Fame is on the California Museum's website at https://californiamuseum.org/vin-scully/.

Contributors

Emma Amaya is a retired computer programmer and analyst who works part-time in the Dodger Stadium team store. She was the 2013 recipient of the Baseball Reliquary's Hilda Award and is a member of the Society of American Baseball Research. In addition to her X (Twitter) social-media account @crzblue, she also posts at @Dodgershaiku with a daily haiku poem about the Dodgers games.

Joe Buck has been the lead NFL play-by-play broadcaster on ESPN's *Monday Night Football* since 2022. The eight-time Emmy Award winner began broadcasting games for the St. Louis Cardinals in 1991, filling in on games for his father, Hall of Fame broadcaster Jack Buck. During his time at Fox Sports (1994–2021), Joe Buck called twenty-three World Series and twenty-one All-Star Games. His 2016 autobiography is titled *Lucky Bastard*. He was the 2020 recipient of the Pete Rozelle Radio-Television Award from the Pro Football Hall of Fame, which his father received in 1996.

Fred Claire was Los Angeles Dodgers general manager from 1987 to 1998. The team made three playoff appearances in those twelve seasons and won the 1988 World Series. He worked in the team's front office in various roles prior to his general manager position. Claire began covering the Dodgers as a sportswriter in the 1950s and '60s, wrote *My 30 Years in Dodger Blue* in 2004, and is the subject of the 2020 book *Extra Innings: Fred Claire's Journey to City of Hope and Finding a World Championship Team*, where Vin Scully is included in honoring Claire's commitment to the cancer-treatment facility.

Ned Colletti was Los Angeles Dodgers general manager from 2006 to 2014. The team made five playoff appearances in those nine seasons. He started in public relations with the Chicago Cubs in 1982 and went to the San Francisco Giants as director of baseball operations and assistant general manager from 1994 through 2005. He served as a studio analyst on Dodgers games for SportsNet LA (2015–22), was hired as a scout for the NHL's San Jose Sharks in 2019, and has taught a sports management course at Pepperdine University in Malibu. He authored the 2017 book *The Big Chair: The Smooth Hops and Bad Bounces from the Inside World of the Acclaimed Los Angeles Dodgers General Manager*.

Bob Costas was the 2017 recipient of the Ford C. Frick Award given by the Baseball Hall of Fame, which recognized his work calling games for NBC, the MLB Network, and TBS. The twenty-nine-time Emmy Award winner spent some of his childhood in the early 1960s living in Southern California and heard Dodgers games broadcast by Vin Scully. In June 1991 Scully had an extended conversation as a guest on NBC's *Later with Bob Costas*. Costas was the 1999 recipient of the Curt Gowdy Media Award by the Basketball Hall of Fame and, in 2013, received the Vin Scully Award for Excellence in Broadcasting by Fordham University. He wrote the 2000 book *Fair Ball: A Fan's Case for Baseball*.

Bryan Cranston is a six-time Emmy Award–winning actor best known for playing Walter White in the AMC crime drama *Breaking Bad*. He has won two Tony Awards and was in the cast of the Academy Award's 2013 Best Picture winner *Argo*. He was born in Hollywood and raised in the San Fernando Valley area of Canoga Park. He chronicled his love of the Dodgers in his 2017 autobiography *A Life in Parts*.

Joe Davis joined the Los Angeles Dodgers' broadcast team in 2016, overlapping for the final season of Vin Scully's career. He joined Fox Sports in 2014 and has been the lead Major League Baseball play-by-play broadcaster since 2022. He started at ESPN in 2012 at age twenty-four and covered the NFL, college basketball, football, and hockey.

Steve Dilbeck was the lead sports columnist for the Southern California News Group from 2001 to 2009. He has also worked for the *Los Angeles Times*, the *San Bernardino Sun*, and Gannett News Service. He started writing professionally in 1977 and has covered the Angels, Dodgers, Lakers, and Rams, plus eighteen World Series, fourteen Super Bowls, thirteen NBA Finals, and five Olympics.

Ann Meyers Drysdale, inducted into the Naismith Memorial Basketball Hall of Fame in 1993, was the first women to receive a full athletic scholarship to UCLA, become a four-time All-American, and have a tryout with an NBA team in 1979. She married Los Angeles Dodgers Hall of Fame pitcher Don Drysdale in 1986 and has three children. She joined the NBA's Phoenix Suns and WNBA's Phoenix Mercury in 2007 as a vice president, as well as a color analyst, for both franchises. Her forty-plus years of broadcasting span six Olympics and have included every major network. Her 2012 memoir is titled *You Let Some Girl Beat You? The Story of Ann Meyers Drysdale*.

Dan Durbin, PhD, is a founder and director of the Annenberg Institute of Sports, Media and Society at the University of Southern California. He is also creator of the African-American Experience in Major League Baseball Oral Histories Project research program, examining the meaning of sport as a rhetorical process.

Bill Dwyre was, in addition to the *Los Angeles Times* sports editor from 1981 to 2006, a three-times-a-week sports columnist from 2006 to 2015. Dwyre won the Red Smith Award in 1996 by the Associated Press Sports Editors for sustained excellence in sports journalism. He was sports editor of the *Milwaukee Journal* from 1973 to 1981.

Chris Erskine is the nationally known humor columnist and a former editor for the *Los Angeles Times* who spent ten years writing about sports during his thirty years at the newspaper from 1990 to 2020. He is the author of four books, including the 2018 *Daditude*, a collection of his favorite *Times* columns on fatherhood. His work can currently be found at ChrisErskineLA .com.

Kevin Fagan created the comic strip *Drabble* when he was twenty-two years old in 1979. It appears in more than two hundred newspapers across the nation. He and his wife are parents of three children and live in Mission Viejo. His work and writing can currently be found at https://Drabble .substack.com and https://twitter.com/drabblecomic.

Bruce Froemming is third all-time with 5,163 games umpired in Major League Baseball during thirty-seven seasons (1971–2007). He holds the record for participating in the most no-hitters as an umpire (eleven, including Nolan Ryan's record-breaking fifth, which Vin Scully called) and most games umpired in the postseason, which includes twenty-two World Series contests. Froemming was the second base umpire for two games Scully said were among his most memorable: Kirk Gibson's 1988 World Series Game One home run and Dennis Martinez's perfect game in 1991, both at Dodger Stadium.

Steve Garvey played nineteen MLB seasons (1969–87), fourteen of them with the Los Angeles Dodgers. He set the National League record for playing in 1,207 consecutive games from 1975 to 1983, won four Gold Gloves, and was the first to be voted into the All-Star Game starting lineup as a write-in candidate, winning the 1974 game MVP the same year he was NL MVP. A ten-time National League All Star, he received MVP votes in nine seasons, finishing second in 1978. In addition to a 1986 autobiography, he wrote *My Bat Boy Days: Lessons I Learned from the Boys of Summer* in 2008.

Dennis Gilbert is one of the managing principals of Paradigm Gilbert, an insurance and financial-services firm. He was cofounder and chair of the Professional Baseball Scouts Foundation to help families of scouts in need. He was cofounder of Beverly Hills Sports Council, where he negotiated thousands of contracts from 1980 to 1999 for more than two hundred athletes, including Mike Piazza, Barry Bonds, Jose Canseco, George Brett, and Bobby Bonilla. Gilbert played professional baseball in the Boston Red Sox and New York Mets organizations out of Gardena High School and LA City College. He has a baseball field named for him at Los Angeles Southwest Community College, which was home of baseball's RBI Youth Program.

Brian Golden was an Associated Press sports editors' award-winning columnist for the Antelope Valley Press, covering Southern California sports on the professional, college, and high school levels for more than four decades through 2020.

Michael Green, PhD, is the department chair of history at the University of Nevada, Las Vegas, specializing in Nevada history, nineteenth-century America, and Abraham Lincoln. He earned his BA and MA at UNLV and his PhD at Columbia. Among the books he has authored are *Freedom, Union, and Power: Lincoln and His Party during the Civil War* in 2004 and *Lincoln and the Election of 1860* in 2011. His works on Nevada include *Las Vegas: A Centennial History* (with Eugene Moehring).

Paul Haddad is a *Los Angeles Times* best-selling author who writes about his native Los Angeles. His 2012 book, *High Fives, Pennant Drives, and Fernandomania: A Fan's History of the Los Angeles Dodgers' Glory Years 1977–1981*, was inspired by his collection of recorded Dodgers broadcasts. His Twitter platform @la_dorkout honors many forgotten aspects of Los Angeles. His website is PaulHaddadBooks.com.

David J. Halberstam is a longtime member of the voting panel for the Ford C. Frick Award, presented annually for excellence in baseball broadcasting by the National Baseball Hall of Fame and Museum. He is a noted historian and columnist on his Sports Broadcast Journal website since 2018. Halberstam called basketball games for more than a quarter century, including for St. John's University and the NBA's Miami Heat. He served as executive vice president and general manager of Westwood One Sports. He has authored two books, including *Sports on New York Radio: A Play-by-Play History* in 1999. He is the creator of the website SportsBroadcastJournal.com.

Derrick Hall became president of the Arizona Diamondbacks in 2006 and its chief executive officer in 2009. He spent twelve years in the Los Angeles Dodgers' front office from 1993 to 2005, including serving as its senior vice president of communications. Prior to that, Hall was a sports broadcaster and hosted a talk show on the Dodgers' XTRA-AM flagship station. He was inducted into the Arizona Sports Hall of Fame in 2019 for his impact on baseball in the state.

Orel Hershiser played eighteen MLB seasons (1983–2000), thirteen of them with the Los Angeles Dodgers. He set the MLB record for consecutive scoreless innings pitched (fifty-nine, in 1988), the same year he won the

National League Cy Young Award and World Series MVP. He posted a 204-150 record in 510 games, won a Gold Glove and a Silver Slugger, and was named to three All-Star Games. He joined the Dodgers' SportsNet LA when it launched in 2014 after working as baseball analyst at ABC and on ESPN's *Sunday Night Baseball* (2010–13). He is the author of *Out of the Blue* in 1989 and *Between the Lines: Nine Things Baseball Taught Me about Life* in 2002.

Jim Hill has been a Los Angeles–based sports anchor at KCBS-TV, KCAL-TV, and KABC-TV since 1976. He was an NFL defensive back from 1968 to 1975. Hill did play-by-play on NFL regional broadcasts from 1980 through 1993 and was the Super Bowl XVIII sideline reporter for ABC. In 2006 he was given a star on the Hollywood Walk of Fame and honored with a Golden Mike Award Lifetime Achievement recognition in 2022. He is a member of the Los Angeles Urban League board of directors.

Gil Hodges Jr., living and working in Palm Beach Gardens, Florida, is the only son of Baseball Hall of Fame first baseman Gil Hodges. He was a first baseman drafted by the New York Mets in 1971 out of Long Island University and played two seasons of Single-A level. He is part of the 2021 documentary *The Gil Hodges Story: Soul of A Champion*.

J. P. Hoornstra has been a multimedia reporter and podcast host covering baseball for the Southern California News Group since 2006, and he also appears on *Access: SportsNet Dodgers* on SportsNet LA. The UCLA graduate is the author of *The 50 Greatest Dodgers Games of All Time* in 2015.

John Ireland has been the NBA Los Angeles Lakers' radio play-by-play broadcaster since 2011. The graduate of UCLA was a sideline reporter for the team's TV coverage from 2002 to 2010 as well as an anchor and reporter for KCAL Channel 9 in LA from 1995 to 2012. He continues to partner with Steve Mason on the *Mason and Ireland* sports-talk show for KSPN-AM radio in Los Angeles. Ireland has also done play-by-play on the Los Angeles Clippers and UCLA football and basketball.

Jaime Jarrin was the 1998 recipient of the Ford C. Frick Award given by the Baseball Hall of Fame, recognizing his eventual sixty-four-year career as the Dodgers' Spanish-language play-by-play radio and TV broadcaster. He began his career in 1959, recreating games in Spanish that were called live by Vin Scully in English. Jarrin worked on broadcasts with his son, Jorge, from 2015 to 2020. The native of Cayambe, Ecuador, retired after the 2022 season. He received a star on the Hollywood Walk of Fame in 1998.

Eric Karros played fourteen MLB seasons (1991–2004), twelve of them with the Los Angeles Dodgers. He won the 1992 National League Rookie of the Year award. The UCLA graduate remains the franchise's Los Angeles leader in career home runs with 270. He has been a baseball analyst for Fox Sports since 2004 and, in 2022, joined the Dodgers' SportsNet LA team. Karros's son Jared, a pitcher out of UCLA, was drafted by the Dodgers in 2022.

Pablo Kay has been the editor-in-chief of *Angelus News*, the news publication of the Roman Catholic Archdiocese of Los Angeles, since 2019.

Tim Klosterman was an associate pastor at St. Monica Catholic Church in Santa Monica from 2008 to 2012, when he joined in celebrating Mass at Dodger Stadium and Angel Stadium. He was director of pastoral formation at the Archdiocese of Los Angeles's St. John's Seminary in Camarillo through 2020.

Ken Korach has been the Oakland Athletics' radio play-by-play broadcaster since 1996. He grew up in West LA and went to college at San Diego State and UC Santa Barbara, graduating in 1975 with a degree in Social Sciences. When he moved to Santa Rosa in the late 1970s to search for a career, he listened to Scully on the Dodgers' Las Vegas affiliate KDWN-AM. He started his career doing MLB games with the Chicago White Sox in 1992. Korach is the author of *Holy Toledo: Lessons from Bill King, Renaissance Man of the Mic* in 2013 and coauthor of *If These Walls Could Talk: The Oakland A's* in 2019.

Will Leitch is a contributing editor at *New York* magazine and the founder of the late sports website Deadspin. He also writes regularly for the *New York Times*, *Washington Post*, NBC News, medium.com, and MLB.com. He is the author of six books, including the 2008 *God Save the Fan: How Preening Sportscasters, Athletes Who Speak in the Third Person and the Occasional*

Convicted Quarterback Have Taken the Fun Out of Sports (And How We Can Get It Back) and the 2010 *Are We Winning? Fathers and Sons in the New Golden Age of Baseball.* His latest novels are *How Lucky* in 2021 and *The Time Has Come* in 2023. His work on the Will Leitch Experience can be found at https://leitch.tumblr.com.

Ken Levine is an Emmy Award–winning writer, director, and producer. During his work on *M*A*S*H*, Levine created a recurring character that appeared in Season Seven named Sergeant Jack Scully, named after Vin Scully. Levine also wrote for *Cheers, Frasier*, and *The Simpsons* and ventured off to become a Major League Baseball play-by-play broadcaster from 1991 through 2012 with Baltimore, Seattle, San Diego, and Los Angeles, where he also cohosted *DodgerTalk* postgame shows on radio with Josh Suchon. Levine's Season Two episode of *The Simpsons* called "Dancin' Homer" created the fictitious Springfield Isotopes baseball team—a nickname the Triple-A Albuquerque team eventually adopted. Levine wrote the 1993 book *It's Gone! . . . No, Wait a Minute . . . Talking My Way into the Big Leagues at 40*. He hosts the podcast *Hollywood and Levine*, and his work can be found at http://KenLevine.Blogspot.com.

Tom Leykis was the host of his own talk-radio show from 1994 to 2009, nationally syndicated on Westwood One, and then from 2012 to 2018, based on the internet and by podcast. He worked at Los Angeles's KFI-AM from 1988 to 1992. His podcast can be heard at http://premiumtom.com.

Jill Painter Lopez is a sports reporter at KCBS Channel 2 and KCAL Channel 9 in Los Angeles and an MLB Network correspondent. She has done live sideline reporting on the MLB Angels and NHL Ducks for Bally Sports West. She was a columnist and reporter for the *Los Angeles Daily News* from 2000 to 2014.

Doug Mann has been a radio and television sports statistician on live broadcasts of the NBA (Lakers and Clippers), MLB (Dodgers and Angels), NHL (Kings), UCLA and USC men's and women's basketball, and Major League Soccer since 1974 and is based in Southern California. His research work has helped Hall of Fame broadcasters Vin Scully, Chick Hearn, and Bob

Miller. Mann has also done NFL, NBA, NHL, and NCAA football and basketball for major networks with Al Michaels, Bob Costas, Dick Enberg, Marv Albert, Kenny Albert, Bob Cole, and Charlie Jones.

Dale Marini, a 1970 graduate of Loyola Marymount University in Los Angeles, received a master's degree in education from the school in 1975. He retired as LMU's associate director of admission in 2014. He also was the official scorer of LMU's men's basketball for forty-four years and was inducted into the LMU Athletics Hall of Fame as a benefactor in 2015. His essay is adapted from a story he wrote for *LMU Magazine* on December 5, 2016, and was reprinted with permission.

Dennis McCarthy has been writing columns for the *Los Angeles Daily News* since 1982 and has been in the Southern California newspaper business for more than fifty years, out of San Fernando Valley State College in Northridge in 1971.

Tim Mead retired as president of the National Baseball Hall of Fame and Museum in 2021 after two years in that role. He spent the previous forty years with the California/Anaheim/Los Angeles organization. From 1999 to 2019 he was the team's vice president of communications. He was also the Angels' assistant general manager from 1994 to '97. He received the MLB's Robert O. Fischel Award for Public Relations Excellence in 2000.

Jessica Mendoza became the first female broadcaster on a Major League Baseball game when ESPN assigned her to that role in 2015. She joined the network's *Sunday Night Baseball* team full-time from 2016 to 2019. The two-time U.S. Olympic softball medalist (Athens gold in 2004, Beijing silver in 2008) was a four-time first-team All-American at Stanford. A past president of the Women's Sports Foundation, she joined the Los Angeles Dodgers' TV analyst rotation in 2022 while continuing work at ESPN.

Al Michaels was the 2021 recipient of the Ford C. Frick Award given by the Baseball Hall of Fame, recognizing his work calling games for NBC and ABC in the 1970s, '80s and '90s, as well as his time with the Cincinnati Reds (1971–73) and San Francisco Giants (1974–76). His most memorable baseball calls include the 1989 World Series interrupted by the San Francisco Earthquake and the 1986 American League Championship Series. For his work covering the NFL, he received the 2013 Pete Rozelle Radio & Television Award from the Pro Football Hall of Fame. He is known for his most famous call, "Do you believe in miracles?" after the U.S. Olympic hockey team upset the USSR in 1980. In 2012 Michaels received the Vin Scully Award for Excellence in Broadcasting by Fordham University. He wrote the 2014 memoir *You Can't Make This Up: Miracles, Memories, and the Perfect Marriage of Sports and Television* with L. Jon Wertheim.

Bob Miller was the 2000 recipient of the Foster Hewitt Memorial Award given by the Hockey Hall of Fame, recognizing his work calling more than 3,300 games with the NHL's Los Angeles Kings from 1973 until his retirement in 2017—the year after Vin Scully retired. Miller's education at the University of Iowa included playing on the school's baseball team. He wrote *Tales from the Los Angeles Kings* in 2006, which was updated in 2013 after the team's first Stanley Cup victory. He has a star on the Hollywood Walk of Fame, plus a statue outside Crypto.com Arena and a banner in his honor inside hanging from the rafters. Miller served as president of the Southern California Sports Broadcasters, which started in 1958 with Vin Scully as one of its first members. In 2018 Miller was given the SCSB's Vin Scully Lifetime Achievement Award.

Patt Morrison has a share of two Pulitzer Prizes as a longtime *Los Angeles Times* writer and columnist. As a public television and radio broadcaster, she has won six Emmys and a dozen Golden Mike awards. She has written *Rio LA, Tales from the Los Angeles River* in 2001 and *Don't Stop the Presses! Truth, Justice, and the American Newspaper* in 2018. She received the lifetime achievement from the Los Angeles Press Club in 2006. Pink's, the renowned Hollywood hot dog stand, named its vegetarian dog the "Patt Morrison Baja Dog" after her.

John Olguin, the principal for JO Sports Strategy, was the vice president of public relations for the Los Angeles Dodgers during his time with the team from 1992 to 2005. He is former senior vice president of marketing and communications for Chip Ganassi Racing.

Kevin O'Malley, the head of operations and MLB ministry coordinator for Catholic Athletes for Christ, is also a senior federal official working on budget and policy issues in Washington DC. He earned a communications and public relations degree with a minor in marketing at the University of Dayton, where he broadcast the Flyers' football and basketball games.

Peter O'Malley took over ownership of the Los Angeles Dodgers' franchise in 1979 after the death of his father, Walter, who had purchased a share of the team in 1950, was the majority owner who moved it to Los Angeles in 1958, and secured full ownership in 1975. Peter was named director of Dodgertown, the team's Vero Beach, Florida, spring training facility, in 1962 right out of college and held executive positions with the Dodgers in the late 1960s, taking over as president in 1970 and retaining that title for twenty-eight years until the franchise was sold to Fox. He partnered with his nephew, Peter Seidler, to purchase the San Diego Padres in 2012.

Mike Parker has been the radio play-by-play voice on Oregon State football, basketball, and baseball since 1999. He called three NCAA championship seasons for the Beavers' baseball team (2006, 2007, and 2018) and was also the voice of the Triple-A Portland Beavers from 1987 to 1992. The six-time Oregon Sportscaster of the Year also hosts a sports-talk show in Corvallis, Oregon, on KEJO-AM. He is a 1982 graduate of the University of Oregon with a degree in rhetoric and communications.

Ben Platt was webmaster of the Dodgers' first official website from April 1996 through 2001. It set the template for how MLB teams established their websites, eventually leading to Platt working a senior correspondent and field producer for MLB.com and MLB Advanced Media from 2000 to 2018.

Ross Porter was the Los Angeles Dodgers' TV and radio broadcaster for twenty-eight seasons, from 1977 to 2004, the fourth-longest tenure in the history of the franchise. The Oklahoma native came to LA in 1966 at age twenty-seven to start as a sportscaster at KNBC Channel 4. In Curt Smith's 2005 book, *Voices of Summer*, Porter is ranked number 58 out of 100 in the game's history, noted for his knowledge and popularity. He continues to tell stories and post interviews on his Ross Porter YouTube channel.

Jeff Proctor has been president of the independent sports production company ProAngle Media since 2005. In the sports television business since 1997, he was an Emmy Award–winning executive producer for Dodgers games on Fox Sports Net West, West 2, and Prime Ticket in Los Angeles, the nation's largest regional sports network. He was vice president of sports for KCBS Channel 2 and KCAL Channel 9 in LA for five years and has been a broadcasting consultant for the Los Angeles Lakers.

Ron Rapoport was a sports columnist for the *Chicago Sun-Times* and the *Los Angeles Daily News* and sports commentator for National Public Radio's *Weekend Edition Saturday* for two decades. He is the author of a number of books on sports and show business, including *Let's Play Two: The Legend of Mr. Cub, the Life of Ernie Banks*. He is a recipient of the Ring Lardner Award for Excellence in Sports Journalism.

Josh Rawitch has been president of the National Baseball Hall of Fame and Museum since 2021. He began working for the Los Angeles Dodgers in 1995 as an intern and became an executive in the communications, public relations, and broadcasting departments. In 2011 he started a decade working for the Arizona Diamondbacks as a senior vice president of content & communications. He was also once an assistant site editor and reporter for MLB.com, covering the Dodgers and San Francisco Giants.

Fr. Willy Raymond served as chaplain to the Los Angeles Dodgers from 2004 to 2014 while he was as associate at St. Monica Catholic Church in Santa Monica. The Maine native has been president of Holy Cross Family Ministries in Easton, Massachusetts, since 2014. He was also the national director of Family Theater Productions in Los Angeles (2000–2014) and has been a board member of Catholic Athletes for Christ since 2005.

Boyd Robertson retired as the stage manager in the Los Angeles Dodgers' TV booth in 2021 after thirty-two years, twenty-eight of them working with Scully. He was a TV stage manager on NBA broadcasts with the Los Angeles Lakers' Hall of Famer Chick Hearn. Robertson also worked at ABC with Jim McKay, Keith Jackson, and the *Monday Night Football* crew of Howard Cosell, Frank Gifford, and Don Meredith.

Andy Rosenberg received seventeen Emmy Awards as a network TV director at NBC Sports (1979–2014). His work included thirteen Olympics; twenty-two Wimbledon Championships; eleven French Opens; twelve NBA Finals; three World Series; thirteen bowl games, including three College Football National Championships; and ten years of many professional golf events.

Sammy Roth is the climate columnist for the *Los Angeles Times* and previously worked at the *Desert Sun* and *USA Today*. He grew up in Westwood. A version of his essay was published in the *Desert Sun* newspaper in Palm Springs, California, in September 2016. His work can be found at https://sammyroth.pressfolios.com.

Joe Saltzman is a professor at the University of Southern California's Annenberg School for Communications and Journalism, beginning as an adjunct lecturer in 1964. He became a full-time faculty member in 1974 when he left CBS to start the university's broadcasting major track. He is director of the Image of the Journalist in Popular Culture (IJPC), a project of the Norman Lear Center. He is the author of *Frank Capra and the Image of the Journalist in American Film* in 2002 and *Heroes and Scoundrels: The Image of the Journalist in Popular Culture* in 2015. His website is JoeSaltzman.org.

Lisa Nehus Saxon teaches media at Santa Monica College and Palisades Charter High School. She wrote for the *Los Angeles Daily News* from 1979 until 1987.

Bud Selig is the commissioner emeritus of Major League Baseball, having served as the game's ninth commissioner from 1998 to 2015, plus six years prior as acting commissioner. He was inducted into the National Baseball Hall of Fame in 2017. He is author of the 2019 book *For the Good of the Game: The Inside Story of the Surprising and Dramatic Transformation of Major League Baseball*.

Harry Shearer has been an Emmy Award–winning character voice on the television series *The Simpsons* since 1983, occasionally playing a baseball announcer that sounds particularly like Vin Scully. In Season Twenty-Eight, Shearer even voices the role of a character named Vin Scully Impersonator in an episode called "The Caper Chase." He cowrote, cocreated, and costarred in the 1984 film *This Is Spinal Tap*. His acting roles include *A Mighty Wind*, *For Your Consideration*, *The Right Stuff*, and *The Truman Show*. He was a writer and cast member on NBC's *Saturday Night Live* from 1979 to 1985—once doing a Scully character during the 1984 World Series. His work can be found at HarryShearer.com.

Brent Shyer was the Dodgers' director of broadcasting, publications and new media from 1988 to 2001. He is currently vice president of special projects for O'Malley Seidler Partners.

T. J. Simers is a sports columnist who wrote for the *Los Angeles Times* from 1990 to 2013. He also wrote for the *Orange County Register*, *San Diego Union*, *Rocky Mountain News*, and the *Commercial Appeal* (Memphis TN). He was named 2000 California Sports Writer of the National Sportscasters and Sportswriters Association.

Josh Suchon has been the play-by-play voice of the Triple-A Albuquerque Isotopes since 2013. He hosted Los Angeles Dodgers' postgame shows with Ken Levine from 2008 to 2011. His play-by-play career includes work for the Single-A Modesto Nuts. He covered the San Francisco Giants and Oakland Athletics for the Bay Area News Group from 1996 to 2007. He is the author of three books, including *Miracle Men: Hershiser, Gibson, and the Improbable 1988 Dodgers* in 2013.

Matt Vasgersian started his MLB play-by-play career in 1997 with Milwaukee and has continued it in San Diego (2002–8) and with the Los Angeles Angels (2021–present). He broadcast games for NBC starting in 2001, was at Fox Sports from 2006 to 2017, and has been with the MLB Network since its launch in 2009. He was the lead play-by-play man for ESPN's *Sunday Night Baseball* from 2018 to 2021.

Paul Vercammen is a five-time Emmy Award–winning Los Angeles–based journalist who worked twenty-six years at CNN, served as news director and anchor at KEYT Santa Barbara, and graduated from, and taught as an adjunct professor at, USC.

Tom Villante, the Dodgers' radio and TV game producer from 1952 to 1958, returned to New York and, in 1968, headed Batten, Barton, Durstine & Osborn (BBDO) Advertising's account as executive director of Major League Baseball's ad campaign. In 1979 he joined Major League Baseball as its executive director of marketing and broadcasting, advising teams on negotiating local broadcasting rights. He helped created the sport's first ad slogan: "Baseball Fever: Catch It!" He lives in New York.

Jon Weisman is the founder and writer of the pioneering baseball website DodgerThoughts.com. He has spent more than thirty years writing about sports and entertainment for the *Los Angeles Times*, *Los Angeles Daily News*, ESPN.com, SI.com, and *Variety*. He was the Los Angeles Dodgers' director of digital and print content from 2013 to 2017 and rejoined the team in 2023 as vice president, communications. He has written two books about the franchise: *Brothers in Arms: Koufax, Kershaw, and the Dodgers' Extraordinary Pitching Tradition* in 2018 and *100 Things Dodgers Fans Should Know & Do before They Die*, last updated in 2021. Weisman's journey to his first interview with Scully is included in the 2009 documentary *Bluetopia: The LA Dodgers Movie*, celebrating the team's fifty years in Los Angeles.

Brian Wheeler called games on radio for the NBA's Portland Trail Blazers from 1998 to 2019. He grew up in Los Angeles until age fourteen, when he moved to Chicago. He is completing his autobiography, titled *It's a Great Day: The Personal and Professional Challenges Overcome to Produce a Dream Career*.

Printed in the USA
CPSIA information can be obtained
at www.ICGtesting.com
CBHW021544140624
10087CB00018B/659/J